"This book is a transformative guide that empowers leaders to break free from self-doubt and find their authentic voice. With practical strategies, expert insights, and a focus on inclusivity, this book is a must-read for anyone looking to amplify their influence and lead with confidence in today's dynamic world."

Jennifer Ptacek, *University of Dayton, USA*

"*Amplifying Your Leadership Voice* is an insightful, empowering guide that speaks directly to the challenges and aspirations of today's professionals. Grounded in research and enriched with personal experience, this book offers a clear, practical roadmap for developing authentic leadership communication skills. Whether you're finding your voice for the first time or looking to refine it, this book delivers the tools and inspiration to lead with confidence and clarity."

Matt Koschmann, *University of Colorado Boulder*

Amplifying Your Leadership Voice

Amplifying Your Leadership Voice is a transformative guide designed to help professionals at all levels to discover, refine, and amplify their leadership voice. This step-by-step, evidence-based approach moves beyond basic communication skills, emphasizing self-awareness, confidence, and authenticity to expand your influence, impact, and presence. Since communication is the primary yardstick by which others assess your leadership—whether or not you have a formal title—the more attention and practice you give to verbal, nonverbal, and written expression, the more confident and effective you'll become. This book empowers you to communicate with intention and lead with purpose.

Through four distinct levels—discover, refine, amplify, and sustain—you'll learn to assess your strengths, identify growth areas, craft compelling stories, navigate difficult conversations, and leverage digital tools. Each chapter offers actionable tips, real-world examples, reflective exercises, and expert insights to help you speak up more often and influence others. Whether you're an emerging leader or an experienced executive, these strategies will help you overcome fear, build resilience, and foster meaningful connections to advance your career and create lasting impact.

If you're ready to move beyond silence and step into your leadership power, this book is your essential guide to sustained growth and success. Ideal for both new and seasoned professionals, it is also an excellent resource for executive education, MBA, and graduate courses in leadership communication.

Dr. Leah M. Omilion-Hodges is Professor of Communication at Western Michigan University, specializing in leader communication, team dynamics, and leader–member relationships. With experience in business and healthcare, she has authored four leadership books and publishes research in leading scholarly journals. She hosts *The Communicative Leader* podcast, offering practical tips for workplace success. Recognized as Distinguished Professor, Dr. Omilion-Hodges is dedicated to empowering employees and fostering healthy, effective work environments.

Amplifying Your Leadership Voice

From Silent to Speaking Up

Leah M. Omilion-Hodges

Taylor & Francis Group

NEW YORK AND LONDON

Designed cover image: Getty Images

First published 2026
by Routledge
605 Third Avenue, New York, NY 10158

and by Routledge
4 Park Square, Milton Park, Abingdon, Oxon, OX14 4RN

Routledge is an imprint of the Taylor & Francis Group, an informa business

© 2026 Leah M. Omilion-Hodges

The right of Leah M. Omilion-Hodges to be identified as author of this work has been asserted in accordance with sections 77 and 78 of the Copyright, Designs and Patents Act 1988.

All rights reserved. No part of this book may be reprinted or reproduced or utilised in any form or by any electronic, mechanical, or other means, now known or hereafter invented, including photocopying and recording, or in any information storage or retrieval system, without permission in writing from the publishers.

Trademark notice: Product or corporate names may be trademarks or registered trademarks, and are used only for identification and explanation without intent to infringe.

Library of Congress Cataloging-in-Publication Data
A catalog record for this book has been requested

ISBN: 978-1-032-99521-2 (hbk)
ISBN: 978-1-032-99519-9 (pbk)
ISBN: 978-1-003-60461-7 (ebk)

DOI: 10.4324/9781003604617

Typeset in Perpetua
by Apex CoVantage, LLC

Access the Support Material: https://www.thecommunicativeleader.com

To my family—your constant love, support, and laughter are the heart of everything that I do. And to my younger self—thank you for your grit and gumption in pushing through those early, nerve-wracking, and often painful presentations. Your resilience has carried you to where you are today.

Contents

Introduction: Unlocking Your Leadership Potential   1

LEVEL 1
Discover Your Leadership Voice   7

1 The Danger of Silence: Why It's Time to Speak Up   9

2 Discover Your Leadership Voice: Assess, Understand, and Grow   23

3 Inside the Leader's Voice: The Anatomy of Influence and Authenticity   46

LEVEL 2
Refine Your Leadership Voice   63

4 Speak with Impact: Master Verbal and Nonverbal Communication Skills   65

5 Write to Lead: Developing Your Digital and Written Communication   89

6 Breaking Barriers: Overcoming Obstacles to Your Leadership Voice   110

7 Communicating across Boundaries: Navigating Cultural Spaces with Confidence   130

CONTENTS

LEVEL 3
Amplify Your Leadership Voice — 155

8 Authentic and Confident: Crafting Your Unique Leadership Voice — 157

9 Command Attention: Elevate Your Presence and Build Your Platform — 180

10 Amplifying with Tech: Harnessing Digital Tools to Elevate Your Voice — 197

LEVEL 4
Sustain Your Leadership Voice — 211

11 Leadership Resilience: The Power of Self-Care and Reflection — 213

12 Your Leadership Muscle: Exercising and Strengthening Your Voice Daily — 227

Index — *239*

Introduction
Unlocking Your Leadership Potential

Have you ever walked into a meeting with a great idea, but the words just got stuck in your throat? That feeling of being unseen and unheard is more common than you think. It's the silent struggle of countless professionals who know they have something valuable to contribute but can't find a way to express it.

You know that speaking up is key to advancing your career and making a meaningful impact. But building the skills to do so can feel overwhelming. We've all been there, feeling like our ideas are being silenced, ignored, or dismissed, or simply unsure of how to get started.

What if I told you there's a way to change this experience? What if you could learn to speak up with confidence, conviction, and clarity, without any fear of rejection or pushback? What if you could become a leader who is heard and respected by others?

Speaking up isn't just about personality or talent; it's a skill that can be cultivated and strengthened. Research shows that employees who voice their opinions are more likely to be seen as leaders[1], enjoy greater job satisfaction[2], and experience faster career growth[3]. But speaking up isn't just beneficial for individuals—it's also great for organizations. When employees feel heard and valued, they're more motivated, engaged, and committed to their work.

FROM BEING SILENT TO SPEAKING UP: MY STORY

So, how do you go from being silent to speaking up? Through a proven four-step system developed by an internationally recognized leadership communication expert. My methods are not only rooted in data, but they were also forged through personal experiences. I wasn't always a confident speaker. In fact, I was once a member of the "silent majority" (more on that in Chapter 1)—an introvert who was a downright terrible public speaker. My journey from being that terrified student to a professor with a popular podcast is proof that your leadership voice isn't just waiting to be unlocked; it can be built and strengthened.

I remember one particularly terrible presentation in college. My hands trembled, my voice cracked, and my legs literally shook. My whole body felt like it was betraying me. The feedback from my peers was brutal: "Stop acting so terrified." "Calm down."

That experience, and the comments I received, didn't magically turn me into a confident speaker. It was a wake-up call that led me on a two-decade journey to master leadership communication. This book is the culmination of that work—a guide to help you find and amplify your leadership voice, so you never have to feel that way again.

That experience has stayed with me, and I often return to it. Most of my other presentations weren't quite as disastrous, but I've certainly had my share of doozies—like the time I was a new assistant professor, and my director attended one of my research talks. By then, I was a practiced speaker, but when I saw her take a seat, my legs started shaking uncontrollably. I ended up walking away from the microphone and into the audience, hoping it would come across as engaging rather than letting my nerves detract from my credibility. Since then, I've dedicated a lot of time and energy to developing my leadership voice. And while I still feel nervous before a presentation, podcast, or meeting a new class, I now know I have the skills to succeed and make a meaningful contribution.

Owning your leadership voice empowers you to do more than just speak up. It provides tools to enhance your presence, infuse leadership into your writing, and become a thought leader in your industry, while also equipping you with the strategies to navigate conflict, address pushback, and productively dissent.

EMBARKING ON YOUR LEADERSHIP COMMUNICATION JOURNEY

Ready to embark on a transformative journey? This book is your personal roadmap, guiding you through four powerful levels of leadership mastery (see Table 0.1):

Table 0.1 Progression of Your Leadership Voice: From Self-Awareness to Sustainable Influence

 Level 1: Discover Your Leadership Voice

Every great leader starts with awareness. In this stage, you'll start to connect with your authentic self—your values, strengths, and unique perspective. It's about recognizing what makes your voice special and beginning to understand the voice you want to amplify. This level includes the following chapters:

INTRODUCTION

- Chapter 1: The Danger of Silence: Why It's Time to Speak Up
- Chapter 2: Discover Your Leadership Voice: Assess, Understand, and Grow
- Chapter 3: Inside the Leader's Voice: The Anatomy of Influence and Authenticity

 Level 2: Refine Your Leadership Voice

With awareness in hand, the next stage includes sharpening your skills and overcoming fears that hold you back. You'll learn to communicate with clarity and conviction, align your actions with your core values, and build confidence in your leadership presence. In Level 2, you'll focus on the following chapters:

- Chapter 4: Speak with Impact: Master Verbal and Nonverbal Communication Skills
- Chapter 5: Write to Lead: Developing Your Digital and Written Communication
- Chapter 6: Breaking Barriers: Overcoming Obstacles to Your Leadership Voice
- Chapter 7: Communicating across Boundaries: Navigating Cultural Spaces with Confidence

 Level 3: Amplify Your Leadership Voice

At this stage, your influence starts to grow intentionally. You learn to scale your voice — telling compelling stories, navigating difficult conversations, and inspiring others. It's about making your leadership impact resonate across teams, organizations, and communities. Chapters in Level 3 include:

- Chapter 8: Authentic and Confident: Crafting Your Unique Leadership Voice
- Chapter 9: Command Attention: Elevate Your Presence and Build Your Platform
- Chapter 10: Amplify with Tech: Harnessing Digital Tools to Elevate Your Voice

 Level 4: Sustain Your Leadership Voice

True mastery is about longevity. In this final stage, you cultivate habits of resilience, continuous learning, and legacy-building. Your leadership becomes sustainable — an authentic force that continues to inspire, uplift, and transform. Level 4 chapters include:

- Chapter 11: Leadership Resilience: The Power of Self-Care and Reflection
- Chapter 12: Your Leadership Muscle: Exercising and Strengthening Your Voice Daily

---

This book is your personal guide, designed to be flexible and adaptable to your unique journey. While the four levels of leadership mastery are designed to build upon one another, you're encouraged to navigate them in the order that best suits your current goals.

This book takes a step-by-step approach to help you improve your leadership communication skills. The journey to confidence is direct and tailored to where you're starting from. If you're reading this and feeling seen for the first time, you're not alone. The fear of speaking up is more common than you think, but it doesn't have to hold you back. This book provides a clear path forward, from the very first step.

And for experienced leaders—CEOs, managers, and seasoned professionals—this journey offers a unique opportunity for reflection and growth. The most accomplished leaders never stop learning, and this book provides the research-backed insights and strategies you need to refine your communication and maintain your edge.

No matter where you are right now, this path offers stepping stones for everyone—from the most apprehensive to the most skilled. Why? There is no single "perfect" leadership communication style. Instead of prescribing a single, rigid approach, we'll explore best practices backed by research and share real-world scenarios to help you discover what feels most authentic to you.

Throughout this book, each chapter will include helpful features designed to deepen your understanding and support your leadership journey. Look forward to these tools and prompts:

- **Actionable Insights**: Practical, easy-to-apply leadership communication tips to help you start amplifying your leadership voice today.
- **Data and Trends**: Inspiring statistics and research-backed trends to guide your leadership development and remind you that you're not alone.
- **Conversations with Leaders**: Exclusive tips from CEOs and industry leaders featured on *The Communicative Leader* podcast.
- **Key Takeaways**: Chapter summaries with three to five actionable lessons—perfect for quick reference.

Each chapter is crafted in a conversational, audience-centered style to respect your limited time. I've integrated infographics, bulleted lists, and other helpful tools to distill complex concepts into practical, easy-to-digest content.

You'll also find complementary materials to enhance your learning. Resources like the *Amplifying Your Leadership Voice: Leadership Blueprint* provide deeper insights and powerful strategies, going beyond the text to help you master leadership communication. These valuable extras are available via a dedicated access box (like the one below) in each chapter.

READY TO PUT THIS INTO PRACTICE?

Amplify Your Leadership Voice Further

When you see this box, it's your cue to explore additional materials that support and deepen your learning. Access all supplemental resources at TheCommunicativeLeader.com.

Throughout this journey, you'll gain the tools and strategies to amplify your leadership voice and make a meaningful impact— at work, at home, and in your community. It is time to stop waiting and start leading. Let's start the journey to unlocking your leadership potential.

NOTES

1 Merchant, N. (2021, August 9). People who speak more are more likely to be considered leaders. *World Economic Forum*. https://www.weforum.org/stories/2021/08/leaders-talk-more-babble-hypothesis/
2 Gallup. (2025). State of the American workplace: Understanding employees, informing leaders. *Gallup.com*.
3 Hilton Segel, L., & Hatami, H. (2023, October 30). *Say what? A leader's guide to communicating clearly*. McKinsey & Company. https://www.mckinsey.com/~/media/mckinsey/email/leadingoff/2023/10/30/2023-10-30d.html

Level 1
Discover Your Leadership Voice

Chapter 1
The Danger of Silence
Why It's Time to Speak Up

WELCOME TO LEVEL 1: DISCOVER YOUR LEADERSHIP VOICE

Welcome to the first step in your leadership journey: discovering your authentic voice. At this foundational stage, you'll begin to uncover the immense power that lies within you—an insightful voice that's been waiting to be heard but, often remains silent.

Think of this as turning on the lights in a dim room. Suddenly, what was hidden becomes clear, and you see the potential that's been there all along. This is your moment to understand why silence can be so damaging and why it's crucial to start speaking up.

- In Chapter 1, "The Danger of Silence," you'll explore the profound impact silence has on your influence, not just for yourself, but for your team and organization. You'll recognize the costs of holding back and discover why your voice matters more than ever.
- Next, Chapter 2, "Discover Your Leadership Voice," invites you to take honest stock of where you stand today. Through reflection and self-assessment, you'll identify your current strengths and gaps, setting the stage for intentional growth.
- Finally, in Chapter 3, "Inside the Leader's Voice," you'll delve into the core elements that make an effective leader's communication compelling—clarity, authenticity, conviction, and emotional intelligence. Understanding these fundamental building blocks will empower you to communicate in ways that are both genuine and impactful.

This first level is about awakening—the moment you realize that your voice is a vital leadership asset waiting to be discovered and cultivated. As you step into this phase, remember: every great leader started exactly where you are now, on the cusp of unlocking their potential.

WHAT'S THE SECRET TO BEING SEEN AS A LEADER?

When I talk to employees from all walks of life, I'm constantly asked: what's the secret to becoming a recognized leader? The answer I share with them often takes them aback, but it's rooted in a universal truth. The key factor others use to measure your leadership ability is not your title, experience, or expertise—it's something much simpler.

It's your communication. Consider this: When good leaders communicate, they are clear about their goals. You leave the conversation with a solid understanding of its purpose and how it relates to you. Good leaders use stories and language that everyone can grasp. Instead of relying on jargon or confusing analogies, they connect with their team on a personal level.

For example, have you ever been in a meeting where the leader felt distant or disconnected? You left feeling unsure about what to do or how to apply the information. That's because they lacked empathy—the ability to see and understand their audience. A true leader acknowledges others' perspectives and feelings, using language that makes you feel heard and valued, like "I understand where you're coming from" or "I can imagine how frustrating that must be."

Take a moment to think about a leader you deeply respect. It could be a coach, mentor, or a public figure who has positively influenced you. What makes them so effective? Let's reflect on their communication style. Do they . . .

- **Use Clarity?** Do they communicate in simple, compelling language and stories that everyone can understand?
- **Show Empathy?** Do they demonstrate compassion and understanding, especially during challenging times?
- **Lead with Authenticity?** Do they stay true to their values and openly admit when they're wrong or uncertain?
- **Maintain an Open Presence?** Do they use an engaged, welcoming body language, like making eye contact and nodding, to build trust?
- **Influence Through Writing?** Are their emails, memos, and social media posts clear, informative, and audience-centered?

Your reflections on these questions likely reveal a consistent truth: great leaders communicate in ways that are genuine, inclusive, and empowering. They aren't perfect, but they're committed to growth and adaptability.

This quick exercise only scratches the surface. In reality, our unique communication styles are shaped by countless nuanced behaviors. Ultimately, our ability to make a lasting impact—at work, in our communities, or at home—is built on three core pillars:

1. **Verbal Communication**: Clear messaging, effective feedback, and active listening.
2. **Nonverbal Communication**: Body language, tone, presence, and proximity.
3. **Written Communication**: Everything from persuasive proposals to concise emails and your digital footprint.

Each of these areas influences how we express ourselves and ultimately, how we drive change.

When it comes to amplifying our leadership voice, the options are virtually limitless. This means that everyone can find a communicative style that feels genuine, allowing us to share ideas confidently while fostering a respectful dialogue.

To get started, here are some foundational skills that are essential for sharing ideas and persuading others:

- **Adapt your style for impact**: Tailor your approach to meet your audience where they are. How you pitch a client is worlds apart from a conversation about a difficult topic with an employee. Context always matters.
- **Harness the power of storytelling**: Make your messages memorable and relatable by sharing stories. They are one of the most powerful tools for creating an engaging atmosphere and forging a deeper connection.
- **Integrate technology wisely**: Use digital tools thoughtfully. While some conversations require a face-to-face approach, emails and texts offer valuable flexibility when used appropriately.
- **Reflect on your personal style**: Understand your communication tendencies and biases. This self-awareness is crucial for personal growth and fostering inclusive, respectful interactions.
- **Practice intentional communication**: Be present and actively listen. It's easy for our minds to wander, but effective leadership requires focus. By intentionally engaging, you model behavior that inspires others to do the same.

In this chapter, we'll explore why speaking up can feel difficult, examine the consequences of staying silent, and highlight the tangible benefits of sharing your voice. Get ready to commit to a practice that will lead to success, both professionally and personally.

Remember, every step you take to improve your communication has the power to make a meaningful difference not just for you but also for those around you.

MOST OF US WERE NEVER TAUGHT . . .

Most of us were never taught the critical communication skills we need to succeed. We've mastered our jobs, but few have received the necessary training to advocate for ourselves clearly, assert our ideas constructively, or navigate the crucial conversations that determine our success. This leaves many avoiding the most stressful areas of communication altogether, such as:

- Handling resistance and staying calm in the face of criticism
- Navigating difficult conversations
- Negotiating conflict

Table 1.1 **Data and Trends: Silent Majority Statistics**

While you might feel alone in your hesitation to speak up, the data tells a different story.

- 75% of employees feel that their voices are not heard at work.[1]
- 60% of employees have not spoken up in the past year due to fear of retribution or retaliation.[2]
- 55% believe that their opinions are not valued.[3]
- 51% of employees report feeling unable to share their opinions freely.[4]
- 17.5% of employees report not speaking up at all in the workplace.[5]

These statistics reveal common concerns many employees face about speaking up and remind us that we're not alone in these feelings.

These challenges are compounded by a rapidly changing work landscape. The shift to hybrid and remote work has left many feeling disconnected, as spontaneous feedback and in-person collaboration have diminished. We now face:

- **Less in-person interaction:** Fewer face-to-face moments can lead to feelings of disconnection and isolation.
- **Reduced collaboration:** Virtual settings can make teamwork less seamless, slowing down innovation.
- **Increased uncertainty:** Economic shifts and resource constraints create a stressful environment, where employees may hesitate to voice concerns.

By recognizing these evolving challenges, we can find new ways to foster meaningful communication. This is no longer a soft skill—it's a requirement for success. You can't afford to stay silent (see Table 1.1).

THE SILENT MAJORITY: WHY WE STAY QUIET

We've all been there: a valuable idea dies in a meeting because no one challenges the status quo, or a promising project stalls for a lack of new ideas. This isn't just a corporate cliché; it's the real-world consequence of a widespread problem: employee silence.

You're not alone in feeling this way. Research shows that 85%[6] of employees feel unable to voice their opinions, often believing it's pointless or fearing professional repercussions. This trend is only growing, with 63% of Generation Z employees reporting a lack of confidence in expressing themselves at work.[7] The "silent majority" may be motivated by self-protection, but their silence holds back both their careers and their organizations.

It's time to understand why we stay quiet, and how these barriers prevent us from sharing our valuable insights.

The Fear of Rejection or Criticism

We worry that our ideas will be dismissed or, worse, ridiculed. This fear can be paralyzing, causing us to hold back and miss crucial opportunities to share our expertise. But if communication is how others assess our leadership, staying silent isn't doing us any favors.

The Fear of Being Seen as Confrontational

We often stay quiet out of fear of being labeled aggressive or argumentative. This hesitation is particularly pronounced for women and minorities, who are more likely to face this stereotype when speaking up.[8,9] As a result, many leaders from underrepresented groups must weigh the risk of being labeled against the necessity of contributing, which often leads to silence. This silence often breeds resentment and disconnect, preventing us from addressing issues and finding solutions. Sometimes, a little conflict is exactly what's needed to move forward.

The Fear of Causing Conflict

Some of us avoid speaking up because we're afraid of rocking the boat. While voicing an opinion can lead to disagreements, growth and progress often depend on these conversations. Staying quiet means missing chances to find real solutions.

The Fear of Imposter Syndrome

We hold back because we doubt our ideas or worry that others will judge us. This self-doubt, or imposter syndrome, can be overwhelming, stifling even the most valuable insights. But your voice matters—and you've absolutely earned your place at the table.

These concerns boil down to communication apprehension. While some feel nervous in every situation, most of us find that nerves are mainly triggered by a specific context, like work or public speaking.

OVERCOMING COMMUNICATION APPREHENSION

Fear of speaking up is universal, but it's not the same for everyone. For some, it's public speaking; for others, it's a new or difficult conversation. The truth is, communication apprehension is often situational. As you begin to reflect on your strengths and growth areas, here are three initial strategies to help you get started on taming that apprehension:

- **Practice self-compassion**: Be kind to yourself. Nerves are normal, and they're a sign that you care. With practice, you can learn to channel that adrenaline to sharpen your focus and strengthen your connection with your audience.
- **Focus on the problem, not the people**: Silence often stems from feeling intimidated by others' titles or authority. Instead of focusing on who's in the room, focus your attention on the problem itself. This shifts the conversation from being a daunting interaction to a collaborative effort to solve a shared challenge.
- **Contribute with questions**: Asking the right questions—like *"What challenges might we face?"* or *"How will we measure success?"*—is a great way to assert your leadership voice and guide meaningful conversations. This strategy allows you to contribute and build confidence without feeling like your ideas are being critiqued or your expertise is being questioned. See Table 1.2 for expert advice on speaking up.

While there are many reasons why we may hesitate to share ideas at work, staying silent has staggering consequences:

- **You stunt your own growth**. When you don't contribute, you lose opportunities to refine your ideas and lead conversations.

Table 1.2 Instant Impact: Leadership Takeaway from Public Speaking Expert, Jacqueline Farrington

Conversations with Leaders: Focus on Being Helpful, Not Good	*Focus on being helpful, not "good."* Public speaking expert Jacqueline Farrington shared this insight with me, and it has transformed my leadership voice. Whether I'm presenting at an international conference, to a group of employees, or teaching undergraduates, aiming to be helpful shifts my focus. It calms my nerves and helps me concentrate on delivering value to my audience—rather than obsessing over every perceived mistake. Jacqueline explores this idea and many more tips in Season 4, Episode 4 of *The Communicative Leader* podcast, available on your favorite streaming platform.[10]

- **Your team and company miss out.** Your silence withholds valuable expertise that could drive collective success.
- **You limit your network.** Speaking up is essential for connecting with others and building the relationships that form the foundation of trust.
- **You can be overlooked.** If your capabilities are unknown, you won't be considered for bigger roles and new opportunities.

When individuals stay silent, it also affects the entire organization. This silent majority can stifle innovation, creativity, and adaptability, hampering an organization's ability to respond to challenges and make informed decisions.

These conditions are the perfect breeding ground for groupthink—a phenomenon where people's desire for harmony outweighs a critical evaluation of options. History offers cautionary tales, from the Titanic crew ignoring iceberg warnings to the Stanford Prison Experiment. Ultimately, groupthink is a serious threat to organizational success. Staying open and encouraging diverse perspectives is vital to avoid its pitfalls.

Employee silence is a widespread issue with staggering consequences. When a silent majority of employees withhold their ideas, it leads to disengaged teams, stifled innovation, and stalled progress. This lack of communication can cause conflicts to escalate and ultimately prevent both individuals and organizations from reaching their full potential.

While employee silence carries serious consequences, the good news is that a culture of engagement can drive real growth. For instance, Gallup reports that organizations with high employee engagement are 21% more profitable than those with low engagement.[11] When employees are involved in decision-making, they're more committed, productive, and invested in the organization's success. People want to feel seen and valued, and organizations thrive when they foster environments that encourage open contributions while also giving employees the skills to communicate respectfully and clearly.

Whatever the reason, it's time to break free from silence. Sharing your voice isn't just a personal choice; it's a professional imperative. It opens new doors to growth, innovation, and success—for both you and your organization. Your voice matters. It's time to use it.

THE POWER OF SPEAKING UP: WHY YOUR VOICE MATTERS IN THE WORKPLACE

Have you ever felt your ideas were ignored, your opinions dismissed, or your voice silenced? It's a frustrating feeling that can make you feel like a passive bystander rather than an active contributor. But your voice is essential to your professional success. When you're heard and valued, you feel more confident, credible, and influential. When you stay silent, you risk disengagement and missed opportunities.

Sharing your thoughts allows you to contribute meaningfully by offering unique perspectives and challenging assumptions. When you don't speak up, you miss chances to learn, build relationships, and grow professionally. Leaders who share ideas and ask questions are seen as engaged and influential, and this isn't just an extrovert's game. Contrary to stereotypes, introverts are often excellent listeners and thinkers; they just need space to share their insights, and they can be just as influential.

You don't have to become the loudest voice overnight. Instead, start with small, low-pressure ways to show your engagement. These simple steps will build your confidence and demonstrate your commitment:

- **Practice active listening**: Be fully present in conversations and seek feedback from colleagues. Asking an expert for their recommendations shows you value their input while also demonstrating engagement.
- **Be prepared**: Do your homework before meetings so you can contribute meaningfully and confidently.
- **Remain respectful**: It's okay to disagree. What matters is fostering open, respectful discussions. Valuing different voices ensures that everyone has a chance to be part of the decision-making process, and that's how real progress happens.

As you follow these tips, you'll build a reputation as a thoughtful, engaged, and influential professional. When you're seen as someone who speaks up and listens, your confidence and credibility will grow too (see Table 1.3).

Table 1.3 Actionable Insights: The Power of Observation

One of the most effective ways to start your speaking up journey is to observe others. Why? Because research shows we learn new skills by watching others model behaviors, and it's a low-stakes way to begin.
Notice people around you who confidently speak up—there's a lot to learn from them.
Body language: When nervous about sharing, our gestures can feel awkward. Watching someone who is comfortable—raising a hand, leaning in, or sharing their idea—can give you a helpful example.
Listen to their language: Do they use "I" statements ("I think") or "we" ("We have a great opportunity")? Notice their tone, pacing, and word choice.
Observe how they handle pushback: Many fear confrontation, but seeing how others stay calm, acknowledge differing views, and keep their voice steady can help ease that fear.
Start by watching—it's a powerful way to build confidence and learn what works.

THE CONSEQUENCES OF STAYING SILENT: THE DEVASTATING EFFECTS OF STAYING SILENT IN THE WORKPLACE

Staying silent at work might seem like a way to avoid conflict, but it often fuels negativity and stagnation. The impact is wide-reaching, hindering personal growth, job satisfaction, and overall well-being. What else happens when we hold back our ideas and concerns?

You Stunt Your Growth

Silence means missing chances to learn, share knowledge, and develop new skills. Without contribution, we can also feel stuck and uninspired.

Progress Stalls

Silence stifles innovation. When crucial insights are lost, important initiatives can stall or fail, directly impacting the organization's performance.

You Feel Undervalued

Staying silent sends a message that our opinions don't matter. Over time, this erodes self-esteem, motivation, and purpose. It can lead to presenteeism—being physically at work but mentally checked out.

You Fuel Stress and Burnout

When you can't express yourself or share your concerns, you may internalize them. This can lead to anxiety, frustration, or other struggles that impact your physical health and overall well-being.

It's time to break the silence (Figure 1.1). Sharing your thoughts, ideas, and concerns fosters a culture of openness, collaboration, and growth. While silence might seem easier, it often leads to regret and stagnation.

Your voice isn't just a tool for personal success; it's a professional and ethical duty. Being present, engaged, and committed is essential for your team's success. When you don't speak up, you risk letting your team fail or allowing others to take credit for your ideas.

Take Steve Wozniak and Steve Jobs: Wozniak famously created Apple 1 but stayed quiet about his role only to see Jobs present it as his own, leaving Wozniak feeling betrayed. While most of us won't face that level of betrayal, it underscores the importance of speaking up. Your voice matters. Don't let others take credit for your contributions or let silence become a barrier to success.

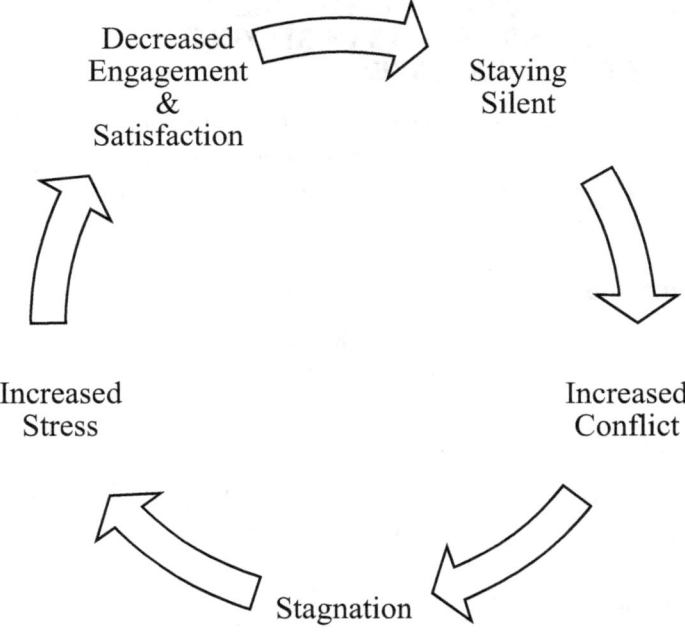

Figure 1.1 The Spiral of Silence illustrates how remaining silent can perpetuate conflict, hinder progress, increase stress, stall career growth, and create a repetitive cycle.

THE BENEFITS OF SPEAKING UP

As a busy professional, you're no stranger to juggling multiple tasks and responsibilities. But in the race to get everything done, don't neglect the power of your voice. When you make it a point to share your thoughts, ideas, and opinions, you unlock a world of benefits that can elevate your career and personal growth (see Figure 1.2).

Boost Your Confidence

Speaking up is a powerful way to build confidence. When you share your expertise, you demonstrate your competence to yourself and your colleagues. This not only increases your sense of self-assurance but also makes you more willing to take on new challenges, which can lead to more opportunities or new projects.

Establish Credibility

Every time you speak up, you establish yourself as an expert in your field. Your colleagues will begin to trust your opinions and value your input, earning you

THE DANGER OF SILENCE

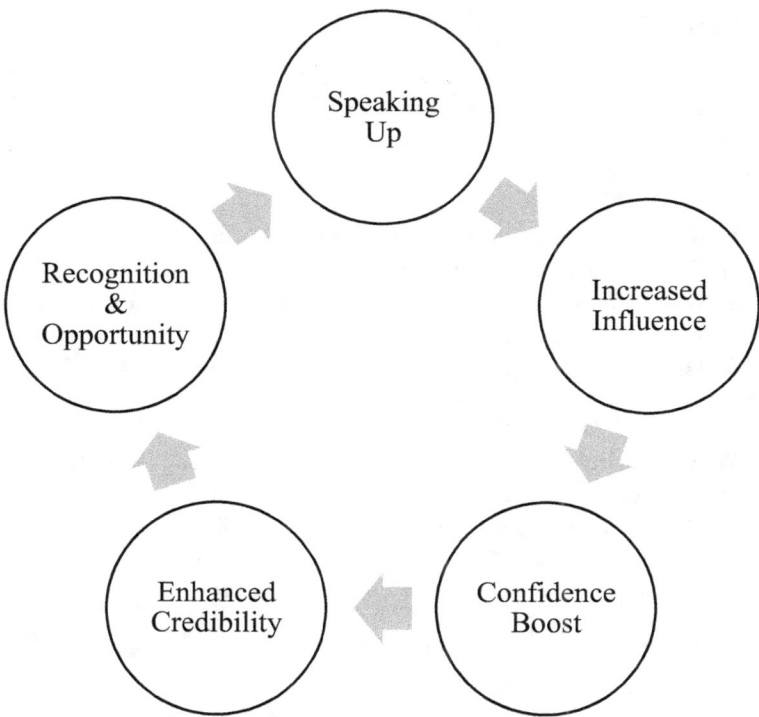

Figure 1.2 The Power of your Leadership Voice: This cycle demonstrates how speaking up can boost influence, build confidence, enhance credibility, and lead to greater recognition and opportunities.

increased credibility and respect. This can open doors to new possibilities, from taking on leadership roles to being approached for mentorship or guidance.

Gain Influence

By sharing your ideas, you gain a greater sense of control and influence over your work. Your thoughts are more likely be considered, allowing you to drive results and make a meaningful impact. This leads to a sense of empowerment and ownership over your professional reputation.

Foster Better Communication

When you speak up, you're not just helping yourself, you're helping your team. When everyone feels heard and valued, teamwork becomes more cohesive and productive. This creates a more positive and supportive work environment, where everyone feels motivated to succeed.

SPEAKING UP QUIZ

As a professional, confidently speaking up is key to leadership and collaboration. To gauge your comfort level, try this quick five-question quiz. It offers insight into your communication strengths and areas for growth. Let's see where you stand!

1. **When you have an idea or concern, do you:**
   a) Share it immediately with your colleagues or supervisor
   b) Write it down and send it to someone, but don't mention it out loud
   c) Keep it to yourself, thinking "it's not important" or "they won't listen"
   d) Talk to a trusted friend or mentor outside of work about it

   Score: a) 3 points, b) 2 points, c) 1 point, d) 0 points

2. **When a colleague presents an idea that you disagree with, do you:**
   a) Speak up and express your concerns respectfully
   b) Listen politely and nod along, but don't contribute
   c) Stay silent, thinking "it's not worth rocking the boat"
   d) Politely disagree and offer an alternative solution

   Score: a) 3 points, b) 2 points, c) 1 point, d) 3 points

3. **In meetings, do you:**
   a) Actively participate and share your thoughts
   b) Contribute occasionally, but only when you're sure your idea is well-received
   c) Listen and take notes, but rarely speak up
   d) Only speak up when directly asked for input

   Score: a) 3 points, b) 2 points, c) 1 point, d) 0 points

4. **When faced with a difficult or uncomfortable situation at work, do you:**
   a) Speak up assertively and advocate for yourself or others
   b) Seek guidance from a supervisor or HR
   c) Try to avoid the situation or hope it resolves itself
   d) Feel anxious or stressed and struggle to find the right words

   Score: a) 3 points, b) 2 points, c) 1 point, d) 0 points

5. **How do you feel about sharing constructive feedback with colleagues or supervisors?**
   a) Comfortable giving and receiving feedback to improve processes and relationships
   b) Hesitant to give feedback, but willing to accept it

c) Prefer not to give feedback, fearing it might seem critical
d) Feel anxious or uncomfortable giving or receiving feedback

Score: a) 3 points, b) 2 points, c) 1 point, d) 0 points

Add Up Your Scores
- **0–4 points:** You're just starting out, and that's fantastic! Every small step you take is building your confidence. Keep going, you're on your way!
- **5–9 points:** You're making great progress! You're comfortable enough to speak up, and with a bit more practice, you'll be even more confident.
- **10–15 points:** You're a natural! Your voice is strong, and you're already making a positive impact. Keep shining; you're inspiring others to do the same!

READY TO PUT THIS INTO PRACTICE?

Amplify Your Leadership Voice Further

After completing the quiz, visit TheCommunicativeLeader.com for detailed insights into your scores and guidance for your next steps in your leadership journey.

KEY TAKEAWAYS

1. **You're in Good Company**: You're not alone in feeling apprehensive about speaking up. Many professionals—even seasoned leaders—struggle with communication apprehension. While this fact won't magically tame your nerves, it can offer comfort in knowing that these feelings are shared. Consider sharing your hesitations with your team; that simple step can break the ice and foster camaraderie.
2. **Leadership Is All About Communication**: Dazzling personality alone does not make a great leader. Neither does having the loudest or most dominate voice. Your ability to communicate is what truly shapes how others perceive your leadership potential. Are you inspiring your team? Breaking down complex ideas into manageable bites? Engaging them in meaningful conversations? Your communication skills are the secret weapon to unlocking your leadership potential!
3. **Silence Has Consequences**: Staying silent carries significant professional consequences. When employees withhold their ideas, they risk feeling undervalued and frustrated, which can erode their confidence and impact their well-being. Additionally, teams miss out on valuable insights, and organizations risk stagnation and high turnover.

4. **Communication Is a Muscle—Flex It!** Communication isn't some elusive skill; it's a muscle that gets stronger with practice. Giving and receiving feedback provide real-time insights, helping you adapt on the spot. Embrace this journey of improvement. Each step will pay off, both personally and professionally. Challenge yourself to try a new communication technique each week—whether it's active listening, reframing a question, or offering constructive feedback. Before you know it, you'll see progress across the board!

NOTES

1 Gallup. (2025). State of the American workplace: Understanding employees, informing leaders. *Gallup.com*.
2 Ethics & Compliance Initiative (ECI). (2020). *The ECI national business ethics survey*. https://www.ethics.org
3 Gallup. (2018). *State of the American workplace*. https://www.gallup.com/workplace/238085/state-american-workplace-report-2018.aspx
4 ISS. (2023). *Belonging in the workplace report*. https://www.issworld.com/en/news/2023/07/06/public-opinion-survey-di
5 Burris, E., McCune, E., & Klinghoffer, D. (2020, November 17). When employees speak up, companies win. *MIT Sloan Management Review*. https://sloanreview.mit.edu/article/when-employees-speak-up-companies-win/#:~:text=We%20found%20that%20relatively%20few,not%20speak%20up%20at%20all
6 Chou, S. Y., & Chang, T. (2020). Employee silence and silence antecedents: A theoretical classification. *International Journal of Business Communication*, 57(3), 401–426. https://doi.org/10.1177/2329488417703301
7 Mental Health America. (2024, October 10). *MHA releases 2024 mind the workplace report, GenZ and Millennials report the poorest work health scores*. https://mhanational.org/news/mha-releases-2024-mind-the-workplace-report-genz-and-millennials-report-the-poorerest-work-health-scores/
8 Motro, D., Evans, J. B., Ellis, A. P. J., & Benson, L. (2022, January 31). The "angry Black woman" stereotype at work. *Harvard Business Review*. https://hbr.org/2022/01/the-angry-black-woman-stereotype-at-work
9 Heilman, M. E., Caleo, S., & Manzi, F. (2024). Women at work: Pathways from gender stereotypes to gender bias and discrimination. *Annual Review of Organizational Psychology and Organizational Behavior*, 11, 165–192. https://doi.org/10.1146/annurev-orgpsych-110721-034105
10 Omilion-Hodges, L. (Host). (2024, January 29). Leadership, change, and communication: A conversation with CEO and former TEDx talk coach Jacqueline Farrington [Audio podcast episode]. *The Communicative Leader Podcast*. https://www.thecommunicativeleader.com/podcast/episode/7eff5c27/leadership-change-and-communication-a-conversation-with-ceo-and-former-tedx-talk-coach-jacqueline-farrington
11 Harter, J. (2018, August 26). Employee engagement on the rise in the U.S. *Gallup*. https://news.gallup.com/poll/241649/employee-engagement-rise.aspx

Chapter 2

Discover Your Leadership Voice

Assess, Understand, and Grow

Level 1.
Discover Your
Leadership Voice

Congratulations on starting the process of discovering the power of your leadership voice. Now, the next step is to gain clarity on where you are today. In this chapter, you will reflect on your strengths, identify areas for growth, and establish a solid foundation for your ongoing leadership development. This honest assessment is designed to help you make purposeful progress on your journey of amplifying your leadership voice.

LEADERSHIP IS COMMUNICATION, AND COMMUNICATION IS LEADERSHIP

The saying, "It's not what you say, but how you say it", is a cornerstone of effective leadership. Your communication skills are the true measure of your leadership. While your results matter, effective communication is what makes them sustainable.

As a manager, supervisor, or director, you're in the spotlight. How you communicate shapes your team's perception of you, directly influencing their engagement and response. Leadership is about influence. If a leader can't clearly articulate a vision, build trust, or actively listen, their time in the role will likely be short-lived. Leaders are responsible for advocating for their teams, and if they can't express their needs effectively, everyone's success is jeopardized.

The bottom line is that communication is the foundation of how your leadership is perceived. As we delve deeper, I'll show you how to effectively harness your communication skills to exert influence in any context. Remember, communication isn't just a measure of leadership; it's also your most powerful tool.

AMPLIFYING YOUR LEADERSHIP VOICE

The best part? You don't need fancy tech or years of training—just intention and reflection.

This chapter uncovers your unique communication strengths and growth areas. Mastering core skills like active listening, public speaking, and conflict resolution elevates your leadership and ensures that your messages truly resonate. By the end, you'll have practical tools to make sure that others not only hear you but also genuinely engage with what you have to say.

IDENTIFYING YOUR NATURAL COMMUNICATION STYLE

As you begin this assessment (Table 2.1), you're taking a vital step toward becoming a more confident, authentic leader. Understanding your unique communication style is the foundation for amplifying your voice and connecting more genuinely with others.

This assessment will guide you through a comprehensive exploration of your communication tendencies, from your comfort with different group sizes to your approach to conflict, negotiation, and nonverbal expression. By examining your emotional intelligence, assertiveness, and adaptability, you can lean into your strengths and identify key areas for growth (see Figure 2.1 for elements of your natural communication style).

Table 2.1 Identifying Your Natural Communication Style Assessment

Instructions: Rate each statement using the following scale:

1—Strongly Disagree: You feel the opposite of what the statement says.

2—Disagree: You mostly do not agree with the statement.

3—Neutral: You neither agree nor disagree; you might feel ambivalent about it.

4—Agree: You mostly agree with the statement.

5—Strongly Agree: You wholeheartedly relate to the statement.

1: Introversion/Ambivert/Extraversion:

1. I feel energized after spending time with a small group of friends or colleagues.
2. I prefer deep conversations with one or two people over a casual chat with a larger group.
3. I often find group settings overwhelming or draining.
4. I enjoy meeting new people and engaging in discussions with strangers.
5. I am comfortable sharing my thoughts publicly in a group setting.

(Continued)

Table 2.1 Continued

2: Conflict Negotiation
6. When faced with conflict, I work to find a solution that meets everyone's needs.
7. When faced with conflict, I prefer to address it in an open and respectful manner.
8. I often find myself avoiding those I am in conflict with instead of engaging with them.
9. I believe it is essential to consider others' feelings during a disagreement.
10. I tend to keep my true feelings to myself to maintain harmony in a conversation.

3: Interaction Preferences:
11. I thrive in one-on-one conversations and prefer them over larger group discussions.
12. I often feel like my ideas are lost in large group discussions.
13. I enjoy brainstorming with a small team and feel comfortable contributing to the discussion.
14. In a large group setting, I usually prefer to listen rather than speak.
15. I find it easier to build rapport and connect with individuals rather than with audiences.

4: Emotional Intelligence:
16. I can easily recognize my emotions and how they affect my thoughts and behavior.
17. I am able to empathize with others' emotions and perspectives.
18. I often take time to reflect on how my words will impact the feelings of others before I speak.
19. I feel comfortable discussing emotional topics with others.
20. I can manage my emotions effectively, even in stressful situations.

Reminder: Rate each statement using the following scale:
1—Strongly Disagree: You feel the opposite of what the statement says.
2—Disagree: You mostly do not agree with the statement.
3—Neutral: You neither agree nor disagree; you might feel ambivalent about it.
4—Agree: You mostly agree with the statement.
5—Strongly Agree: You wholeheartedly relate to the statement.

5: Assertiveness:
21. I feel comfortable saying "no" to requests that I cannot accommodate.
22. I express my needs and wants clearly in conversations.
23. I think it is important to assert my opinions even when they differ from the majority.
24. I frequently seek feedback from others to validate my viewpoints.
25. I feel confident advocating for myself in situations where I feel my rights are being challenged.

(Continued)

Table 2.1 Continued

6: Adaptability:

26. I adjust my communication style based on the audience or individual I am interacting with.
27. When new information arises, I am willing to change my perspective or approach.
28. I am comfortable with ambiguity and can navigate conversations without a clear direction.
29. I seek to understand differing viewpoints rather than consistently defending my own.
30. I notice when others are uncomfortable during a conversation and try to address it.

7: Active Listening:

31. I make a conscious effort to fully concentrate on what others are saying during conversations.
32. I often paraphrase or summarize what others have said to ensure I understand their message.
33. I avoid interrupting others while they are speaking.
34. I ask clarifying questions to engage with the speaker and show interest.
35. I can recall details from past conversations with people, indicating that I listened attentively.

8: Other-Oriented Focus:

36. I actively consider others' viewpoints before sharing my own opinions.
37. I often adjust my communication approach based on how the other person is feeling.
38. I strive to create a comfortable environment for others to express themselves.
39. I prioritize team goals and collaboration over individual recognition in group settings.
40. I feel a strong sense of responsibility to ensure that others feel heard in conversations.

Reminder: Rate each statement using the following scale:

1—Strongly Disagree: You feel the opposite of what the statement says.

2—Disagree: You mostly do not agree with the statement.

3—Neutral: You neither agree nor disagree; you might feel ambivalent about it.

4—Agree: You mostly agree with the statement.

5—Strongly Agree: You wholeheartedly relate to the statement.

(Continued)

DISCOVER YOUR LEADERSHIP VOICE

Table 2.1 Continued

9: Nonverbal Communication:
- 41. I am aware of how my body language impacts my communication with others.
- 42. I use eye contact to show engagement or interest during conversations.
- 43. I can interpret others' nonverbal signals to gauge their feelings or attitudes.
- 44. I often mirror the body language of the person I'm talking to in order to build rapport.
- 45. I adjust my tone to match the emotional context of conversations.

10: Feedback Giving and Receiving:
- 46. I find it easy to provide constructive feedback to others.
- 47. I actively seek feedback on my performance and communication from peers.
- 48. I approach giving feedback with sensitivity to others' feelings.
- 49. I view constructive criticism as an opportunity for growth rather than a personal attack.
- 50. I feel comfortable receiving feedback without becoming defensive or upset.

Figure 2.1 This diagram highlights key aspects of your natural leadership communication style, including areas like conflict negotiation, emotional intelligence, assertiveness, and active listening—revealing strengths and opportunities for growth.

Learn More About Your Natural Communication Style

These questions are designed to help you better understand your communication tendencies to support your personal growth. While the previous survey provides a broad view, these open-ended questions can offer deeper, more personal insight. You are encouraged to answer thoughtfully, focusing on the items most relevant to you.

1. **When are you most comfortable speaking up?** Describe a recent situation where you felt at ease sharing your thoughts. What was the context, and what factors contributed to your comfort?
2. **How do you handle conflict?** Provide a specific example of how you typically approach disagreements or conflicts.
3. **When have you adapted your style?** Think of a time when you had to change your communication style for a specific person or situation. What did you change, and why was it effective?
4. **What's your biggest communication challenge?** Reflect on a time you struggled to communicate an idea. What contributed to that difficulty, and what changes can you make for future situations?
5. **How do you make others feel heard?** Describe a situation where you successfully helped someone feel supported. What strategies did you use?

Understanding Your Assessment Score

Now, let's take a moment to understand how to interpret your scores. This will help you gain insights and identify areas for growth. For each statement in the assessment, you rated yourself on a scale from 1 to 5, where:

1 *Strongly Disagree:* You feel the opposite of what the statement says.
2 *Disagree*: You mostly do not agree with the statement.
3 *Neutral*: You neither agree nor disagree; you might feel ambivalent about it.
4 *Agree*: You mostly agree with the statement.
5 *Strongly Agree*: You wholeheartedly relate to the statement.

Now that you've completed the assessment, you will have a series of scores across different categories. Here's how to interpret them:

1. **Introversion/Ambivert/Extraversion:**
   - **What to look for**: Individual item scores of 4 or 5 suggest an extroverted tendency, where you likely thrive in social environments. Scores of 2 or 3 indicate an ambivert tendency, meaning you find balance in both social and solitary settings. Scores of mostly 1 and 2 suggest

introverted tendencies, indicating a preference for smaller, more intimate interactions.
- **Your strength**: Recognizing your natural energy sources, such as a large group of people or smaller-scale interactions, can help you choose environments that enhance your comfort and effectiveness.
- **Leadership voice growth opportunity**: If your score on extroversion is lower, try engaging in larger group settings occasionally to build confidence and expand your network—perhaps by aiming to speak up at least once during each team meeting. If you scored higher on extroversion, take a moment to check in with your active listening. Use your social strengths to help include and support those who may be more reserved.

2. **Conflict Negotiation:**
   - **What to look for**: Higher scores on items addressing a shared solution (e.g., statements 6, 7, and 9) suggest a more collaborative conflict negotiation style, while higher scores on avoidant items (8, 10) indicate a tendency to shy away from conflict or tension.
   - **Your strength**: Understanding your conflict style can help you navigate tough conversations with respect. While avoiding conflict might feel easier, collaboration is healthier for relationships and long-term work harmony.
   - **Leadership voice growth opportunity**: If you lean towards an avoidant style, you may consider how to embrace a more collaborative approach. Focusing on shared goals can help to diffuse tension, paving the path for joint problem-solving.

3. **Interaction Preferences:**
   - **What to look for**: Higher scores in smaller group settings (11, 13, and 15) and discomfort in larger groups (12, 14) highlight your preference for smaller interpersonal interaction compared to larger group settings. Lower scores of 1 and 2 suggest that you likely prefer and thrive with larger audiences.
   - **Your strength**: This awareness helps you structure your networking and brainstorming sessions in ways that maximize your comfort and natural strengths.
   - **Leadership voice growth opportunity**: If larger groups are challenging for you, consider developing strategies for contributing to these environments, such as preparing points in advance or suggesting tasks are completed in smaller groups and then shared with the whole team.

4. **Emotional Intelligence:**
   - **What to look for**: Higher scores on all items on this scale indicate well-developed emotional intelligence.

- **Your strength**: This skill set enhances your relationships and communication by allowing you to connect authentically with others.
- **Leadership voice growth opportunity**: If you scored lower in certain emotional intelligence areas, take time to reflect on those items. Maybe you're a skilled listener but find sharing your own experiences more challenging. That is okay! The goal is to lean into your strengths while taking small but meaningful steps to grow. For example, acknowledging when you're unsure about a decision or asking for clarification shows honesty and can build trust and openness.

5. **Assertiveness:**
    - **What to look for**: Higher average scores on direct expression (21, 22, 23, and 25) suggest that you excel at asserting your opinions.
    - **Your strength**: Being aware of your assertiveness helps you confidently express your needs and opinions while also honoring others' perspectives.
    - **Leadership voice growth opportunity**: If assertiveness feels challenging, practice setting boundaries in lower-stakes situations to build confidence for more challenging scenarios. For example, try saying "no" when your schedule is full. If a firm "no" feels just out of reach, you might say: *"I'd love to, but I'm currently working on X,Y, and Z. Is there someone else on the team that has capacity?"*

6. **Adaptability:**
    - **What to look for**: Higher scores, think 4s and 5s, reveal a more adaptable communication approach.
    - **Your strength**: Adaptability allows you to effectively navigate diverse conversations and changing contexts. Adaptability is also a great way to build trusting relationships because you meet people where they are instead of expecting them to bend to your preferred style.
    - **Leadership voice growth opportunity**: Make a habit of exploring new ideas and perspectives, practicing flexibility in both your thinking and actions. A simple way to develop this skill is by observing others. For example, if you have a client who prefers email over calls, try adapting to their communication style. Even if you usually prefer phone calls, meeting your client where they are can foster a more productive and trusting relationship over time.

7. **Active Listening:**
    - **What to look for**: Scores of 4 and 5 across items show a tendency to engage deeply with others and confirm understanding through paraphrasing and clarifying questions.
    - **Your strength**: Strong active listening skills foster trust and collaboration in your interactions. Bonus: it also makes others feel more psychologically safe![1]

- **Leadership voice growth opportunity**: If your listening skills could use a boost, try simple techniques like summarizing what you've heard before responding. This small step can make a big difference in your engagement. We'll explore more active listening best practices later in this chapter.

8. **Other-Oriented Focus:**
    - **What to look for**: Higher scores on considerations of others' feelings (36, 37, 40) suggest a strong other-oriented focus.
    - **Your strength**: This focus enhances teamwork and rapport-building by making others feel heard and valued.
    - **Leadership voice growth opportunity**: If considering others' perspectives is challenging, make a conscious effort to seek out diverse viewpoints and express appreciation for them. Valuing different insights from clients and stakeholders can lead to better outcomes, as it helps us leverage unique experiences to find innovative solutions that meet everyone's needs.

9. **Nonverbal Communication:**
    - **What to look for**: Higher scores on these items indicate that you are aware of both your own nonverbal communication and others'.
    - **Your strength**: Being attuned to nonverbal signals can bridge gaps in understanding and create deeper connections.
    - **Leadership voice growth opportunity**: If nonverbal cues are an area for growth, practice becoming more aware of your own body language and try different expressions to strengthen your communication. Notice yourself tuning out in meetings? Check your posture. I bet you're not leaning in or nodding. Often when we disengage, we hunch or divert our gaze to a screen or agenda. You might not be saying, "*I'm not paying attention,*" but your body is sending that message.

10. **Feedback Giving and Receiving:**
    - **What to look for**: Higher scores on giving constructive feedback (46, 48) suggest an ability to navigate feedback interactions positively. Scores of 4 and 5 on receiving feedback items (47, 49, 50) reveal that you actively seek feedback, whereas lower scores on these items may indicate that this is a growth area.
    - **Your strength**: Comfort with feedback promotes personal and professional growth, both for yourself and for others.
    - **Leadership voice growth opportunity**: If feedback conversations feel challenging, try role-playing these scenarios with a trusted colleague or friend to build confidence. Understanding the grace it takes to accept feedback can also guide how you deliver it in thoughtful, other-oriented ways. For additional insights, check out Season 3, Episode 5 of The

Communicative Leader podcast, where Executive Coach Aneace Haddad shares valuable perspectives on feedback, leadership, and mindfulness.[2]

APPLYING YOUR COMMUNICATION INSIGHT

The journey of cultivating your leadership voice is ongoing. Embrace your unique communication strengths and let them guide you toward becoming an even more impactful leader! Take a moment to reflect on the following key insights:

- **Leverage your strengths:** Recognize your natural strengths and consider how to apply them across different communication settings. For example, active listeners often excel at mediating conflict.
- **Spot your patterns:** Identify emotional triggers or recurring tendencies that reveal your style, such as being assertive, reserved, expressive, or analytical.
- **Acknowledge growth areas**: Be honest about where you can improve; acknowledging these areas is the first step toward meaningful growth.
- **Set an achievable goal:** Commit to a focused, measurable goal, such as sharing your opinion at least once a week with colleagues.
- **Practice and reflect:** Commit to ongoing practice and regular reflection. Revisit your responses over time to track your progress and celebrate your leadership development!

> **READY TO PUT THIS INTO PRACTICE?**
>
> **Amplify Your Leadership Voice Further**
>
> For a deeper, personalized reflection on your natural leadership communication strengths, explore the Amplifying Your Leadership Voice: Leadership Blueprint available at TheCommunicativeLeader.com.

IDENTIFY AND ADAPT: RECOGNIZING AND TAILORING YOUR COMMUNICATION TO MEET OTHERS' STYLES

A common theme in many of these communication tendencies is an other-oriented approach (see Table 2.2). These skills are interconnected and mutually reinforcing, focusing on how we can genuinely connect with, understand, and support others. When we communicate in ways that consider both our needs and those of others, we foster more effective interactions and stronger relationships, leading to better outcomes for everyone.

This is where communication accommodation theory (CAT)[3] comes in. CAT is a valuable tool for enhancing leadership communication and building strong

Table 2.2 Actionable Insights: Learning from Others

Just as your communication strengths are different from mine, popular leaders' communication styles vary too. This helps us to see that there is no one "right" way to use our communication to lead.
Former U.S. President, Barack Obama—Inclusive language, Storytelling, and Pacing. Obama's speeches emphasized unity and collective action by integrating "we" and "us" to create shared purpose. He also incorporated personal anecdotes and stories that made complex issues relatable.
Former New Zealand Prime Minister, Jacina Ardern—Authenticity, Empathy, and Digital Engagement. Ardern was lauded for her leadership during the 2020 global pandemic, specifically for her down-to-earth communication, which includes sharing her own feelings and connecting with the experiences of others. Ardern is also known for being active on social media to communicate directly to the public, making her accessible and relatable.
Television Host and Comedian, Jimmy Kimmel—Humor, Vulnerability, and Emotional Intelligence. Kimmel may seem like a surprising choice, but he leads by masterfully using humor, vulnerability, and emotional intelligence. Kimmel shares his personal experiences, is not afraid to show emotion, and expertly adjusts his communication style to connect with guests and his audience.

team dynamics. By understanding and applying its principles, you can tailor your style to better meet the diverse needs of your team and clients. This flexibility deepens relationships, boosts collaboration, and increases motivation.

KEY PRINCIPLES OF COMMUNICATION ACCOMMODATION THEORY

Principle 1: Active Listening

Effective leadership begins with the ability to actively listen. This means giving your full attention to others to truly understand their perspective.

Pay Attention to Verbal and Nonverbal Cues

- **Tone of voice**: Is it calm and steady or raised and shaky? Rapid speech may indicate anxiousness or excitement, while slower speech can suggest reflection or sadness.
- **Word choice**: Are they using positive language indicating agreement and enthusiasm or does their language signal dissatisfaction, stress, or disagreement?
- **Hesitations and fillers**: Frequent "ums" and "ahs" may suggest uncertainty or discomfort with a topic, and vocal fillers such as "like" or "you know" can reveal nervousness. However, vocal fillers can be a sign that someone feels comfortable with you and therefore takes a more relaxed approach. Staying present while listening helps you to recognize these cues.

Make Eye Contact and Give Validation

- **Eye contact**: Committing to eye contact helps to signal engagement and can quickly build rapport and goodwill.
- **Nonverbal cues**: Demonstrate active listening through your body language—nod your head, lean slightly forward, and keep your arms uncrossed to show openness and attentiveness. My introverted friends, this is a great way to show you're engaged without having to vocalize it.

Ask Questions, Paraphrase, and Summarize

- **Avoid close-ended questions**: Questions that can be answered with a simple "yes" or "no" shut down a conversation. If that's not your goal, stick with an open-ended question, one that requires a more substantive response.
- **Paraphrase and summarize**: Repeat back what you've heard in your own words to illustrate active listening. This can be as simple as saying "*What I hear is . . .*" This helps to clarify understanding *and* this can also help to prevent miscommunications or misunderstandings.
- **Avoid interruptions**: This one will be tough, especially if you were raised in a family that shows their love by talking loudly and at the same time. While it may feel just about impossible, it is important to allow the speaker to finish their thoughts. Resisting the urge to interrupt shows respect and reinforces your commitment to listening.

Active Listening Example: In a team meeting, a peer discusses a challenging project. As an engaged colleague, you can demonstrate active listening by maintaining eye contact and using nonverbal cues like nodding. When there is a natural pause in the conversation, you can summarize their points by saying, "*What I hear you saying is . . .*" This not only shows that you value their contributions to the team, but it also fosters trust and encourages open dialogue.

Principle 2: Flexibility in Style

An effective leader adapts their style to meet the needs of their audience. This is the core of an other-oriented approach—the ability to be flexible and meet others where they are.

Be Willing to Flex

Ask yourself, "What does this situation call for?" You also want to reflect on your audience and their needs. When you reflect on the goals of the situation as well as the questions posed above, you will likely lean into one or more of the following styles:

- **Professional or casual**: While it's important to maintain a professional tone during formal requests or when delivering difficult news, many workplace interactions allow for a more casual approach. The key is to understand your audience and context, knowing when to shift from a formal presentation to a casual, collaborative meeting.
- **Empathy and warmth**: In sensitive conversations, such as those involving personal issues or conflict, adopting a warm and empathetic tone can demonstrate understanding and provide reassurance. This can be conveyed by saying *"I'm so sorry to hear you're going through that; how can I help you to find a solution?"* during a sensitive conversation.
- **Clear and direct**: There are times when you need to convey important information, like the consequences of a policy violation. This does not mean raising your voice, but rather using strong, declarative sentences such as *"This behavior will not be tolerated according to Section C of the Employee Handbook. The next steps are . . ."* This approach ensures that your message is clear and understood while avoiding blame or shame.

Positive Body Language and Humor Are Your Friends

- **Tailored language**: Adjust your word choice to connect with your audience. In specialized conversations with experts, jargon might be appropriate, but in broader settings, accessible language helps ensure understanding. For example, how I speak with peers at conferences differs from my communication in a corporate consulting environment or with students. Being mindful of your audience allows your message to land more effectively.
- **Use relatable examples**: When addressing complex ideas, incorporate familiar analogies or references. These can come from popular culture, everyday workplace challenges, or family dynamics. For example, I often draw references from movies, sports, and music when working with employees and students, which helps bridge understanding and makes ideas resonate more effectively.

Flexibility Example: During a team debrief, if you notice tension whenever the project deadline is discussed, instead of diving straight into serious talk, consider starting with a lighthearted comment about how stressful deadlines can be. Sharing a personal story or recalling a time you faced a similar challenge can help ease tension and create a space where everyone feels safe and willing to share. Small shifts like this can transform the tone and foster a more productive, connected conversation.

Principle 3: Solicit Feedback

To truly lead with influence, you must know whether your message is being received as intended. Regularly seeking feedback is a critical skill for building trust and staying informed.

- **Implement regular check-ins**: Regular individual meetings are a manager's best tool for building rapport and staying informed about projects and employee progress. They don't need to be long—20 to 30 minutes is plenty—and can be scheduled weekly, monthly, or quarterly based on your needs. Use this time to genuinely ask how your team members are doing and practice active listening. It's also an ideal opportunity to set up recurring feedback sessions, inviting employees to share their thoughts and ideas.
- **Foster open dialogue:** Incorporate opportunities for feedback into your team gatherings. Use open-ended questions like "What do you think about our current communication approach?" or "How can we improve our communication?"
- **Empower your team:** Empower your team by including them in decisions about how communication is handled. This fosters ownership and invites valuable ideas.

Soliciting Feedback Example: During a team meeting, after discussing project updates, you might invite feedback by saying, "I'd love to hear your thoughts on how we communicate as a team. What's working well? What can we improve? Let's take 5 minutes for an informal check-in and then discuss any insights that come up." This simple project fosters an environment ripe for sharing and discussion.

Figure 2.2 offers practical strategies to help you put the principles of Communication Accommodation Theory into action. While adopting an other-oriented approach requires effort, the return on investment is significant. The following strategies will help you implement these principles and unlock the related benefits.

Having explored the key tips and benefits of Communication Accommodation Theory, it's clear how powerful adapting our communication style can be for building stronger connections. By aligning how we speak and express ourselves, we can reduce misunderstandings, bridge social gaps, and strengthen relationships both at work and in our personal lives.

As we transition to the next part of this chapter, let's pause to reinforce a critical point: while assessing your leadership voice is important, laying a solid foundation and strengthening your existing skills are essential. This ensures that as we work to amplify your leadership throughout the book, those core skills are well established.

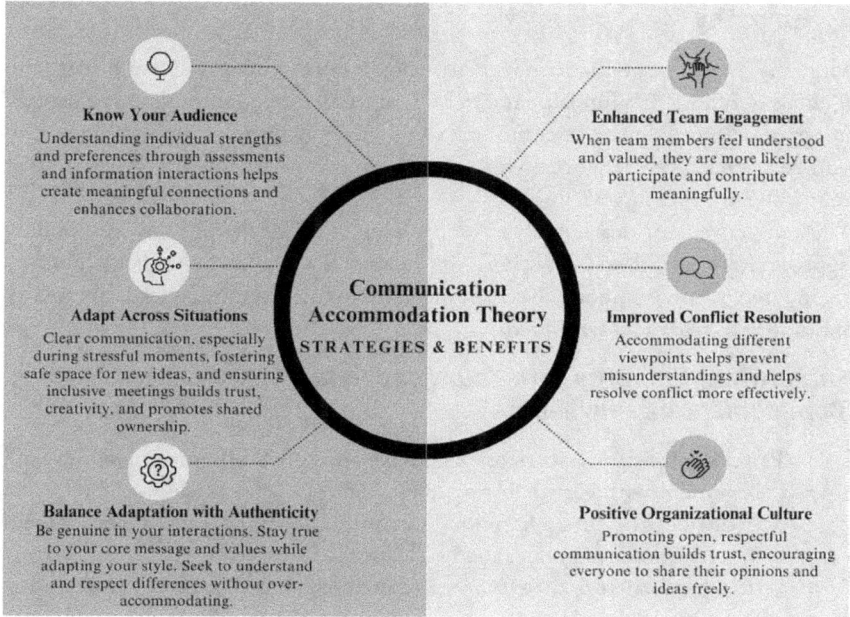

Figure 2.2 This graphic presents strategies from Communication Accommodation Theory alongside their benefits, showing how adapting communication fosters engagement, understanding, and positive team outcomes.

It's time to roll up our sleeves and explore five foundational communication skills essential for effective leadership. I've included practical tips and exercises to help you sharpen these skills, so when you step into your leadership role, you're not just heard—you're truly understood.

FOUNDATIONAL COMMUNICATION SKILLS

Great leaders have a secret weapon: foundational communication skills. These aren't just "soft skills"; they're essential tools for connecting with others and ensuring that your voice is heard. In this section, we'll explore five powerhouse skills: empathy, clarity and conciseness, successful conflict negotiation, giving constructive feedback, and public speaking. As you revisit your communication style assessment, you may discover that these skills either confirm your strengths or point to new opportunities for growth. Embracing these skills will supercharge your leadership voice and make you more poised and impactful.

1. Empathy

Empathy is the bridge that connects us, allowing us to understand and share the feelings of others. It's fundamental to building authentic relationships and fostering trust within any team or community. When you communicate with empathy, you're not just hearing words; you're tuning into emotions and perspectives that may differ from your own.

At its core, empathy involves recognizing, understanding, and responding appropriately to others' emotions. It combines a cognitive understanding—seeing things from someone else's perspective—with an emotional connection—the ability to truly feel with them.

Integrating Empathy Into Your Leadership Communication Playbook

- **Practice active listening** by giving your full attention and showing engagement with verbal acknowledgement like, "*I hear you.*"
- **Validate emotions** without judgment. For example, say, "*It's understandable to feel frustrated in this situation.*"
- **Ask open-ended questions** to encourage sharing. Try, "*How are you coping with this?*" or "*What do you need from me right now?*"
- **Share your perspective** when appropriate, relating a similar experience or expressing understanding by saying, "*I've felt that way before too.*"

Empathy in Practice

Imagine a tough conversation with a colleague about a recent change. Approach it with empathy by actively listening and acknowledging their emotions. You could say, "*I understand this change has been challenging. Let's discuss how we can make this transition smoother.*" This approach aligns with Communication Accommodation Theory, as you're adjusting your style to match their emotional needs, which deepens your connection and enhances your persuasiveness.

2. Clarity and Conciseness

Clarity and conciseness are your trusty sidekicks in effective communication. When you organize your thoughts and express them simply, your message shines instead of getting lost in jargon or unnecessary details.

Clarity means presenting ideas in a way that is easily understood, while conciseness involves expressing your messaging succinctly without sacrificing meaning.

Integrating Clarity and Conciseness Into Your Leadership Communication Playbook

- **Plan your message**: Before you speak or write, identify your main idea. Ask yourself, "What is the key point I want to share?"

- **Simplify your language**: Use plain, direct language instead of jargon whenever possible.
- **Organize your thoughts**: Present information logically. Start with your main idea and then add supporting details. Remember, you have to lay the foundation before you can build the house.
- **Limit unnecessary details**: Focus on what truly matters; cut out fluff that might distract your audience.
- **Use visuals or examples**: Incorporate visuals, metaphors, or concrete examples to clarify complex ideas.

Clarity and Conciseness in Practice

When preparing for a presentation or team update, aim to distill your message to its essentials. Instead of saying, *"We are currently in the process of evaluating various options to improve our workflow, which involves considering multiple factors and gathering input from different departments,"* try, *"We're evaluating options to improve our workflow, considering input from all departments."* This respects your audience's time and makes your message more impactful.

Remember, tailoring your message to your audience's level of understanding, whether they're experts or newcomers, helps ensure clarity. Being concise not only respects their time but also increases the chances your message will be understood and remembered.

3. Successful Conflict Negotiation

Conflict may seem intimidating, but it's a powerful opportunity for growth, understanding, and collaboration. Instead of viewing disagreements as setbacks, try to see them as signals that others are invested. When people share differing opinions, it shows they care deeply and want to contribute—an essential ingredient for effective teams.

Think of conflict negotiation as a dance: an exchange where each person shares their thoughts, feelings, and ideas. It's about engaging in open, respectful dialogue to address differences, find common ground, and reach mutually beneficial solutions. It involves managing emotions, understanding diverse viewpoints, and working collaboratively.

Integrating Conflict Negotiation Into Your Leadership Communication Playbook

- **Approach openly**: Enter discussions without assumptions or defensiveness. Be willing to listen and understand others' perspectives.
- **Foster safety**: Create an environment where everyone feels comfortable sharing opinions without fear of judgment. Remember, respectful disagreement is a sign of engagement.
- **Identify common interests**: Focus on shared goals such as *"We both want this project to be successful, even if we have different ideas on how to achieve it."*

- **Reframe conflict**: View disagreements as opportunities to innovate and discover new solutions, rather than obstacles. You might say, *"I'm glad we're discussing this because our different perspectives could lead to a creative solution."*

Conflict Negotiation in Practice

When disagreement arises, start by actively listening and acknowledging the other person's emotions and viewpoints. For example, *"I understand you're concerned about the deadline, and I appreciate your honesty."* Then, work together to find common ground by exploring mutual interests. This helps diffuse tension and lays the foundation for constructive dialogue.

4. Constructive Feedback

Constructive feedback is a gift that fosters growth, collaboration, and continuous improvement. When delivered with kindness and helpful insight, it encourages honest dialogue and empowers others to learn from their experiences.

Think of feedback as a bridge, not a wall. When shared thoughtfully, it opens the door to breakthroughs and innovation. Effective feedback is clear, specific, and focused on behaviors or outcomes, never on personal traits. The goal is to guide improvement in a supportive way that motivates development.

- **Be specific and focused**: Highlight particular actions rather than making broad statements. Instead of *"You need to communicate better,"* say, *"In our last meeting, I noticed you didn't share your ideas on the project timeline. Sharing your insights could really help the team."*
- **Use a kind, supportive tone**: Deliver feedback with empathy, emphasizing your intent to support growth. Phrases like *"I appreciate your effort, and I think we can improve by . . ."* foster a positive environment.
- **Balance positives with areas for improvement**: Start with what's working well before addressing improvements to keep motivation high.
- **Tailor your style**: Apply Communication Accommodation Theory by adjusting your feedback to match the recipient's preferences. Some may prefer directness, whereas others may prefer a gentler approach.
- **Encourage a growth mindset**: Frame feedback as an opportunity for development. For instance, *"This is a chance to develop your skills further,"* rather than *"You're doing this wrong."*
- **Invite dialogue**: Ask questions like, *"What do you think about this?"* to foster open exchange.

DISCOVER YOUR LEADERSHIP VOICE

- **Be open to receiving feedback**: Demonstrate a growth mindset by accepting feedback graciously and asking clarifying questions if needed. This shows your commitment to continuous improvement.

Constructive Feedback in Practice

Instead of saying, "*You're always late and unreliable,*" try "*I've noticed that arriving on time has changed recently and it is impacting our team's workflow. Let's work together to find a solution that helps you arrive promptly so we can keep our projects on track.*" This specific, behavior-focused feedback emphasizes collaboration and support, turning a potential confrontation into a growth opportunity.

When given and received with empathy, clarity, and respect, feedback creates an environment where everyone feels safe, valued, and motivated to improve. This culture of open communication nourishes trust, connection, and collective growth (see Table 2.3).

Table 2.3 Instant Impact: Leadership Takeaway from Communication Experts, Dr. Julien Mirivel and Dr. Alex Lyon

Conversations with Leaders: Don't Just Exchange Information, Build Connections	"*Communication is not just about exchanging information; it's about building connections,*" says Dr. Julien Mirivel. Alongside Dr. Alex Lyon, he highlights that strong relationships rooted in positive communication are the foundation of effective leadership.
	Alex emphasizes, "Effective leadership emerges from understanding the individual voices within your team. When we listen deeply and adapt our communication, we create an environment where everyone feels valued and empowered."
	Both experts advise actively seeking to understand your team's unique communication styles and adjusting your approach accordingly because tailored communication enhances collaboration and trust. Julien reminds us, "A leader who prioritizes relationships lays the groundwork for trust, engagement, and innovation."
	For deeper insights, listen to Season 4, Episode 9 of *The Communicative Leader* podcast, available on your favorite streaming platform.[4]

5. Public Speaking

Public speaking can feel like walking a tightrope, but it's more than just delivering words; it's your platform for sharing ideas, shaping narratives, and connecting meaningfully with others. Effective public speaking allows you to bring your vision to life and rally others around your ideas. Embrace the nerves because they're a sign that you care.

Integrating Public Speaking Into Your Leadership Communication Playbook

- **Know your audience**: Tailor your message to their interests and understanding for greater impact.
- **Share stories and examples**: Use personal anecdotes or relevant stories to illustrate your points, making your message memorable and engaging.
- **Be authentic**: Be yourself and let your personality shine through. Authenticity builds trust and rapport with your audience.
- **Use clear, expressive language**: Speak with clarity, varying your tone and pace to keep your audience interested. Avoid jargon unless appropriate with your audience.
- **Channel nervous energy**: Recognize that feeling nervous is natural. Channel that energy into enthusiasm and passion for your topic.
- **Engage with eye contact and body language**: Make eye contact, use purposeful gestures, and move with confidence to connect with your audience.
- **Practice and prepare**: Rehearse your speech to boost confidence and ensure smooth delivery.
- **Be relatable**: Share your authentic self. Your warmth can turn a speech into a heartfelt conversation. For instance, I often share my early public speaking mishaps as a way to connect with the audience and demonstrate the power of practicing and refining your leadership communication skills.

Public Speaking in Practice

Remember, it's okay to stumble. What matters is your authenticity and passion. When you're relatable and true to yourself, your warmth can turn a speech into a meaningful connection.

With public speaking as part of your communication toolkit, you'll grow, inspire, and motivate those around you. Every opportunity to speak is a chance to influence and create change. Step up with confidence—you've got this (see Table 2.4)!

Table 2.4 Data and Trends: Our Communication Strengths and Growth Areas

Here are some fascinating insights into how we connect at work, including our strengths and growth areas.

Our Communication Superpowers:

1. **Listening Skills:** About 85% of what we learn comes through listening.[5] Active listeners are magic makers at work. They foster collaboration and help squash misunderstandings faster than you can say "miscommunication."
2. **Nonverbal Cues:** Much of our communication is conveyed through body language, facial expressions, and tone. Many adults have a natural knack for picking up on these cues, which is fantastic news!
3. **Digital Communication:** 30% of adults are almost constantly online,[6] whether it's using email, social media, and messaging apps. Our digital communication game is strong!

Where We Can Level Up:

1. **Conflict Resolution:** On average, adults spend over 4 hours weekly dealing with conflict at work, with 65% of employees reporting that their managers could do more to help resolve it.[7]
2. **Public Speaking:** The vast majority of adults report some jitters when it comes to public speaking.[8] Confidence is crucial for sharing ideas and advancing leadership.
3. **Feedback:** 63% of employees want more regular feedback on their work performance.[9] If we're not great at giving or receiving feedback, we're effectively putting the brakes on our own growth.
4. **Communicating Across Generations:** Let's face it—baby boomers, Gen X, millennials, and Gen Z all have unique communication styles. These differences can cause a big mess of misunderstandings.[10] This is why we need to focus on accommodating our communication to meet others where they are!

Wrapping It Up

While we have solid communication strengths, there's always room for growth. Recognizing this helps us focus on continuous improvement—because we're all in this together!

KEY TAKEAWAYS

1. **Communication Is Your Leadership Superpower**: Effective leadership fundamentally depends on clear and purposeful communication. Your words serve as powerful tools to inspire, clarify, and motivate. Investing time in refining your elevator pitch can significantly enhance your ability to convey your message with impact. Practicing in front of trusted colleagues or mentors can further build your confidence, ensuring that your introductions and key messages leave a memorable and positive impression.

2. **Know and Refine Your Communication Style**: Self-awareness is a wonderful gift for a leader. By understanding your unique communication style, you can genuinely connect with others and foster more meaningful relationships. Embrace your idiosyncrasies, but stay open to feedback and growth. Consider asking a trusted colleague about your strengths and blind spots. This can deepen your understanding of yourself and your ability to continue to grow your leadership voice.
3. **Master the Art of Active Listening**: Building trust starts with the simple yet profound skill of active listening. When you truly listen to your team, you show them that their voices matter, and that can work wonders for morale. Practice reflective listening by using phrases like *"What I hear you saying is . . ."*—it's a small but powerful way to validate their feelings and open the door to deeper conversations. Your attention makes a big difference!
4. **Transform Conflict Into Collaborative Opportunities**: Conflict is a natural part of teamwork, and approaching it with an open mind can lead to creativity and innovation. Instead of dodging tough conversations, embrace them as opportunities to grow and innovate. When tensions arise, suggest a friendly brainstorming session to turn "I disagree" into *"Let's explore this together."* This not only diminishes conflict but also fosters a collaborative spirit where new ideas can flourish.
5. **Empathy as Your Leadership Cornerstone**: Empathy is at the heart of strong leadership and meaningful connections. By tuning into the feelings and perspectives of your team, you foster a nurturing environment where everyone feels valued and heard. Beginning meetings with a simple check-in, such as by asking, *"How is everyone feeling today?"* demonstrates that you care about their well-being. This warm approach sets a supportive tone for the discussion ahead, encouraging openness and collaboration.

NOTES

1 Itzchakov, G., Weinstein, N., Vinokur, E., & Yomtovian, A. (2023). Communicating for workplace connection: A longitudinal study of the outcomes of listening training on teachers' autonomy, psychological safety, and relational climate. *Psychology in the Schools*, 60(4), 1279–1298.
2 Omilion-Hodges, L. (Host). (2023, October 9). Leadership & mindfulness: A conversation Aneace Haddad [Audio podcast episode]. *The Communicative Leader Podcast*. https://www.thecommunicativeleader.com/podcast/episode/7db216c5/leadership-and-mindfulness-a-conversation-with-aneace-haddad-executive-coach-and-advisor-to-the-c-suite
3 Giles, H. (2016). Communication accommodation theory. In *The international encyclopedia of communication theory and philosophy* (pp. 1–7). John Wiley & Sons.

4 Omilion-Hodges, L. (Host). (2024, March 4). A blueprint for effective leadership communication: Building relationships, implementing strategies and fostering self-awareness: A conversation with Dr. Julien Mirivel and Dr. Alex Lyon [Audio podcast episode]. *The Communicative Leader Podcast.* https://www.thecommunicativeleader.com/podcast/episode/7b5f0dfb/a-blueprint-for-effective-leadership-communication-building-relationships-implementing-strategies-and-fostering-self-awareness-a--conversation-with-dr-julien-mirivel-and-dr-alex-lyon

5 International Listening Association. (2024, August 28). *What role does active listening play in effective communication skills development?* https://vorecol.com/blogs/blog-what-role-does-active-listening-play-in-effective-communication-skills-development-146146

6 Perrin, A., & Atske, S. (2021, March 26). About three-in-ten U.S. adults say they are "almost constantly" online. *Pew Research Center.* https://www.pewresearch.org/short-reads/2021/03/26/about-three-in-ten-u-s-adults-say-they-are-almost-constantly-online/

7 The Myers-Briggs Company. (2022). *Conflict at work: A research report from the Myers-Briggs Company.* https://www.themyersbriggs.com/en-US/Programs/Conflict-at-Work-Research

8 Furmark, T., Tillfors, M., Everz, P. O., Marteinsdottir, I., Gefvert, O., & Fredrikson, M. (1999). Social phobia in the general population: Prevalence and sociodemographic profile. *Social Psychiatry and Psychiatric Epidemiology, 34,* 416–424. https://doi.org/10.1007/s001270050163

9 Eagle Hill Consulting. (2022). *Nearly half of remote and hybrid employees say team performance has improved during the past two years.* https://www.eaglehillconsulting.com/news/employees-say-team-performance-improved-during-pandemic/

10 Berkeley Executive Education. *Enhancing interactional communication: Bridging the gap in global and dispersed teams.* https://executive.berkeley.edu/thought-leadership/blog/enhancing-intergenerational-communication

Chapter 3
Inside the Leader's Voice
The Anatomy of Influence and Authenticity

**Level 1
Discover Your
Leadership Voice**

Having assessed where you are today, you're now ready to explore what makes a leadership voice truly compelling. In this chapter, you will uncover the core elements—clarity, authenticity, conviction, and emotional intelligence—that form the foundation of an effective and authentic leadership communication style. Understanding these building blocks will empower you to craft a voice that resonates and inspires.

Having explored the critical role of communication in leadership, it's time to dig into the heartbeat of effective leadership—the anatomy of a leader's voice. How you communicate isn't just a reflection of your personality; it's the lifeblood of your influence and your ability to rally people around your vision.

So, what makes a leader's voice truly resonate? Think of it as a blend of clarity, conviction, and authenticity, with a hefty dose of emotional intelligence. Each component not only shapes how your message lands but also determines whether your audience is inspired or disengaged. In this chapter, we'll uncover what these components are and provide actionable steps to develop them.

As we dive in, we won't overlook the emotional and psychological factors that can shake the foundation of our communication. From the fear of criticism to the perfectionism that can stifle authentic expression, these influences are real. We'll explore solutions like psychological safety, and I'll share proven strategies from mindfulness to self-compassion, to combat these barriers.

WHAT IS A LEADERSHIP VOICE?

A leadership voice is the distinct style that makes your communication impactful and memorable. It's the unique blend of clarity, conviction, authenticity, and emotional intelligence that resonates with others and sets the tone for effective leadership. There's no one-size-fits-all formula; the key is to embrace your natural communication style and adapt it in ways that serve you best.

Your leadership voice is built and sustained through three foundational practices. By focusing on these areas, you can ensure your communication is heard and respected.

1. **Self-Awareness**: This is your ability to understand your own emotions, strengths, weaknesses, and communication style. Cultivating self-awareness helps you recognize how your voice comes across to others. To develop it, reflect on your interactions and seek feedback to gain insights.
2. **Intention**: Communication without intention can lead to a muddled message. Before any conversation or presentation, define your objectives. Ask yourself: What do I want to achieve? And who is my audience? This intentional focus ensures that your communication aligns with your goals and resonates with others.
3. **Practice**: Just like any top-notch athlete or musician, honing your leadership voice requires time and effort. Start small by rehearsing your key messages. Join groups that focus on public speaking, like Toastmasters, or take on leadership roles in team projects. Your intention will guide your practice, making it focused and purpose-driven.

These foundational elements work in conjunction with the specific components of effective communication: clarity, conviction, authenticity, and emotional intelligence. In the upcoming section, we'll dive deep into each component with practical tips and exercises to help you cultivate them.

WELCOME TO LEADERSHIP COMMUNICATION 101
The Four Essential Ingredients for a Leader's Voice!

Let's face it, leading a team or even a project is usually not a walk in the park. You can't just shout orders from your high horse and expect everyone to fall in line. The magic recipe? It's all about clarity, conviction, authenticity, and emotional intelligence.

1. Clarity

Clarity is about providing a clear vision and direction. This means articulating goals, expectations, and tasks in a straightforward manner. Leaders who communicate with clarity minimize confusion and ambiguity, which not only builds trust but also fosters a culture of transparency and shared purpose.

Workplace Example

Imagine a project kickoff meeting where the leader outlines the project goals, timelines, and individual responsibilities with precision. As a result, every team member knows exactly what they need to do and when, reducing the chances of miscommunication and delays. This also empowers employees to spearhead their respective responsibilities without fear of stepping on someone else's toes while avoiding inadvertent redundancy.

Warning

Clear communication isn't just a nice-to-have; it's the backbone of successful projects. When messages are muddled or unclear, misunderstandings flourish, morale plummets, and even the most promising initiatives can fail spectacularly. Just look at the infamous New Coke launch in the 1980s: Coca-Cola underestimated the power of clear messaging. They changed their formula but failed to transparently explain why. The result? Confusion, outrage, and a massive backlash that forced them to quickly revert to the original recipe. This cautionary tale underscores a vital lesson: for success, clarity in communication is not an option—it's a necessity.

Leadership Tip: To make sure your messages hit the mark, apply the "RACI" model: Responsible, Accountable, Consulted, and Informed.

Understanding the RACI Model:
- **Responsible**: The person or people who directly perform the task.
- **Accountable**: The individual who holds ultimate responsibility for the decision and the success of the task.
- **Consulted**: Those whose input is sought prior to making a decision.
- **Informed**: Individuals who need to be kept updated on decisions and progress.

- **Outline Tasks**: Before implementing the RACI model, it's important to identify the specific tasks involved. This includes all the individual steps and milestones necessary to achieve the project's overall success, including the smaller actions that lead there.

- **Create a RACI Chart**: For each task, assign roles:
    - Who is Responsible?
    - Who is Accountable?
    - Who needs to be Consulted?
    - Who should be Informed?

- **Share, Discuss, and Present**: Present the chart to the team, ensuring everyone understands their roles. Keep the chart in a shared location accessible to all team members.

- **Review and Adjust Regularly**: Like so many tips in this book, this is not a one-time task. Revisit and update the RACI chart regularly, especially as the project progresses or priorities change.

2. Conviction

Conviction breathes life into your vision. Conviction entails having strong beliefs and a passionate commitment to your goals, which inspires confidence and motivates others. When leaders exhibit conviction, they become rallying points for their teams, encouraging collective effort toward shared goals.

Workplace Example

During a challenging financial quarter, a leader passionately emphasizes the importance of a strategic pivot. By articulating their deep belief in the team's potential to succeed, they energize their team to adapt, innovate, and strive for success despite the odds.

Warning

A lack of conviction can create a sense of disconnection and apathy within a team, undermining trust and morale. In 2001, Enron's leadership exhibited a lack of conviction in ethical practices, leading to a massive corporate scandal that fueled the company's collapse. This powerful reminder shows how vital conviction is. Conviction doesn't just guide our decisions, but it also builds trust and commitment that helps to sustain an organization through both challenges and successes.

Leadership Tip

Identify your core values and the vision that drives you (tip: we cover this extensively in Chapter 8). Write them down and reflect on them regularly. Reinforce these beliefs in team meetings to create a shared sense of urgency and purpose. Ready to cultivate your conviction?

- **Identify what matters**: Reflect on the core principles that truly inspire you. Think of them as your guiding light. Write them down and revisit them regularly.
- **Infuse passion**: Use your core values to create connections in your team meetings. Reinforcing these beliefs can help to spark more innovation and shared vision. This can be as simple as pulling in aspects of your organization's mission into discussion when making decisions.
- **Lead by example**: Walk the walk! Show how your conviction manifests in your daily work and decision-making. I have seen many a leader claim to be empathetic and employee-centered just to turn and yell at or shame an employee. It is crucial that your actions align with your values (see Table 3.1).

Table 3.1 Instant Impact: Leadership Takeaway from Body Language Expert, Dr. Richard Reid

	In our fast-paced digital world, meaningful communication can be a challenge. Dr. Richard Reid, an organizational psychologist and body language expert, recommends slowing down to promote deeper engagement.
Conversations with Leaders: Slow Down to Promote Deeper Engagement	1. **Use strategic pauses:** After someone speaks, pause instead of filling the silence. This creates space for reflection and contributes to a richer discussion. 2. **Ask open-ended questions:** Encourage a richer dialogue by posing open-ended questions like "*Can you share more about your perspective?*" 3. **Reflect and validate:** Listen actively, then paraphrase to confirm understanding and validate others' contributions.
	Richard expands on this idea in Season 6, Episode 8 of *The Communicative Leader* podcast.[1]

3. Authenticity

Authenticity involves being genuine and transparent in your interactions. Leaders who are authentic create real connections with their followers, fostering trust and rapport. This quality makes it easier for team members to relate to and feel comfortable approaching their leader, which can enhance collaboration and loyalty.

Workplace Example

A leader shares their own personal challenges and failures during a team meeting, opening up about lessons learned. This vulnerability encourages team members to share their own struggles, creating an environment where everyone feels valued and understood.

Warning

Inauthenticity can lead to distrust, disengagement, and high turnover rates. Elizabeth Holmes, founder of Theranos, projected an image of confidence and innovation but was ultimately found to be a fraud. The fallout from her lack of authenticity severely damaged her reputation and led to legal consequences, emphasizing how detrimental it can be to not be true to one's values. Moreover, Holmes's actions have cast a long shadow of doubt over the credibility of female entrepreneurs, who now face additional challenges in overcoming the stigma associated with her deception.

Leadership Tip

Engage in self-reflection to identify what makes you unique. Share your journey, including successes *and* failures, with your team. Remember, you're sharing personal insights, such as information about your experiences and perspectives that are intended to build connection and trust. However, always be mindful of boundaries and avoid revealing private or sensitive details. Ready to cultivate your authenticity muscle? Here are some actionable steps to get you started:

- **List key experiences**: Reflect on key moments that have shaped you, including accomplishments and challenges alike!
- **Identify themes**: Review your list of key experiences for patterns or recurring traits that highlight your values.
- **Craft your story**: Create a narrative with a beginning (your background), middle (key experiences), and end (lessons learned and growth).
- **Make it a habit**: Dedicate 15 minutes weekly to reflect on your experiences, noting what went well, any personal missteps, or inspiring leadership you observed.

4. Emotional Intelligence

Emotional intelligence (EI) is the ability to recognize, understand, and manage your own emotions, as well as those of others. Leaders with high EI are adept at navigating the complexities of team dynamics, responding to emotional cues, and motivating individuals in meaningful ways. They create an environment where team members feel valued and understood (see Table 3.2).

Table 3.2 Actionable Insights: Emotional Intelligence on the Big Screen

Emotional intelligence is one of those concepts that is better understood through observation, and one powerful way to see it in action is in films. Here are some recommendations: • **Good Will Hunting (1997)**: This film explores the significance of self-awareness and mentorship in personal development, emphasizing that leaders must acknowledge their own vulnerabilities while supporting others. • **Draft Day (2014)**: Following a professional football team manager on draft day, this film illustrates the ability to manage stress and make critical decisions that weigh both emotional and practical factors. • **Hidden Figures (2016)**: This film tells the true story of three African American women at NASA during the early 1960s, showcasing their roles as mathematicians and engineers in making the 1962 orbital flight possible despite facing racial and gender challenges. • **CODA (2021)**: Centered on Ruby, the hearing daughter of deaf adults, this film explores identity, empathy, and communication while highlighting the complexities of interpersonal dynamics and leadership.

AMPLIFYING YOUR LEADERSHIP VOICE

Workplace Example

A leader notices a team member is unusually quiet in a meeting. Afterward, they check in one-on-one, asking if everything is okay. This proactive approach not only addresses any concerns but also shows the team member that their emotions and well-being are valued.

Warning

Ignoring emotional intelligence can result in unresolved conflicts, low morale, and weak team cohesion. After the 2008 financial crisis, many leaders showed a lack of emotional intelligence when communicating layoffs and reductions. Companies like Lehman Brothers faced backlash and mistrust because their leaders failed to empathize with their employees' emotional turmoil, which further damaged their reputation.

Leadership Tip

Develop your emotional intelligence by practicing active listening. Active listening is a foundational leadership skill that you've seen mentioned multiple times in this book, and for good reason. It's a powerful, multifaceted skill with significant benefits for a leader. By focusing entirely on the speaker and paying close attention to their tone and body language, you can deepen your understanding of their emotions and enhance your response strategies. This simple practice builds trust and strengthens connections, making you a more effective and influential leader. Here are some steps to put your emotional intelligence into action:

- **Commit to active listening**: I promised we'd revisit this! When you're fully engaged and free of distractions, you not only absorb more, but also build rapport—a true win-win.
- **Notice nonverbal cues**: Remember, it is not just what you hear—it's also about what you see. Pay attention to body language, facial expressions, and tone. For instance, someone saying they're fine, but crossing their arms or avoiding eye contact may be signaling otherwise. Let's be real—sometimes, actions speak louder than words.
- **Ask open-ended questions**: Promote thoughtful dialogue with questions like *"Can you tell me more?"* or *"What might that look like?"* to empower your conversation partner.
- **Pause before responding**: Take a moment to process what's been said and tune into their emotions. Are they excited, upset, or a mix of both? By taking their emotional temperature, you can respond with intention and empathy.

An influential leadership voice is built on four core components (see Figure 3.1). Think of clarity as your GPS—without it, your team risks losing direction. Add

INSIDE THE LEADER'S VOICE

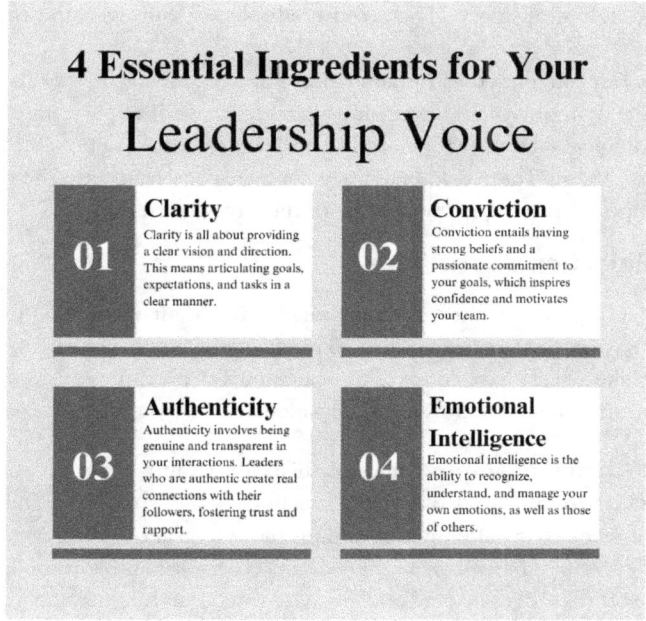

Figure 3.1 This graphic highlights four key ingredients of your leadership voice—clarity, conviction, authenticity, and emotional intelligence—and their role in inspiring and influencing others

conviction, your unwavering belief in your vision, and others will follow with wholehearted commitment. Authenticity is your secret weapon for building trust; when your team perceives genuine transparency, they'll stand with you through any storm. Finally, emotional intelligence is your leadership superpower, helping you read the room with finesse and know when to celebrate, comfort, or challenge. Together, these elements create a powerful voice that delivers results while fostering loyalty and resilience to overcome any challenge.

THE FACTORS THAT CAN SILENCE YOUR LEADERSHIP VOICE

Your ability to communicate authentically greatly influences your impact—whether you're collaborating with colleagues, supporting your team, or engaging with leaders. No matter your role or title, everyone has a leadership voice that matters. Yet, many find this voice silenced by emotional and psychological barriers lurking beneath the surface. These barriers include fear of rejection or criticism, a desire for control or perfection, insecurity, self-doubt, and environments lacking psychological safety. These can easily drown out even the most confident voices.

So, how can you quiet these inner critics? For every obstacle, there's a strategy to reclaim and amplify your voice. In this section, we'll explore the emotional and psychological factors that can hold you back and learn actionable strategies to rise above them. The world benefits when everyone leans into their ability to inspire, empower, and uplift regardless of their role or title.

Fear of Rejection or Criticism

Fear of rejection isn't just an anxious thought; it's a gut-wrenching feeling that makes you second-guess every idea. This nagging worry whispers, "What if they don't like what I have to say?" and can paralyze even the most experienced employees, stifling ideas before they can shine.

- **Workplace example**: Imagine this: you're in a team meeting with a new idea for a project that could transform your workflow. You feel your pulse race, your palms sweat, and just as you're about to speak, you catch a side-eye from a colleague. Self-doubt creeps in, and you think, "They'll just roll their eyes at me too." So, you bite your tongue, and your game-changing idea is lost.
- **Why conquering this challenge matters**: If you stay silent, you risk missing out on vital opportunities for innovation and collaboration. Speaking up doesn't just empower you; it also helps to foster a culture where ideas can thrive. When you don't share your voice, you're sending the message that your insights don't matter. But they do. Your voice is the key to unlocking new solutions and contributing to a more dynamic, successful team.
- **Long-term stakes**: Allowing fear to dictate your communication habits can have detrimental long-term effects. You may find yourself stuck in the same position; your career stalled because others aren't aware of your potential. Over time, this fear can lead to feelings of frustration and resentment, not just towards your colleagues but also towards yourself.

Need for Control and Perfectionism

The need for control and perfectionism can feel like an insatiable hunger that demands every detail be flawless before a single word leaves your lips. This overthinking and relentless pursuit of perfection can lead to procrastination that frustrates everyone around you, and let's face it, no one has time for that!

- **Workplace example**: Imagine a team member who has critical feedback that could significantly improve a colleague's work. But instead of sending a quick note, they spiral and obsess over the perfect wording. They might

even pull up a thesaurus to search for just the right synonym, all while deadlines loom. As this member dwells on crafting the perfect email, the opportunity for timely feedback slips away, causing delays and frustration among teammates.
- **Why conquering this challenge matters**: Ah, perfectionism—the dream killer of collaboration! Embracing a "good enough" mindset can push us all forward with vigor. Clarity and punctuality will always win over perfection. When you support each other in sharing ideas and feedback openly, you're not just keeping the wheels turning; you're creating a dynamic, productive environment where everyone feels they can contribute without the pressure of being a perfectionist.
- **Long-term stakes**: If perfectionism drives your work and communication, you risk burnout and chronic stress. The constant pursuit of unreachable standards can lead to dissatisfaction and cause you to be seen as a bottleneck, delaying projects and frustrating colleagues. Over time, the fear of inadequacy may foster self-doubt and create a workplace where others feel like they must tread carefully around your high standards.

Insecurity and Self-Doubt

Insecurity and self-doubt simmer beneath the surface, gnawing at your confidence and leaving you hesitant to express your ideas or assert your opinions. It's that sneaky little voice that tries to convince you that you're not good enough or that everyone else is more capable.

- **Workplace example:** There you are, seated in a team meeting, asked to share your progress on a project. You've worked hard and reached some impressive milestones, but self-doubt kicks in. As you begin to present, your mind races with thoughts like, "Did I explain that well?" or "What if they think it's not enough?" Instead of celebrating your achievements, you instinctively downplay them. Afterward, you replay the meeting in your mind, second-guessing every word, leaving you trapped in a cycle of insecurity.
- **Why conquering this challenge matters**: Acknowledging our insecurities isn't just about boosting self-esteem; it's about fostering an environment where everyone feels seen. When we share openly, we validate our own experiences and inspire colleagues to do the same. A team where everyone feels confident speaking up fuels innovation and generates unique solutions that drive success.
- **Long-term stakes**: Allowing insecurity and self-doubt to dominate your professional life can lead to missed opportunities, stalled career growth, and feelings of being undervalued. Projecting uncertainty may cause others to overlook your potential, preventing you from reaching your goals.

A Psychologically Unsafe Work Environment

A psychologically unsafe work environment is like walking on eggshells. No one feels comfortable expressing themselves for fear of being shot down, ridiculed, or reprimanded. In these settings, ideas and concerns remain unspoken, often leading to resentment and disengagement. We may also hesitate to highlight potential errors or risks, worried about the retribution that might follow.

- **Workplace example**: Imagine you have a burning question about a project that could likely prevent a costly mistake. Instead of asking for clarity, you stay quiet, worried that your manager will get frustrated or see the question as a challenge to his authority. Because they often react angrily when they perceives questioning, you bury the concern, hoping it resolves itself. Spoiler alert: it won't! Instead, you become a silent observer with your worries rumbling in the background.
- **Why conquering this challenge matters**: We all play a part in creating an environment where communicating feels safe. When everyone feels secure enough to share ideas, voice concerns, and suggest solutions, the workplace becomes more vibrant and successful. Open communication boosts morale, fosters collaboration, and drives higher performance.
- **Long-term stakes**: Failing to build a psychologically safe environment can lead to high turnover, low morale, and a culture of fear. When team members don't feel they can speak up, they may disengage or tune out altogether. Over time, this can breed distrust, making colleagues feel isolated, anxious, and undervalued.

> **READY TO PUT THIS INTO PRACTICE?**
>
> **Amplify Your Leadership Voice Further**
>
> For additional guidance and a deeper reflection on assessing and overcoming these obstacles, explore the Amplifying Your Leadership Voice: Leadership Blueprint available at TheCommunicativeLeader.com.

NURTURING YOUR LEADERSHIP VOICE: OVERCOMING THE SILENCING CULPRITS

Now that we've had our little heart-to-heart about the sneaky culprits that can silence our leadership voice, it's time to flip the script! If those pesky fears and doubts are the villains of our leadership story, then it's time to become the superheroes of our own narrative. This section is all about nurturing your unique leadership voice.

Mindfulness Practices for Managing Fear and Anxiety

Imagine this: Staying composed and unruffled amid the chaos of work's trials and obstacles. For me, that might be managing a lecture hall with over 100 undergraduate students. Unless you've experienced it, you can't quite grasp the sheer volume of noise—excited, anxious, and confused students all packed into a small, enclosed space.

Practicing mindfulness becomes your hidden strength in such moments, helping to quiet that inner storm. By incorporating these techniques into your routine, you cultivate a greater sense of awareness and create space to pause before reacting to stressful situations. It's about finding that calm center amid the noise and using it to respond with clarity and confidence.

- **Deep breaths**: Start your day or prep for a challenging meeting with a few slow, deliberate breaths. Inhale through your nose, then gently exhale through your mouth. This quick practice can calm nerves and reduce anxiety.
- **Consider meditation**: Even five minutes with apps like Calm or Headspace can clear your mind, bring a sense of peace, and boost your focus.
- **Try a grounding technique**: Notice 5 things you see, perhaps a favorite photo or your coffee mug. Touch 4 objects nearby to anchor yourself. Listen for 3 sounds, breathe in 2 familiar scents, and taste something that brings you joy—like a sip of tea or a piece of chocolate. This simple practice reminds you that you're safe and present. While it won't solve problems instantly, it reassures you that you're not facing immediate danger.

Long-Term Benefits of Mindfulness

When you make mindfulness a regular part of your routine, you'll notice a gradual decrease in stress and a greater ability to manage your emotions, which helps you stay centered even in tough moments. Over time, this practice can build a resilient foundation, empowering you to face challenges with calm and confidence. Plus, mindfulness nurtures clearer thinking and better decision-making, making your workday feel more manageable.

Boost Your Confidence with Positive Self-Talk

Our inner thoughts can be our worst critics, but what if we could transform that inner critic into a coach? It's not a fantasy. With practice, positive self-talk has the power to transform your mindset and give you the courage needed to confront challenges head-on.

Positive self-talk is a proven tool for building confidence and resilience. By consciously replacing self-doubt with affirmations, you can rewire your brain to support your goals rather than sabotage them. This simple practice can be a game-changer for your professional growth and help you tackle difficult conversations with greater confidence.

- **Affirmations**: A simple way to activate your inner coach is to remind yourself of your strengths. For example, affirmations like, "I am confident," "I am capable," or "My voice matters" will lead to a positive shift in how you see yourself.
- **Celebrate little victories**: Whether it's crossing tasks off your to-do list or finally tackling that lingering project, these moments matter. I like to spend a few minutes on Friday afternoons reflecting on my weekly wins. Just 5 minutes can transform how you view success. Instead of only celebrating major milestones like publications or big podcast weeks, I also value a meaningful conversation with an advisee or the time spent planning future research. Think of it like planting seeds—without planting, there's no tree to enjoy. And here's a bonus: when you're feeling down, revisit your list. It's a powerful way to channel your inner coach and remind yourself of your capability and worth.
- **Envision achievement**: Picture yourself nailing that presentation or speaking confidently in your next team meeting. See the smile on your face and feel the pride of a job well done. The more you visualize success, the more it fuels your confidence and prepares you to perform at your best.

Long-Term Advantages of Positive Self-Talk

Cultivating the habit of speaking kindly to yourself can boost your confidence and help you see challenges differently. Obstacles no longer need to feel like insurmountable mountains. Instead, they become opportunities for growth and learning. This shift empowers you to step up, share your voice, and embrace new challenges with greater ease.

Reframing Negative Self-Talk

Transforming your inner dialogue from harsh criticism to gentle encouragement can truly change how you experience life. While positive self-talk is valuable, reframing involves intentionally turning self-criticism into compassionate and constructive words. This gentle shift nurtures self-compassion and encourages a proactive, kind-hearted approach to obstacles. By reshaping your inner voice in this way, you create space for growth, resilience, and a more hopeful outlook.

- **Recognize negative thoughts**: Start by noticing those negative thoughts. When a critical thought pops up, pause and ask yourself two questions: "Is this thought really true?" and "Would I ever say something so harsh to a friend?" By developing this gentle awareness, you can quiet your inner critic and cultivate a much kinder inner voice.

- **Reframe with self-compassion**: Swap judgment for kindness. Instead of saying, "I messed up," try, "I learned something new." This small shift can lighten your mental load and quiet the constant negative chatter that plays on repeat in your mind.
- **Use problem-solving language**: When challenges arise, view them as opportunities to grow. Ask yourself, "What can I learn from this?" or "What's a different approach I could try next time?" This mindset embraces curiosity and resilience over criticism.

Long-Term Benefits of Reframing Negative Self-Talk

Reframing your inner monologue is an investment with a huge payoff. Over time, you'll build resilience, boost your emotional intelligence, and develop a much kinder view of yourself. This positive shift won't just improve your work life—it will also strengthen your well-being and relationships outside the office. Let's now explore how a psychologically safe environment can help these positive changes take root.

BUILDING A FOUNDATION OF PSYCHOLOGICAL SAFETY

Building a truly cohesive, high-performing team requires psychological safety. When team members feel free to speak up and share ideas without fear of judgment, they foster an environment of trust and openness that drives innovation. What's more, when psychological safety is a priority, team members are more willing to own their mistakes. This allows the team to proactively address issues and prevent problems from negatively impacting key stakeholders or processes.

Your Role in Creating a Psychologically Safe Workplace

- **Encourage open dialogue**: Invite colleagues to share their opinions or experiences to foster collaboration. For example, say, "*Johnny, I know you led that initiative—I'd love to hear more about your experience,*" or "*Hadley's effort last time was a huge success—what should we keep in mind?*" These conversations promote sharing, celebrate team members, and lead to better outcomes.
- **Practice active listening**: Show genuine interest by paraphrasing what you hear and asking open-ended questions. This not only deepens understanding but also builds trust and rapport. (Don't worry, we're not done with active listening!).
- **Share experiences**: Be open about your own challenges and lessons learned. Saying "*This project is feeling overwhelming right now*" encourages others to share and supports a culture of openness. It's not about revealing deep secrets but about fostering connection.
- **Celebrate contributions**: Simple acts of appreciation—like a quick "thank you" or public shout-out during a meeting—can make a big difference. Celebrating contributions helps people feel valued, reinforces psychological safety, and cultivates a positive, supportive workplace culture (see Table 3.3).

Table 3.3 Data and Trends: Psychological Safety in the Workplace.

In today's fast-paced workplace, psychological safety is no longer a nice-to-have; it's essential for employee engagement and retention. Research by the Boston Consulting Group found that employees who feel safe to speak up and take risks report[2]:

- 2.1 times higher motivation
- 2.7 times higher happiness
- 3.3 times greater ability to reach their full potential in the workplace

In contrast, employees with low psychological safety levels are 12% more likely to quit within a year, while only 3% of employees with high psychological safety harbor these intentions.

If these stats seem promising, it's time to prioritize empathy. Empathetic leaders are most likely to create psychologically safe workplaces, and when they do, everyone feels valued, heard, and safe to contribute.

Calling All Leaders: Create a Culture of Psychological Safety

- **Vulnerability starts at the top**: Leaders set the tone for the entire team by being open about their own challenges and stumbles. When employees see that perfection isn't expected, they feel safe to take risks and share their own lessons learned. Acknowledging shortcomings without fear or criticism is essential for fostering a culture of innovation and trust.
- **Seek feedback**: Environments lacking psychological safety often persist because employees are afraid to speak up. Leaders can change this by actively asking for feedback and providing multiple channels like check-ins, anonymous surveys, and performance reviews to stay informed and adjust as needed.
- **Respond to concerns with empathy**: Address concerns the way you'd want yours to be addressed: with curiosity, not judgment. Offer support and work together with employees to find solutions that ease their worries. This collaborative approach shows that you value their perspective and are committed to finding a resolution.
- **Provide professional development**: Educate your team about psychological safety. A great starting point is sharing Amy Edmondson's TED Talk on Building a Psychologically Safe Workplace.

Long-Term Benefits of Fostering a Psychologically Safe Workplace

Prioritizing psychological safety leads to lasting improvements in collaboration, creativity, and morale. Over time, you'll likely see increased productivity, lower turnover, and a more engaged workforce, setting the stage for greater success.

Incorporate these positive habits into your daily life, and you'll see a noticeable difference. It reminds me of Dan Harris's book *10% Happier*. After starting a meditation routine, Harris felt about 10% happier. Maybe not a huge leap, but who doesn't want to tame their inner critic and feel calmer and more empowered?

Remember, discovering and strengthening your leadership voice is a marathon, not a sprint. You don't have to adopt all these practices at once. Begin small, maybe with a five-minute guided meditation after lunch, and gradually build from there. Once it becomes second nature, you can add another habit to your routine.

KEY TAKEAWAYS

1. **You're Not the Only One Who Gets Cold Feet**: Let's get real—everyone, from the intern to the CEO, grapples with the fear of speaking up from time to time. It can feel like you're the only one stuck in silence, while everyone else is chatting away. So, how do you break the silence? Share your own butterflies with your team! This simple act creates a sense of belonging and just might inspire others to find their voices too.
2. **Communication Is Your Leadership Superpower**: Want to lead like effectively? Communication is your ticket. It's not about being the chattiest in the room; it's about crafting a message that resonates. Are you making your colleagues feel empowered and engaged, or are you just throwing jargon around and hoping someone else will take the lead? Learn how to inspire and watch your influence grow! Schedule regular "communication check-ins" where your team can share their thoughts on your messaging—trust me, they'll appreciate it, and you'll improve faster than you can say "feedback."
3. **Silence Stifles Creativity**: When you choose to stay mum, you're not just muting your voice, you could be pushing great ideas into hiding as well. If you hold back, you risk derailing your confidence and hampering your team's creativity too. Talk to your team about ideas and concerns openly to create a culture of innovation, not inhibition. Introduce an "open-door policy" and host brainstorming sessions or round-robin sharing that brings out even the most hesitant voices.
4. **Practice Makes Better:** Just like you wouldn't enter a marathon without training, you shouldn't expect to nail aspects of communication without putting in the reps. Leadership communication is a muscle, and it needs to be exercised. So, embrace every opportunity to share feedback, practice public speaking, or ask tough questions. Challenge yourself monthly to try a new communication technique.
5. **Nurturing Your Leadership Voice Takes Time**: Crafting a leadership voice worthy of a TED Talk is not an overnight gig—it's a journey.

Be patient and deliberate in refining your elements of clarity, conviction, authenticity, and emotional intelligence. Each time you assess and practice, you're working to amplify your voice. Find a mentor who's done the grind and learn from their lessons; an experienced set of eyes can make all the difference.

NOTES

1 Omilion-Hodges, L. (Host). (2025, March 31). The charismatic edge: Mastering the science of influence—a conversation with Dr. Richard Reid [Audio podcast episode]. *The Communicative Leader Podcast.* https://www.thecommunicativeleader.com/podcast/episode/7db5e923/the-charismatic-edge-mastering-the-science-of-influence-a-conversation-with-richard-reid
2 Yousif, N., Dartnell, A., May, G., & Knarr, E. (2024, January 4). *Psychological safety levels the playing field for employees.* The Boston Consulting Group. https://www.bcg.com/publications/2024/psychological-safety-levels-playing-field-for-employees

Level 2

Refine Your Leadership Voice

Chapter 4

Speak with Impact
Master Verbal and Nonverbal Communication Skills

WELCOME TO LEVEL 2: REFINE YOUR LEADERSHIP VOICE

Welcome to a crucial phase in your leadership journey: refining how you communicate. Now that you've awakened your voice, it's time to sharpen your skills, including learning to speak with impact through both words and body language. This chapter will guide you in mastering verbal and nonverbal cues that influence, motivate, and inspire others.

You've just wrapped up the first step—Discovering Your Leadership Voice—and now it's time to put that newfound knowledge into action. Think of this chapter as your personal coaching session for communication because, let's face it, even the most experienced of leaders need a little polish and check-in from time to time. In this section, Refine Your Leadership Voice, you will:

- In Chapter 4, "Speak with Impact," you'll explore techniques to communicate confidently and effectively, ensuring your message is heard, understood, and remembered.
- Next, Chapter 5, "Write to Lead," will help you develop compelling digital and written communication skills, allowing your influence to extend beyond spoken words.
- Afterwards, Chapter 6, "Breaking Barriers," will focus on overcoming obstacles that hinder your leadership voice so you can speak freely and authentically.
- Finally, in Chapter 7, "Speaking Across Boundaries," you will learn how to navigate various cultural spaces with confidence.

EFFECTIVE COMMUNICATORS DRIVE THE WORKPLACE

If you want to be truly seen and heard at work, developing your communication skills is essential. Why? Because it's not about titles, it's about your actions: Listening actively, speaking honestly, and engaging meaningfully. This includes intentional body language, adapting to different audiences, and fostering an environment where everyone feels valued and heard.

Today's effective leaders are approachable, relatable, and encourage ideas from others—they are no longer the loudest or most authoritative voices in the room. Strong communication helps resolve conflicts, build trust, and foster respect. Being open to feedback and applying what you learn reinforces your credibility as a leader. That, my friends, is truly what defines leadership.

Having seen why communication matters, let's explore practical strategies to improve your verbal and nonverbal skills. We'll cover written and digital communication in the next chapter. From confidently speaking up in meetings to managing pushback, you'll strengthen your leadership voice—regardless of your formal title.

VERBAL COMMUNICATION SKILLS

We'll start with verbal skills because they're often the most immediate and memorable. For some, this comes naturally and is a source of pride and confidence fueled by a love of connecting with others. For others, speaking up can feel like a knot in the stomach—fearful and intimidating. Most of us fall somewhere in between: not necessarily thrilled about speaking in meetings but not paralyzed by fear either. No matter where you are on that spectrum, sharpening your verbal skills, such as handling conflicts and accepting feedback gracefully, is key to strengthening your leadership presence. Your spoken words serve as a powerful example to others. The way you speak shapes how you're perceived and impacts the relationships you build. Even if you're not aiming for a formal leadership position, we all want to be seen as competent, confident, and composed. Ready to take your communication to the next level? Here are some practical strategies to improve your verbal communication skills.

CONFIDENCE IN SHARING YOUR IDEAS: MOVING FROM THINKING TO SHARING

Sharing your ideas is a skill that gets better with practice. If you hesitate to speak up, you're not alone; 70% of employees report feeling afraid to share ideas in meetings, worried about how their contributions will be received.[1] However, research shows that teams encouraging diverse viewpoints and active participation make better decisions, with a 22% increase in decision quality.[2]

In other words, although many of us fear speaking up, fostering a culture that values open discussion benefits everyone (see Table 4.1). So, how can you start using your leadership voice to ensure everyone is heard?

Prepare

Ever walked into a meeting unprepared? It happens to everyone. Forgetting to open an agenda or double-check notes isn't a sign that you're an imposter—it's a sign you're human. The key is to see these moments as the exception, not the rule. Moving forward, whether it's a high-stakes or routine meeting, consider taking these steps:

- **Review the agenda**: Take a few minutes to understand the key topics and objectives before you join a meeting. If the agenda is long or has required reading, use an AI tool like ChatGPT or Gemini to get a quick summary. This simple preparation prevents you from frantically scanning the documents and allows you to focus on listening and contributing instead.
- **Gather relevant information**: Have key stats, reports, or background materials ready, especially if you're discussing a project you're involved in. Reviewing previous meeting notes can also help you connect past discussions and contribute meaningfully.
- **Be Concise**: Nervousness can cause rambling. Being prepared with your main points helps keep your message focused. When sharing updates, consider what others need to know—such as how the project impacts stakeholders, budgets, or timelines—and tailor your message accordingly.

Table 4.1 Instant Impact: Leadership Takeaway from Visionary Business Leader, Jimi Gibson

Conversations with Leaders: Three-Step Communication Check	Jimi Gibson, VP of Brand Development at Thrive Agency, stopped by *The Communicative Leader* to share practical, tested insights on becoming an effective, influential communicator.
	Here's his three-step process to double-check that your message is clear:
	1. Distill your ideas into a single sentence a 10-year-old can understand.
	2. Ensure that this message is repeatable. Instead of "*We're spearheading an initiative to synergize efforts across the hierarchy to reduce redundancy and increase output,*" say, "*A new process is going to save you time and the organization money.*"
	3. Ask someone to repeat what you said to confirm your message is understood.
	Jimi expands on these ideas and shares a wealth of other professional communication tips in Season 7, Episode 6 of *The Communicative Leader* podcast.[3]

Present Your Research

Research isn't just for academic papers. Any time you gather information—from a quick web search to exploring your company's shared drive or monitoring competitors—you're doing research. It all counts. Yet, many of us do this research daily but fail to share our findings. Sharing your research strengthens your suggestions and highlights your valuable contributions. For example, I once provided my manager with key statistics, timelines, and upcoming expectations for inclusion on the agenda. When I presented the project overview, colleagues had the relevant information at their fingertips, which boosted transparency and allowed me to focus on the big picture without juggling details.

SHARE WITH CONFIDENCE

While Chapter 6 is about building your confidence, it's helpful to start laying the foundation now. If you're introverted or have faced challenges speaking up, it might feel overwhelming and like confidence is out of reach. I've been there, and I promise, with the right strategies and consistent practice, you can excel. Here's how:

- **I statements**: "I" statements help you express your feelings and needs, allowing you to advocate for yourself without pointing fingers or damaging relationships. Pretty powerful, huh? I statements encourage you to reflect on your emotions rather than blaming someone else for their actions, which can be especially helpful in times of conflict.

    For example, imagine a colleague takes over a presentation that you were meant to lead. Instead of saying, "*You stole the show and embarrassed me,*" try this: "*I was hoping to lead this meeting as we discussed, and I felt a bit sidelined.*"

    If your comments are dismissed, you might add, "*I appreciate your input, but aligning with a plan beforehand helps me contribute effectively.*" This approach allows you to express how someone's actions affect you without blaming them, often leading to a productive conversation.
- **Lead with benefits**: Another way to build confidence when speaking up is to lead with the benefits. If you're tasked with spearheading a new initiative, use your speaking time to highlight how it will help save time, reduce costs, or otherwise benefit stakeholders. Messages that show a clear positive impact are more likely to resonate and receive a warm response.
- **Use examples**: Concrete examples make your points clearer and more relatable. Instead of saying "*the new software integration is going well,*" say "*the new software has allowed us to successfully launch a campaign two weeks ahead of schedule because it made task assignment and deadlines clear, so collaboration was easier, and we weren't bogged down by confusion with decision-making.*" Both examples convey that the new software is helpful, but the second illustration

contains concrete examples that enable listeners to better grasp the impact of the new integration. Beyond using specific examples, you can make your message clearer using tools like metaphors, similes, and contrasts.

Metaphors: A metaphor directly compares one thing to another, helping your audience understand your idea by relating it to something familiar. For example, you might say *"our team is a well-oiled machine"* to convey efficiency and collaboration.

Similes: A simile uses either "like" or "as" to make a comparison, which can help paint a clearer picture for your audience. If you know a new initiative is not necessarily going to be well received, you might say *"Getting everyone on board with this project will be like herding cats"* to emphasize the anticipated challenge.

Contrasts: You can pick two opposing ideas or situations to help clarify your point. For example, you may say *"While traditional methods we've used have been very time-consuming and rigid, this new approach offers us both speed and flexibility,"* to emphasize the advantages of the new approach.

- **Sharing Bad News**: When it comes to delivering difficult news, the key is timeliness and transparency. While discussing budget cuts or layoffs is never easy, presenting the facts clearly—like timelines, support options, and next steps—can help soften the impact.

For example, if you're announcing layoffs, start by acknowledging the difficulty of the situation: *"I understand this news is unsettling. Due to budget constraints, we must reduce our workforce. By Friday, we will share a timeline for the transitions and provide severance packages, along with career counseling services to support those affected."* Being honest about what is known and offering support demonstrates empathy. Clear, compassionate communication helps everyone navigate tough moments more smoothly.

TIPS FOR RECEIVING FEEDBACK

Receiving feedback is essential for collaboration and growth, yet it often feels intimidating. Many people hesitate to ask for it, fearing criticism or rejection. However, feedback is a powerful tool for improvement. It offers valuable insights that can refine your ideas, strengthen relationships, and foster personal and professional development. The best leaders don't just accept feedback; they actively seek it out.

Remain Open-Minded

This takes practice, but it's worth it. It is tough to welcome critiques on work you've deeply invested in. In my academic career, for example, I spend months on research and writing, only to get multipage reviews from anonymous experts. It's easy to get defensive, but I've learned that every publication has improved because of that feedback. While not every suggestion is a fit, the process forces me to think more critically and make my work stronger. This is the key takeaway for all feedback: Focus on your ultimate goal, and you can turn frustration into professional growth.

Ask Clarifying Questions

Asking questions is a great way to make receiving feedback easier. This isn't about challenging what is being said – it's about deepening your understanding so that you can improve your work. Here are a few clarifying questions to use during your next feedback session:

- *Thanks for the suggestion. As a follow-up, what would success look like for this project?*
- *Is there a timeline for implementing these suggestions? What steps would you suggest prioritizing?*
- *Thanks for the feedback. Can you help me see how this suggestion relates back to the project's overall goals?*
- *I appreciate your comments. Can you provide some examples to help me better understand your suggestions?*
- *Thanks for your ideas. What specific area do you think needs improvement so I can focus my efforts there?*
- *How would you approach this differently?*
- *I appreciate that idea. What resources are available to help me integrate that suggestion?*

Asking clarifying questions helps you better understand feedback and provides actionable insights for your next steps. It can also foster deeper discussions among team members, encouraging consideration of resources, priorities, and potential alternatives.

Consider Alternatives

Inviting feedback not only opens you to suggestions for improvement but also creates space for exploring alternative solutions. Here are some ways that considering alternatives can lead to better outcomes:

- **Encourage new opinions**: Inviting feedback encourages team members to share new viewpoints and ideas, which can foster a culture of collaboration and open dialogue.
- **Take a "what if" approach**: A "what if" approach involves structured discussions focused on exploring different options. For example, asking *"what if we approached this project from a completely different angle?"* can reveal insights that might not have emerged otherwise.

MASTERING CONVERSATIONS

In the previous section, we explored receiving feedback. Now we'll focus on another aspect of verbal communication that can cause many of us anxiety: starting and maintaining conversations. We'll discuss strategies for facilitating effective conversations ranging from hallway chats to establishing ground rules for meetings. We're also going to explore how to cultivate a positive conversation culture in your workplace.

Strategies for Effective Conversations

Some people seem to have the gift of gab. Whether they're naturally extroverted or simply enjoy social interactions, they often leave conversations energized. Others, on the other hand, might find the idea of starting or maintaining a conversation draining. Below, you'll find practical strategies to help you spark meaningful conversations and keep them flowing comfortably.

Conversation Starters

Having a few go-to conversation starters can make it easier to engage with others. Think about these in categories such as:

- **Work-related**: *"Hey, how's that project you've been working on coming along?"*
- **Shared interests**: *"Did you catch the game last night?"* or *"I remember you liked hiking too—have you been on any good trails lately?"*
- **Upcoming events**: *"Are you planning on going to the company picnic next week?"*
- **Casual observations**: *"Have you tried that new coffee shop down the street?"*

While these categories can be helpful go-to strategies, don't underestimate the impact of casual check-ins because sometimes a simple question, like *"how's your week going?"* can lead to a meaningful conversation.

Practice Active Listening

This suggestion should sound familiar, I hope! One of the easiest and most impactful things you can do for your leadership communication game is to actively listen to others. Engage in eye contact, avoid distractions, ask follow-up questions, and nod to show you're listening. Additionally, this approach can be especially helpful for introverts or those who prefer not to be the focus of the conversation since great listeners often attract great talkers.

Wrapping Up a Conversation

Conversations may start organically and encourage natural exchange, but how do we wrap these up gracefully? You can summarize the key points to show you listened. This might look like *"I really enjoyed hearing about your project updates and weekend plans. It sounds like you have a lot going on." You can also introduce a natural transition, such as *"It was really great to chat, but I need to head back to my desk to prep for the next meeting."*

> **READY TO PUT THIS INTO PRACTICE?**
>
> **Amplify Your Leadership Voice Further**
>
> Visit TheCommunicativeLeader.com to access The Leadership Blueprint, your essential guide to sharpening your verbal communication skills. Unlock strategies to speak with confidence, influence others, and lead with clarity. We're here to support your growth as a powerful, authentic leader!

FACILITATING MEETINGS

Now that you have some tricks in your toolbox for informal conversations, let's think about how to flex those leadership communication skills during meetings and other formal conversations.

Setting Ground Rules

Setting ground rules helps you establish norms for what is expected in the meeting. While this might feel a little clunky or forced at first, with time this can set your team up to engage in open, respectful, and efficient communication.

- **Establish respect and inclusivity**: This can be as simple as stating *"Let's be creative and pause judgment so we can explore some new ways to approach this."*
- **Time management**: To keep meetings on track, consider setting time expectations based on agenda length or topic sensitivity. For passionate discussions, allocating a maximum of three minutes per person can be effective. You might also assign time limits for each agenda item to help everyone stay on schedule.
- **Stay focused**: Don't let your meetings get sidetracked. When a great idea comes up that's not on the agenda, create a "parking lot" for it. Write the idea down so it's not forgotten, then quickly guide the conversation back to the main topic. This simple practice keeps the meeting productive and respects everyone's time.

Encouraging Participation

Who has been in meetings where you hear the same voices over and over again? To their defense, they may also feel tired of "carrying" the conversation. Luckily, there are simple strategies to encourage broader participation.

- **Round robin.** Set the expectation that everyone will share or weigh in. This ensures all voices are heard and gives quieter voices a chance to practice sharing their ideas.
- **Open-ended questions.** Oftentimes meetings turn into one or more people taking turns reporting out updates. While information sharing is important, this shared time can also be used to get a better idea of how people are doing. For example, an open-ended question like *"What challenges do you all foresee with this proposal?"* can go a long way in provoking a thoughtful discussion that engages multiple areas and groups.
- **Breakout groups.** To engage all participants, especially the quieter voices, try using breakout groups. By dividing the team into smaller groups to discuss specific topics, you create a less intimidating environment that encourages more thoughtful input and builds collaboration. Afterward, each group can share their key insights, fueling a richer discussion for the entire team.

Summarizing Key Points

Another strategy for facilitating an effective meeting includes summarizing key points, takeaways, and action items. Here are some ways to do so:

- **Real-time notes.** Designate a note taker for the meeting minutes. My department rotates through this task alphabetically. While meeting minutes are often shared after the meeting concludes, sharing these in real-time on a screen or whiteboard can be helpful for immediate summaries and to catch any potential oversights or inaccuracies.
- **Wrap-up summaries.** Before moving to the next agenda item, it can be helpful to summarize the discussion, including action items and responsibilities. For example, *"To summarize, Tom offered to lead the project, and we'll follow up with feedback for him by end of day on Tuesday."* While this may seem minor, it helps keep everyone on the same page and reduces misunderstandings.
- **Feedback loop.** At the end of meetings, invite feedback on the conversation process. Ask questions like *"What worked well today, and what could be improved for our next meeting?"*

NAVIGATING DIFFICULT CONVERSATIONS

Ready to move beyond sharing ideas? Let's get into the tough stuff: navigating pushback, handling criticism, and managing conflict. This section offers practical strategies to help you manage resistance and resolve conflicts with skill. We'll also explore how to create a culture where honest feedback and healthy disagreements are encouraged. The goal? To give you the tools you need to approach any conversation with confidence.

Handling Pushback and Criticism

Pushback or resistance often comes from a natural hesitation to resist change or differing opinions. Criticism, on the other hand, typically involves evaluating work and highlighting areas for improvement. While pushback and criticism might not always seem helpful at first glance, both can be valuable when approached thoughtfully.

- **Respectfully acknowledge concerns.** Few things are more discouraging than summoning the courage to share an idea and then being met with a barrage of "no"s. Remember, you're a strong communicator with insightful ideas. It's natural to feel defensive and want to respond with counterarguments, but these knee-jerk reactions can shut down dialogue and create frustration.
- Instead, pause, take a breath, and listen with empathy and respect. You might say, "*I appreciate you sharing your thoughts; I can understand why you might feel that way.*" Validating feelings fosters openness and collaboration. This approach encourages constructive dialogue and positions you as a considerate colleague who values diverse perspectives. Attentive listening helps address concerns early and sets the stage for more successful outcomes.
- **Maintain composure.** Staying calm when faced with pushback is crucial for constructive conversations. Instead of reacting defensively or showing frustration, in a calm voice, say, "*I see where you're coming from, and I appreciate your honesty.*" Remember, your tone matters, so keep it steady and even. Also, pay attention to your body language: uncross your arms and lean slightly forward to demonstrate engagement and openness. With practice, maintaining composure becomes easier and sets a positive tone for productive discussions.
- **Focus on collaborative solutions.** Receiving pushback doesn't mean your idea is off the table; it signals that there are concerns to address. Engage your colleague in problem-solving with statements like, "*Thanks for sharing those concerns. Your experience will be valuable as we refine this. When can we schedule a follow-up to continue the discussion?*" This approach helps you move your ideas forward while gaining valuable insights and turning resistance into an opportunity for collaboration.

Strategies for Responding to Criticism

Criticism is a tough pill to swallow, but it's a vital part of professional development. It's an opportunity to get better. This section will show you how to respond to feedback with an open mind and use it as a powerful tool for building resilience. Let's explore some strategies that can help you turn even the toughest criticism into a catalyst for growth.

- **How to stay calm.** It is easy to get flustered when criticism surprises you. But if we lose our cool, we may miss a valuable learning opportunity. To stay centered, try a simple breathing exercise: inhale for 4 seconds, hold for 4, then exhale for 6. Focusing on your breathing helps settle your nerves and keeps you grounded.
- **Focus on the issue, not the person.** It's easy to get distracted by who's criticizing you or how they're saying it, especially if you have a difficult history with them. For example, imagine after a well-researched presentation, your colleague Ryan says, "*Too bad the market shifted since you started.*" Your initial reaction might be to feel defensive or angry. But if you can detach from Ryan's tone, you'll see that his comment contains valuable information. Remind yourself that your goal is to improve your work, not to win an argument. Focus on the issue and use the comment as an opportunity for growth. We'll continue with this example to show you how.
- **Redirecting the conversation**. With your eyes on the prize, it's time to redirect the conversation. Let's continue with Ryan's criticism and a productive response:

    "*Thanks for the feedback, Ryan. Can you help me to understand which specific market trends have been overlooked?*" This approach keeps the conversation focused on the issue, helping you avoid getting distracted by personal feelings while maintaining a constructive dialogue.
- **Encouraging dialogue**. After redirecting the conversation, get the whole team involved. By asking open-ended questions, you can turn a critique into a group problem-solving session. For example, try saying:

    "*Thanks for identifying the specific market trends you were concerned about. I think it could be really valuable to hear from the rest of the team as well. Are there other trends we should consider? How might these trends impact the project's feasibility and success?*"

    You may also consider other open-ended questions like "*What are some alternative strategies we might consider?*" "*How can we integrate different perspectives on this issue?*" and "*What potential challenges do you foresee and how might we overcome them?*"

    Remember to practice active listening as you go. Summarize what you hear to ensure everyone is on the same page. This keeps the conversation moving and helps you stay present so you can focus on the solution, not the initial critique.
- **Take time if needed**. While some situations, like during meetings, require immediate responses, others allow for a pause. For example, if a student approaches me at the end of class upset about a grade, I'll suggest we discuss it during office hours. This naturally inserts a "cool down" period. This pause helps the student calm and gives me a chance to review the assignment and prepare for our conversation. Having a few phrases ready can help facilitate constructive conversations. Here are a few for you to consider:

    "*Thank you for your feedback. I'd like some time to reflect on it before we discuss it further. Can we schedule a meeting for Thursday?*"

"I appreciate your input. I think I need some time to process this. Can we revisit this conversation tomorrow?"

"I value your perspective and want to give it the consideration it deserves. Can we plan to discuss this again in a couple of days?"

"I hear your concerns, and I want to address them fully. Can I follow up via email on Tuesday?"

Navigating Conflict

So far, you've learned how to deal with pushback and criticism. But what happens when conversations escalate into conflict? In this section, you will get the tools you need to approach conflict with confidence and navigate toward a resolution. Let's start with a workplace example.

Imagine a team working on a new marketing campaign. Two members, Jerry and Dawn, have fundamentally different ideas on how the campaign should be executed. Jerry favors a data-driven approach focused on analytics and targeted advertising, while Dawn champions a creative strategy centered on storytelling and emotional connection. This disagreement has created tension in meetings, stalled progress, and increased frustration, with both sides becoming more entrenched. Now, let's explore best practices for navigating this kind of conflict, then look at how to resolve the tension and find common ground.

- **Active listening**. Active listening is a nonnegotiable skill. To help Jerry and Dawn understand each other's perspectives, encourage them to practice this skill. Each should take turns fully articulating their ideas without interruption. Before responding, they should paraphrase what they heard to ensure genuine understanding. This simple practice shifts the tone from defensiveness to understanding, fostering respect and collaboration even amid disagreement.
- **Identifying triggers**. We all have a few hot buttons—those moments that make us react emotionally. Maybe we raise our voice when we feel ignored or become defensive when our achievements are downplayed. In our example, Jerry might feel frustrated if ideas are dismissed without supporting data, while Dawn may feel undervalued if her creative input isn't acknowledged. Identifying these triggers in yourself and your teammates builds empathy and self-awareness, which helps everyone approach the conversation with more patience.
- **Seeking common ground**. A powerful way to navigate criticism and tension is to focus on shared goals. In this case, both Jerry and Dawn care about the success of the campaign. Reminding them of their shared dedication and the bigger objective—making a meaningful connection with their audience—can open the door to collaboration. Highlighting overlapping goals helps shift the conversation from opposition to a partnership, where Jerry and Dawn can seek solutions that honor both perspectives (see Table 4.2).

Table 4.2 Data and Trends: Conflict Makes Us Antsy.

Uncomfortable with conflict? Rather avoid it and look the other way than attempt to resolve it? You're not alone. Let's look at some statistics related to workplace conflict.

- According to The Myers-Briggs Company,[4] 49% of workplace conflict stems from personality clashes, with 34% resulting from workplace stress, followed by heavy workloads (33%).
- Acas Research[5] found that nearly 500,000 employees resign annually as a result of conflict.
- Niagara Institute[6] found that most adults, over 50%, prioritize harmony when resolving conflict even at the expense of their own needs. They also found that nearly 90% of respondents are willing to compromise if it means breaking a deadlock.

Most of us were never explicitly taught how to navigate conflict well, and if we're honest, it can be uncomfortable. If you're interested in more statistics related to workplace culture, check out: https://pollackpeacebuilding.com/workplace-conflict-statistics.

Resolving Conflict

Now that you've navigated the early stages of conflict, it's time to resolve it. Remember, resolving conflict is often a process that can take time. Sometimes quick apologies clear misunderstandings, but other times, like with Jerry and Dawn, it may require patience. That's perfectly okay. The key is to approach resolution with clear communication, genuine empathy, and an openness to understanding.

- **Focus on interests, not positions**. When we shift our attention to shared interests—like creating a successful campaign—we naturally loosen our hold on rigid positions. This continues the idea of finding common ground. By framing the conversation around what truly matters to everyone, like engaging the audience, we encourage collaboration rather than competition. For example, a team leader might say, "*We all want this campaign to be a success and connect with our audience. Let's focus on how we can work together to make that happen.*"
- **Seek creative solutions**. Encourage the team to brainstorm solutions that blend storytelling with data. For example, they might develop a dual approach where they use analytics for targeted ads while weaving in

compelling narratives to engage the audience. Combining different perspectives can create a stronger, more innovative campaign.
- **Celebrate engagement**. Resolving conflict creates a more collaborative and innovative environment. When Jerry and Dawn reach a solution, celebrate their teamwork as a success. This is also a good time to remind your team that strong opinions are a good thing; it shows they're engaged and care about the outcome. By reframing conflict as a positive, you can turn challenges into opportunities for growth.

While the Jerry and Dawn example shows how common ground can emerge naturally, not all conflicts are so straightforward. Sometimes resolution takes longer, or shared understanding remains elusive. That's okay. With patience, active listening, focusing on shared interests, and separating the person from the problem, you can keep the focus on solutions rather than personalities. Remember, conflict is often a catalyst for progress.

Dissenting

Dissenting is simply when we express disagreement or opposition, whether about ideas, decisions, policies, or practices. Because it involves pushing back, it can feel uncomfortable, especially for those of us who value harmony or worry about conflict. It's natural to hesitate; sometimes resistance feels personal or awkward to handle (see Table 4.3).

Table 4.3 Immediate Impact: Leadership Takeaway from Communication Expert, Dr. Ryan Bisel

Conversations with Leaders: Avoid a Bad Apple Barrel	Dr. Ryan Bisel, Professor of Communication at Oklahoma University, is an expert in leadership, employee voice, and dissent. He reveals why many employees stay silent: **Fear.**
	Employees fear retribution—exclusion, punishment, and shame. Yet the cost of silence is even greater. When we rationalize ethical breaches or overlook policy issues, we risk creating a **bad apple barrel**.
	Ryan explains: "*A bad apple is a single employee who engaged in unethical, immoral, or illegal behavior. A bad apple barrel is an environment ripe for corruption.*"
	By fostering an environment where dissent is safe and constructive, organizations can prevent the barrel from rotting and unlock the power of honest, ethical dialogue.
	Ryan expands on this idea and offers practical strategies for sharing your voice in the workplace in season 3, episode 7 of *The Communicative Leader* podcast.[7]

But here's the good news: when dissent is expressed constructively, it becomes a powerful tool. It helps improve decision-making, fosters trust, and creates a healthier, more innovative workplace. Speaking up with respect and clarity not only brings diverse perspectives to the table but also shows that you value open dialogue. Remember, differing opinions, when shared thoughtfully, can lead to better outcomes.

- **Constructive versus destructive dissent**. Let's clarify the difference. Constructive dissent means disagreeing in a way that aims to improve the situation. You present a well-reasoned argument supported by data and suggest alternatives. It's about offering solutions, not just pointing out problems. Destructive dissent, however, can disrupt the workplace. It's often less thoughtful and more emotional and can lead to tension or damaged relationships. It might involve dismissive comments, personal attacks, or disruptive behavior that escalates conflict rather than resolves it. See Table 4.4 for examples of what to do and what not to do when raising concerns.
- **Benefits of dissent**. When done well, constructive dissent can be incredibly valuable. It brings different viewpoints to the table, sparking creativity and better decision-making. It helps identify potential issues early, preventing bigger problems later on. Plus, when employees feel safe sharing their ideas and concerns, they become more invested in their work. This openness boosts organizational learning and overall effectiveness.

Think back—have you ever held back your concerns? Imagine how things might have been different if you had voiced them earlier. Could you have avoided an unintended mistake or uncovered a better approach? Reflecting on these moments can encourage you to speak up more confidently next time. Now let's think about how to practice constructive dissent.

How to Practice Constructive Dissent

- **State your concern clearly and respectfully**. When you engage in constructive dissent, your goal is to have a thoughtful conversation aimed at improvement, not conflict. Frame your dissent around the issue, not personal traits or motives.
- **Support your point with evidence**. Back up your concerns with relevant data such as market trends, performance metrics, stakeholder feedback, or industry reports. This shows that your perspective is grounded in facts, not emotions.

The art of dissent isn't just about saying "*I disagree*," it's about doing so with grace and grit. Next time you feel the urge to speak up, remember you're helping to fine-tune the engine, making your workplace more thoughtful and resilient. Constructive dissent isn't an obstacle; it's your ticket to better solutions and stronger teamwork.

Table 4.4 Actionable Insights: Constructive Versus Destructive Dissent in the Workplace

Workplace Example: Your company is proposing a new remote work policy that requires employees to come into the office at least three days a week.

Constructive Dissent (What to Do)

You disagree with the new policy due to concerns about commuting and its impact on your productivity and work–life balance.

1. **Identify key concerns:** Gather data showing that employees are more productive and report more work–life balance while working remotely.

2. **Offer solutions:** Instead of just saying "no," propose an alternative that allows for more flexible work options, such as coming in any ten days during the month, and cite examples from other companies that have successfully implemented similar policies.

3. **Request a meeting:** Request a meeting with management to discuss your perspective in a calm and respectful manner.

4. **Engage in dialogue:** During the meeting, actively listen to management's reasoning behind the policy while also presenting your evidence in a constructive manner.

Destructive Dissent (What NOT to Do)

Your colleague disagrees with the new policy but expresses their dissent in a destructive way.

1. **Negative remarks:** Your coworker vents their frustration to everyone who will listen, often making sarcastic comments about management's competence and the fairness of the policy.

2. **Gossiping:** Your coworker spreads discontent among team members, encouraging others to complain instead of seeking constructive solutions.

3. **Undermining authority:** Your peer disregards the policy by continuing to work remotely and encourages others to do the same, which creates confusion and resentment.

4. **Personal attacks:** During a team meeting, your coworker blames specific managers for the decision, suggesting they don't care about employee well-being.

Key Differences

Constructive dissent aims to improve a situation or decision through respectful, thoughtful feedback. In contrast, destructive dissent creates conflict, disrupts teamwork, and damages morale. While constructive dissent fosters growth and collaboration, destructive dissent leads to division and frustration.

NONVERBAL COMMUNICATION SKILLS

As we shift from focusing on words to understanding nonverbal cues, it's important to recognize that what you say is only half the story; how you say it can make all the difference. Nonverbal signals like eye contact, body language, and posture can amplify your message or inadvertently send mixed messages. For example, a warm "I agree" can be undermined by slouched shoulders or distracted glances that suggest disinterest.

Let's explore how to use these powerful nonverbal elements with intention Mastering your nonverbal communication can elevate your leadership presence and help you connect more authentically.

SIGNAL THAT CONFIDENCE: BODY LANGUAGE

Welcome to the world of body language, the unsung hero of communication. Without a single word, our nonverbal cues—from posture and gestures to eye contact—can speak volumes. These signals are incredibly powerful tools for conveying trust, confidence, and engagement, often more effectively than words alone.

In this section, we will explore the essentials: body posture, facial expressions, gestures, and most importantly, eye contact. Mastering your nonverbal communication is especially beneficial for quieter voices, helping you convey enthusiasm and connect with others effortlessly. To show you what that looks like in action, let's compare an example of less effective body language with a more engaging and approachable posture.

Figure 4.1 shows an employee whose body language isn't quite aligned with engaging communication. His arms are crossed, and his neutral expression suggests he's not fully tuned into his audience. While this isn't necessarily negative body language, it highlights an important point: if we're not checking in with ourselves, we might inadvertently be sending a message we don't intend—such as disengagement or defensiveness—without realizing it. This can cause us to miss valuable opportunities to connect beyond just our words.

In contrast, Figure 4.2 demonstrates much more positive body language. The man is using thoughtful hand gestures, maintaining an open posture, and turned toward his conversation partner—traits that invite engagement. He's smiling and making eye contact, which convey warmth and confidence. The woman he's speaking with, although her arms are crossed, is smiling and leaning slightly in, showing she's engaged and receptive.

These two examples set the stage for the upcoming sections on facial expressions, eye contact, gestures, mirroring, proxemics, tone, and haptics.

AMPLIFYING YOUR LEADERSHIP VOICE

Figure 4.1 Overlooking the Subtle Signals: The Importance of Nonverbal Communication Often Goes Unnoticed

Figure 4.2 Embracing the Silent Language: Harnessing Nonverbal Cues to Connect and Communicate More Effectively

They serve as visual anchors you can return to throughout your communication journey, helping you understand and practice effective nonverbal cues in every interaction.

The Power of Posture

Want to instantly convey confidence? Start with your posture. Without saying a word, your stance can signal authority and approachability. Being mindful of your posture can completely change how others perceive you and how you feel in any room. It's a simple adjustment with a big impact on your leadership presence.

- **Convey confidence.** Standing tall with your shoulders back and your head held high is the universal sign of confidence. This posture not only projects self-assurance but also can actually help you feel more confident. Research shows that adopting a powerful stance can reduce tensions and anxiety, all while signaling competence.
- **Establish influence.** An open posture—like uncrossing your arms and facing your audience—creates a welcoming atmosphere. It signals approachability and a willingness to connect, helping you establish influence and build rapport with others.

- **Practice makes better**. Regularly check in with your posture during meetings and interactions. Are you standing tall with a straight back and open shoulders? Avoid crossing your arms, as it can unintentionally signal defensiveness, disinterest, or resistance. Instead, keep your arms open to foster approachability and engagement.

Facial Expressions

Like posture, many of us don't think much about what our facial expressions convey. But if we're not mindful, we might send mixed messages. Here are some key expressions that can boost your communication, build rapport, and foster a positive workplace atmosphere.

- **Genuine smile**. A real smile—one that reflects genuine happiness—goes a long way. It signals warmth and approachability, especially when greeting colleagues or meeting new people. Research shows that a sincere smile makes you appear 20% more trustworthy[8] and 10% more attractive[9] and enhances perceptions of competence and confidence[10] both in everyday interactions and during interviews.
- **Nodding**. Nodding is a simple yet powerful way to show agreement and encourage a speaker. It demonstrates active listening and invites others to share more. Just be mindful, as excessive nodding can undermine your authority or become distracting. A few well-timed nods—especially when the speaker is seeking affirmation—reinforce engagement and strike the right balance.
- **Raised eyebrows**. Raising your eyebrows can express surprise or curiosity or emphasize a point during a discussion. It's a simple way to show interest and connect with peers, making conversations feel more engaging and genuine.
- **Neutral expression**. During sensitive or serious conversations, a neutral facial expression can boost your credibility and show you're fully present. It signals engagement without exaggeration, helping you come across as approachable and credible. Be mindful of "resting b&% face," which can be misinterpreted as disinterest or judgment. If you've gotten this feedback, try these tips:
    - **Relax your facial muscles**: Consciously release tension in your forehead, eyebrows, jaw, and mouth to appear more approachable.
    - **Monitor your eyebrows**: Aim to keep your eyebrows relaxed and in a neutral position. Furrowing or lowering them can unintentionally create a harsh or unapproachable appearance.

Eye Contact

Eye contact is a powerful nonverbal tool that can significantly enhance your workplace communication.

- **Establish connection**. Use eye contact to create a genuine connection, whether speaking to an individual or a group. It shows you're present, attentive, and truly engaged.
- **Adapt to your audience**. Different cultures and organizations have varying norms around eye contact. Pay attention to your audience's comfort level and adjust accordingly. In some settings, too much eye contact may feel intrusive; in others, it's expected. Want more tips on communicating across cultures? Check out Chapter 7.
- **Break it up**. Constant eye contact can be intimidating. Instead, periodically shift your gaze to signal that you're thinking. Then, return your focus to the audience to maintain connection.

Gestures

Gestures are a crucial component of nonverbal communication, playing a large role in how we convey messages, express emotions, and project competence.

- **Types of gestures**. Gestures can be a powerful tool in communication. Here's a quick breakdown of some of the most common types:
  - **Emblems**: Gestures with specific, culturally understood meanings (e.g., a thumbs-up).
  - **Illustrators**: Gestures that enhance verbal messages, such as using your hands to show size or direction.
  - **Regulators**: Gestures that help manage the flow of conversation, such as raising your hand to signal for a pause.
  - **Affect displays**: Gestures that convey emotions without words. For example, throwing your hands up in frustration at another driver during rush hour is a common way to show annoyance nonverbally.
- **Controlled movements**: Every gesture you make matters. Avoid fidgeting, wringing your hands, or picking at cuticles, as these gestures (known as adaptors) signal anxiety and can distract from your message. Instead, use intentional, controlled movements to reinforce your message and show you're composed.
- **Signal key points**: Use hand movements to guide discussions and highlight important information. For example, you can raise your hand to invite a colleague to speak or gesture toward a key slide during a presentation. When you're not emphasizing a point, keep your hands resting on the table or at your sides to convey confidence and maintain composure. This is also a great bonus for those of us who tend to have shaky hands when nervous.

Mirroring

Mirroring is a powerful nonverbal technique that involves subtly matching the behaviors, posture, and facial expressions of your conversation partner. The key word here is *subtly*. When done effectively, mirroring enhances rapport by fostering trust and a genuine sense of connection.

Pay close attention to your partner's nonverbal cues—if they lean in, you can lean in slightly; if they smile, reflect that warmth; if they show concern with a frown, acknowledge it with a gentle response. It's not about copying every reaction like a robot but about aligning your cues in a natural, empathetic way that demonstrates engagement and understanding. This simple practice can make you more likable, deepen your relationships, and elevate your leadership presence.

Proxemics: Personal Space

Understanding personal space is essential for effective communication. The distance you maintain with others influences perceptions of trust, authority, and connection. Being mindful of these invisible boundaries can enhance your leadership presence and foster a comfortable environment.

- **Respect personal space**. Different cultures and individuals have varying comfort levels with proximity. In casual conversations with colleagues, maintaining an arm's length distance typically shows respect and fosters connection. Standing too close can feel intrusive, while standing too far away can create distance—literally and figuratively. Aim for that comfortable middle ground where everyone feels at ease.
- **Use proximity strategically**. You can use proximity to guide a conversation. For example, in a team meeting, subtly moving closer to quieter individuals can signal that you value their input and encourage them to participate. Conversely, when interacting with senior leadership, taking a respectful step back demonstrates deference and acknowledges their authority.
- **Practice awareness**. Continuously observe your surroundings. Is your audience leaning in, indicating engagement? Or pulling back, signaling discomfort? Reading these nonverbal cues allows you to adjust your distance appropriately, creating a more effective and comfortable communication environment.

Tone and Paralinguistic Cues

Your tone can make or break your message. Words are simply the vehicle for communication; it's your tone that guides the direction and amplifies the impact of your message. Paralinguistic cues such as pitch, volume, tempo, and rhythm add depth and nuance, conveying emotions and intentions that words alone may not fully express.

- **Mind your pitch and volume.** A strong, assertive tone conveys confidence and can motivate your audience. Conversely, lowering your voice when discussing challenges can signal urgency and help focus attention. Adjusting your pitch and volume allows you to effectively communicate confidence, concern, or enthusiasm as the situation demands.
- **Pay attention to tempo.** The speed at which you speak communicates urgency or thoughtfulness. Slowing down your pace can emphasize important points, while a faster tempo can convey excitement and energy. Be sure to match your speaking rate to the context and content of the conversation.
- **Utilize variety.** Nobody wants to listen to a dull, monotone voice. "Bueller, anyone?" Instead, vary your tone—use inflection to highlight key ideas, build suspense, or shift emotions. The right variety transforms a routine message into something memorable and powerful.

Haptics: Touch

Touch, or haptics, is one of the least discussed yet most powerful forms of nonverbal communication. When used appropriately, it can significantly strengthen your connections with colleagues. However, understanding the nuances of physical contact is crucial.

- **Respect cultural norms.** Be mindful that different cultures and individuals have varying comfort levels with proximity and touch. A handshake may be appropriate in some cultures but considered too forward in others. Pay attention to your colleagues' cues—if someone seems hesitant, a warm smile or nod can convey friendliness without crossing boundaries.
- **Use touch strategically.** You can use touch to make a strong first impression or foster camaraderie. A firm handshake can signal confidence, while a gentle touch on the shoulder during a casual conversation can build rapport. However, always consider the context; when in doubt, less is more. Always prioritize professionalism and comfort. If a teammate leans away or seems uncomfortable, adjust your approach accordingly. Respecting personal boundaries fosters a respectful environment and demonstrates that you genuinely care.

The Power of Silence

Silence is a potent communication tool. In a world filled with noise, intentional pauses create space for reflection, emphasize key points, and convey emotion more effectively than words alone.

- **Embrace pauses.** Use deliberate pauses during conversations or presentations. A brief silence allows your audience to process information, builds anticipation, and underscores important messages.

- **Use silence to foster engagement**. Resist the urge to fill every moment with words. Allowing moments of quiet encourages participation, especially from hesitant colleagues, and gives everyone space to share their thoughts.
- **Indicate contemplation**. When discussing complex topics or making decisions, a pause signals that you're thoughtfully considering the matter. It demonstrates respect for the conversation and invites others to reflect and contribute.

KEY TAKEAWAYS

1. **Communication Is Your Leadership Cornerstone:** Want the 'leader' label with or without the position? You've got to flex those communication muscles! Approachability and relatability are your secret weapons. Encourage diverse viewpoints because teams that champion open discussions make better decisions! Remember, while speaking up is important, active listening is essential to be able to contribute in meaningful ways.
2. **The Power of Preparation:** Rolling into a meeting unprepared? That's like going to an interview without knowing about the company! Take charge by thoroughly reviewing the agenda, gathering relevant facts, and organizing your thoughts. A well-prepared communicator projects confidence and clarity, making it easier to contribute effectively to the discussion. You want your ideas to shine, not get buried by a lack of clarity.
3. **Embrace Constructive Dissent:** Dissenting doesn't make you a rebel without a cause; it makes you a savvy problem-solver who is committed to excellence. When you express disagreement, do so with the aim of improving decisions. Frame your input around facts and insights, and back it up with evidence. Remember: constructive dissent invites innovation and fosters an environment where creativity thrives. Your voice matters, so use it to solve problems and innovate!
4. **Master Nonverbal Communication:** What you say is important, but how you say it is crucial. Nail your body language, facial expressions, and eye contact because your nonverbal communication speaks even louder than your words. Stand tall, maintain eye contact, and keep an open posture. A genuine smile can set the tone for approachability and warmth, while gestures can emphasize essential points. Harness the power of nonverbal cues, especially my naturally quieter friends, as they can help you convey engagement and influence.
5. **Cultivate a Feedback Culture:** Feedback doesn't have to feel like nails on a chalkboard; think of it as a fast track to personal growth. Cultivate a culture where team members feel empowered to exchange feedback

openly. This not only enhances collaboration and trust but also reinforces a culture of open communication where everyone is committed to learning.

NOTES

1. Edmondson, A. C. (2018). *The fearless organization: Creating psychological safety in the workplace for learning, innovation, and growth*. John Wiley & Sons.
2. Van der Meer, L., Maat, M., & Van den Bosch, F. A. J. (2018). The role of shared leadership in decision quality: A student of team dynamics and decision-making in interdisciplinary teams. *Organizational Behavior and Human Decision Processes*, *148*, 162–171. https://doi.org/10.1016/j.obhdp.2018.05.002
3. Omilion-Hodges, L. (Host). (2025, March 24). The magic of leadership communication: How to captivate, influence, and inspire your team: A conversation with Jimi Gibson [Audio podcast episode]. *The Communicative Leader Podcast*. https://www.thecommunicativeleader.com/podcast/episode/7c6f30d7/the-magic-of-leadership-communication-how-to-captivate-influence-and-inspire-your-team-a-conversation-with-jimi-gibson
4. The Myers-Briggs Company. (2022). *Conflict at work: A research report from the Myers-Briggs Company*. https://www.themyersbriggs.com/en-US/Programs/Conflict-at-Work-Research
5. Acas. (2021, May 11). *Estimating the costs of workplace conflict*. https://www.acas.org.uk/research-and-commentary/estimating-the-costs-of-workplace-conflict/report
6. Bennet, M. (2022, August 11). *Workplace conflict statistics: How we approach conflict at work*. https://www.niagarainstitute.com/blog/workplace-conflict-statistics
7. Omilion-Hodges, L. (Host). (2023, October 23). Leadership, business ethics, and speaking up: A conversation with Dr. Ryan Bisel [Audio podcast episode]. *The Communicative Leader Podcast*. https://www.thecommunicativeleader.com/podcast/episode/7bd031c3/leadership-business-ethics-and-speaking-up-a-conversation-with-dr-ryan-bisel
8. Rule, N. O., & Ambady, N. (2008). The face of trustworthiness: Physiognomy and the uncanny valley. *Social Influence*, *3*(1), 26–43. https://doi.org/10.1080/15534510802216016
9. Walker, M. (2010). Smiling makes you more attractive. *Journal of Experimental Social Psychology*, *46*(2), 181–188. https://doi.org/10.1016/j.jesp.2009.09.002
10. McGowan, M. (2018). The power of a smile: How smiling affects people's the opinions of you in a job interview. *Washington State University Journal of Communication*, *25*(1), 45–60.

Chapter 5
Write to Lead
Developing Your Digital and Written Communication

**Level 2.
Refine Your
Leadership Voice**

Having strengthened your spoken communication, the next step is to learn how to craft compelling digital and written messages. In this chapter, you will discover how to articulate your ideas clearly and persuasively across various platforms, expanding your influence beyond face-to-face interactions.

Building on our exploration of a leader's authentic voice in the last chapter, we now turn to the backbone of effective communication—written and digital skills that cut through today's fast-paced, distraction-filled world. Mastering the art of clear, concise messaging is essential; it transforms your words into powerful tools that resonate with your audience whether you're drafting an email, delivering a presentation, or engaging in a virtual meeting. In this chapter, you'll discover how to craft messages that are not only heard but also remembered, helping you capture attention and prompt action.

Effective communication begins with simplicity: using direct language, avoiding jargon, and focusing on key messages that respect your audience's time. In the realm of written communication, storytelling plays a vital role by connecting facts with emotions to foster relatability and memorability. We'll explore narrative structures, emotional appeals, and real-world examples to elevate your writing. Beyond crafting messages, how we deliver them in digital spaces matters just as much, so we'll cover strategies for engaging virtual audiences, encouraging quieter voices, and making every interaction meaningful. These practical skills can be learned and improved over time, enabling you to communicate clearly, inspire action, and foster authentic connections.

WRITTEN COMMUNICATION ESSENTIALS
Rule 1. You're Writing for Your Audience: Not for Yourself

Many people find this surprising because we often see ourselves as central to our writing. While the act of writing originates with you, your main goal is to communicate with others. Before putting pen to paper—or fingers to keyboard—take a moment to ask yourself these helpful questions:

Who is my audience?
- What are their ages, backgrounds, and interests?
- Are they experts or casual readers?

What is the purpose of the document?
- Are they looking for information, a call to action, or motivation?
- Do I want to inform, persuade, or inspire them?

What do they need and expect?
- What do they already know about this topic?
- What do I want them to take away?

How familiar are they with the subject?
- Should I include background details or technical info?
- How much depth is needed?

What tone and style will best connect with my audience?
- Should I be formal or casual?
- Should the document be informational, persuasive, conversational, or professional?

In addition to these basics, consider your audience's values and beliefs, how they will use the information, and their preferred format. While this list might seem a bit overwhelming at first, think back to a recent email you sent or a memo you drafted; you probably handled many of these aspects automatically, without consciously realizing it. For those of you who write frequently as part of your work, this process may feel like second nature. If writing is more occasional for you, it's helpful to revisit this list to remind yourself: focus on your audience, not just yourself. Let's look at an example:

Workplace Example

A manager drafting a quarterly report doesn't use technical jargon or detail-oriented language if presenting to a nontechnical board of directors. Instead, they focus on the overall performance and key metrics that align with business objectives, ensuring the audience understands the implications without getting lost in technical details.

Rule 2. Embrace Simple, Direct Language

It can be really easy to get lost in technical details. When we're using specialized language day in and day out, it can be difficult to think about how to translate the ideas into simpler messaging. Also, while you may be excited about specific nuances and details as they relate to your area of expertise, by returning to Rule 1 and writing for your audience, it is important to remember to provide only the content that impacts your audience directly.

Workplace Example

An HR professional sends out a communication about new benefits. Instead of saying, "*We are implementing a novel holistic health insurance plan that aims to enhance the overall wellbeing of employees across physical and emotional dimensions,*" they write, "*We are introducing a new health insurance plan that will give you better benefits.*"

Rule 3. Avoid Jargon

Let's be real: jargon can throw a monkey wrench in understanding and engagement. If you want everyone to understand what you're saying rather than just nodding along with confused looks, drop the lingo and keep it simple. Clear communication not only keeps things efficient, but it also shows you respect your audience.

To illustrate, consider this experience: Thirty minutes into my first day as a marketing specialist at a hospital, I was in a meeting and felt completely lost. I understood maybe 20% of what was being said, and I vividly remember thinking that I'd have understood more if the discussion had been in Spanish, despite my shaky grasp of the language. My next thought was, "What have I done? Did I really make a career change for this?"

The jargon and acronyms were overwhelming. This experience taught me a valuable lesson: clarity always trumps confusion. Simple, straightforward communication truly makes a world of difference.

Workplace Example

A project manager emails team members about an upcoming client presentation. Instead of saying, "*We need to leverage our synergies to meet our KPIs,*" they say, "*We need to work together to meet our deadline for the client presentation.*" This makes the message accessible and also helps the audience process the message more quickly and with less risk of misunderstanding.

Rule 4. Focus on Key Messages

When communicating about complex projects, it's easy to get lost in the details. Taking a step back to identify the key message is crucial to effective, audience-centered communication. Those outside of your project team don't need every detail in one email. If you're not sure where to get started, consider these clarifying questions:

- What is the most important message I want to convey?
- What action do I want my audience to take?
- What information is necessary for the audience to understand the context of the message?

I always suggest having a colleague review your message before you send it. When I chaired a recent committee, I asked members to review my emails before sending them to the faculty. Their feedback helped me more clearly reflect the group's sentiment and communicate our message more clearly.

Even with a PhD in Communication and while writing a book on leadership communication, I still make it a point to ask colleagues to periodically review my messages. It's a good reminder that no matter how experienced you are, it's easy to get caught up in jargon and details and lose sight of the main point. Sometimes, fresh eyes make all the difference.

Workplace Example

A sales director is sending out a memo about performance targets. Instead of outlining every single metric for the year, they focus on the top three goals for the next quarter, using bold text and bullet points to highlight them, ensuring that the team can quickly grasp what's most important.

Rule 5. Read Twice, Send Once

Today's workplaces move at lightning speed, making quick communication tempting and error-prone. Taking a moment to read your message twice can save you from misunderstandings and unintended missteps (see Table 5.1).

Table 5.1 Instant Impact: Leadership Takeaway from Writing Expert, Pam Hurley

Conversations with Leaders: Writing Is Leadership	Meet Pam Hurley: With 30 years of coaching corporate clients, she specializes in transforming technical experts' writing and speaking skills.
	Many see writing as just another task to get done. But Pam redefines it as problem solving, turning communication into an activity that demands strategy, expertise, and savvy.
	If you're documenting processes or sharing project updates, remember you're engaging in crucial problem solving, not just checking a box.
	Learn more from Pam's insights in Season 4, Episode 8 of *The Communicative Leader* podcast.[1]

On the first read, focus on the overall flow: Are your main points clear? Is the tone appropriate for your audience? Look for areas where clarity could be improved or jargon might cause confusion.

On the second read, review the details: grammar, typos, formatting, and the accuracy of dates and figures. Catching these small errors preserves your credibility and professionalism.

Workplace Example

In 2021, NASA tweeted that it was "sending a spacecraft to Uranus." While the statement was accurate, the phrasing led to a flood of jokes and memes across social media, prompting the agency to clarify that it meant to refer to a mission involving the planet's rings and moons.

Rule 6. Be Authentic

When you write, embrace your true voice. Authenticity builds trust and makes your message relatable. Share your insights and experiences instead of defaulting to jargon or corporate speak because your perspective is what makes your communication impactful. Don't be afraid to show vulnerability or admit when you don't have all the answers; honesty fosters openness and collaboration. Ultimately, being authentic lets your personality shine, creating a more engaging and meaningful connection with your audience.

Workplace Example

A CEO writes a personal note to the staff during a challenging time, sharing their own feelings and experiences rather than adopting a formal corporate tone. By expressing vulnerability and solidarity, they foster a sense of community and trust within the organization.

Rule 7. Use Active Voice

Using active voice is key to clear, effective workplace writing. It makes sentences more direct and easier to understand by showing who's performing the action. For example, instead of "The report was completed by the team," try "The team completed the report." This not only clarifies responsibility but also grabs the reader's attention. In business, active voice enhances persuasiveness, promotes accountability, and fosters collaboration. Ditch passive constructions. Embracing active voice will elevate your writing and might even keep your old English teacher happy!

Workplace Example

Instead of writing, "The project was approved by the department manager," you would write instead, "The department manager approved the project." In the active voice example, the department manager performs the action of approving the project. This direct approach focuses on the action and those performing it, making the communication clearer and more engaging. Simple yet effective, this small tip can boost your credibility and influence.

Rule 8. Bullet Points and Lists Are Your Friends

Many of us hesitate to use bullet points or numbered lists because we're used to writing in full paragraphs. While complete sentences have their place, there's a time and a purpose for lists. When drafting an agenda or email, focus on the key messages you want to highlight and make them easy for readers to find. Just as journalists are taught not to bury the lead, we shouldn't hide important details like action items or deadlines inside lengthy paragraphs. Lists improve clarity and help your main points stand out.

Workplace Example

When outlining the agenda for a team meeting, a manager uses bullet points to clearly list the topics to be discussed:

- Project updates
- Client feedback
- Upcoming deadlines

This format enables team members to prepare effectively for the meeting.

Rule 9. End with a Call to Action

A recent survey shows that the average office worker receives around 120 emails a day,[2] plus over 300 messages daily if you include instant messaging, Slack, and other mediated platforms.[3] With so much information vying for attention, it's essential that your audience knows exactly what to do next.

The best way to ensure this? Always end your message with a clear call to action.

Workplace Example

After presenting a new marketing strategy, a marketing manager concludes the email with, "*Please review the attached presentation and share your feedback by Friday so we can finalize our approach.*" This outlines the next steps for recipients and specifies when the action should be completed.

Rule 10. Know When to Use Visuals

Visuals can transform dense or forgettable messages into memorable, engaging ones. The key is to use them strategically. Consider incorporating visuals when:

- **Handling complex data**: Charts, graphs, and tables can simplify complex information, like statistics, making it easier to understand.
- **Making comparisons**: Bar graphs or side-by-side images can make differences and similarities more apparent, such as when you're showing performance targets over multiple periods.
- **Explaining processes**: Flowcharts and diagrams can illustrate steps more effectively than verbal instructions alone.
- **Highlighting key takeaways**: Infographics effectively summarize information in an eye-catching and memorable way.

Workplace Example

A financial analyst is preparing a report on budget allocations for the department. They include visuals like pie charts to illustrate spending categories and bar graphs for budget trends over the last three years, making the data easier to understand at a glance, particularly for those who may not have a strong background in finance.

Great written communication starts with truly understanding your audience and speaking their language. By focusing on your core messages; using simple, direct language; and thoughtfully incorporating visuals, you can make your messages more engaging and meaningful. The final steps—proofreading and ending with a clear call to action—ensure that your message lands and inspires the right response.

Next, we'll look at storytelling. It's a powerful way to make your messages more engaging and memorable.

READY TO PUT THIS INTO PRACTICE?

Amplify Your Leadership Voice Further

For a deeper reflection on your written communication strengths, explore the Amplifying Your Leadership Voice: Leadership Blueprint available at TheCommunicativeLeader.com

---

THE ROLE OF STORYTELLING IN WRITING

Karen Eber, CEO, author, and speaker, challenges the idea that storytelling is just for childhood. She highlights that in the workplace, storytelling is a powerful leadership tool—making messages memorable, building trust, and deepening connections. Unlike dry reports, stories engage more of the brain, enhancing understanding and retention while fostering psychological safety and energizing teams.

On *The Communicative Leader* podcast, Karen shared a four-question framework to incorporate storytelling into your leadership voice.

1. **Who am I talking to?** Make your story relevant. For example, linking a well-known sports victory story to overcoming obstacles or teamwork makes it memorable.
2. **What do I want them to take away?** Be clear with a call to action—leave your audience ready to act.
3. **What's their current mindset?** Understand if your team feels overwhelmed or energized and meet them there.
4. **What obstacles might arise?** Anticipate challenges like pushback or deadlines and prepare solutions.

Taking a few minutes to answer these questions before a meeting can transform your communication—whether verbal, written, or digital—by truly putting your audience first.

Karen's approach reminds us that storytelling isn't just about sharing; it's about sparking connection, trust, and enthusiasm. When you understand your audience and clarify your message, each story becomes an opportunity to inspire beyond data alone.

Up next, we'll explore practical tips and engaging examples to turn routine memos and reports into compelling, clear messages your team actually reads.

MASTERING THE MESSAGE: WRITING INFLUENTIAL WORKPLACE DOCUMENTS

In today's busy workplace, clear and thoughtful writing, whether in memos, meeting notes, presentations, or social media, can set you apart as a confident and impactful leader. For introverts, these channels offer a special space to reflect, craft authentic messages, and share insights that might otherwise go unheard. By honing your clarity, organization, and storytelling, you can turn everyday communication into a powerful tool for influence, allowing your ideas to resonate and elevate your leadership one well-crafted sentence at a time.

Effective Email

In today's digital workplace, email reigns supreme. Amid this flood of messages, a thoughtfully crafted email can stand out and cut through the noise. Yet, many of us default to hurried replies or generic templates that fail to convey our true voice (refer Table 5.2 for an example of what not to do). But don't worry! Below we're going to look at common pitfalls to avoid and simple strategies to elevate your email skills.

Table 5.2 Email Example: What Not to Do.

Email Example 1: What NOT to Do
Subject: Project Update

Hi Team,

I hope everyone is doing well and that you are all ready for another week of productive work on our project. I wanted to touch base regarding the status of the various tasks we've been discussing over the past few weeks, including the initiation of Phase 2 of the project, which encompasses the redesign of our user interface, updates to our database architecture, and finalization of the marketing strategy. Please make sure to review your sections thoroughly and confer with your peers if you have any questions. The deadline is approaching fast, so I expect everyone to step up their game and meet the expectations previously outlined in our roadmap documentation. For those who missed the last meeting, we had a lengthy discussion about the integration metrics and user feedback that should be incorporated into our product enhancements. Let's all ensure we're on the same page by the end of this week. Also, don't forget to format the documents according to the style guide we shared, and make sure to keep any external sources properly cited.

Thanks!

Best,
Mike Manager

We've all sent a message that's a bit of a "fishing expedition"—full of details that bury the main point. The problem is, when readers have to search for your key message, it can lead to confusion and unnecessary back-and-forth. If your communication requires a magnifying glass to find the point, it's a signal to try a different approach. Let's explore how to make your message stand out.

Table 5.3 Email Example: What to Do.

Email Example 2: What to Do
Subject: Project Update and Action Items for Phase 2

Hi Team,

I hope you're doing well!

I'm writing to share updates and action items for Phase 2.

> As a reminder, this phase involves a three-pronged approach:
>
> 1. Redesigning the user interface
>
> 2. Updating the database
>
> 3. Finalizing our marketing strategy
>
> Key Updates:
> - **Phase 2 Initiation**: We are officially beginning next Monday.
> - **Integration Metrics**: Incorporate user feedback into our product enhancements.
>
> Action Items:
> 1. **Review Your Sections**: Please review your assigned sections by **Friday**.
> 2. **Peer Collaboration**: Please meet with your group for a Phase 2 check-in by **Wednesday**.
> 3. **Format Documents**: Ensure your documents follow the style guide and cite external sources.
>
> Let's aim to be aligned by the end of this week. If you missed our last meeting, please catch up on the notes shared in the project folder.
>
> Thank you for your continued hard work. Please reach out if you have questions or need support.
>
> Best,
> Lizzie Leader

Key Updates

Let's look at the key differences between the two emails:

- **Subject Line**: The first email's subject is vague, while the second clearly indicates the content and includes action items.
- **Greeting and Tone**: The second email adopts a friendly, positive tone that encourages engagement.
- **Structure and Readability**: With headings, bullet points, and spacing, the second email is easier to read.
- **Clarity of Action Items**: The second email clearly outlines what is needed, making expectations straightforward.

- **Avoiding Jargon**: Using simple language, the second email is accessible to all team members.

By applying these techniques, the second email effectively communicates the necessary updates and creates a more reader-friendly experience. Taking a few extra minutes to craft impactful emails can save you from answering the same questions repeatedly. It's a small step that makes a big difference.

Effective Proposals

A well-crafted proposal is your golden ticket to winning over clients or securing support for your projects.

What to Do

Begin with a compelling executive summary that grabs attention, like opening with a surprising industry statistic related to the problem your proposal addresses. Clearly articulate your objectives, like boosting efficiency, and outline your approach with actionable steps. For example, if proposing a new software solution, include a timeline for implementation and explain its impact on different organizational units. Use visuals to clarify complex ideas and provide a thoughtfully prepared budget that highlights value. Together these elements enhance understanding and make your proposal more accessible.

What NOT to Do

Steer clear of excessive jargon, which can alienate readers; remember, clarity is just as important to your finance team as to your marketing colleagues. Lastly, don't use a generic, one-size-fits-all approach. Tailoring your proposal to your specific audience shows effort and understanding. A one-size-fits-all approach screams, "I didn't put in the effort!"

Effective Presentations

An engaging presentation can transform a dull meeting into a captivating experience, leaving your audience informed and inspired.

What to Do

Start with a strong hook like a personal story or an intriguing anecdote related to your topic. Keep slides uncluttered; for example, use one powerful image related to your data rather than several. Practice your delivery with colleagues or record yourself to ensure a natural, confident connection with your audience. Remember to highlight both successes and areas for improvement to keep your audience engaged.

What NOT to Do

Avoid reading directly from your slides; it's a surefire way to disengage your audience. Don't let slides become overly cluttered with text or complex graphics by taking a less-is-more approach. Instead of listing everything your team accomplished, say, "Here's what we achieved," and then add context. Transition from bullet points to engaging stories to better illustrate your points and maintain interest.

Effective Newsletters

A well-designed newsletter keeps your audience informed and engaged, serving as a valuable connection between you and your readers.

What to Do

Start with a catchy subject line that might include a timely tip or insight, like "Maximize Your Productivity This Week with These Tools." Segment your content into easily digestible sections, such as team highlights or upcoming events. Incorporate visuals, such as a photo from the last team-building event, coupled with compelling stories about employees' achievements, and finish with clear calls to action, inviting feedback or engagement.

What NOT to Do

Avoid overwhelming readers with lengthy articles; instead, keep content concise and relevant, such as how you'd communicate pivotal information in a quick team meeting. Don't forget to proofread; typos can undermine your credibility and turn your colleagues off in an instant. Also, steer clear of a monotonous layout because a bland newsletter goes right into the digital recycling bin!

Effective Meeting Minutes

Meeting minutes are the unsung heroes of effective communication, providing clarity and accountability after discussions.

What to Do

Capture key points, decisions, and action items, including who is responsible and deadlines. For example, if your team discussed a new project timeline, specify who is accountable and when deliverables are due. Keep minutes clear and concise because no one wants to wade through pages of transcripts. Send the minutes promptly, ideally within 24 hours, to keep everyone aligned and facilitate quick follow-up. For more tips on effective meeting minutes, check out Table 5.4.

Table 5.4 **Actionable Insights: Effective Meeting Minutes**

Taking effective meeting minutes can be more nuanced than it seems.

From choosing the right formatting to determining the appropriate level of detail, it often takes time to develop your rhythm, especially with a new team or group.

Scour the Shared Drive: Before volunteering or being assigned to record minutes, review previous examples to understand the expected format and detail level.

Pro Tip: Save a recent example with the current date to streamline the process and maintain consistency across meetings.

Hot Topic? My first experience capturing minutes was during a tense, finger-pointing meeting. In that moment, I made eye contact with a trusted senior colleague and followed her lead on what to include. If you're unsure, routing your draft minutes to a colleague for review can help ensure accuracy and professionalism.

What NOT to Do

Don't transcribe everything said. Instead, focus on the key points and action items relevant for future reference. Avoid unclear abbreviations or jargon that might confuse readers later. Instead of vague phrases like "We'll circle back," be specific, noting the exact follow-up meeting time and highlighting action items. Lastly, don't forget to confirm attendance!

Effective Social Media Posts

Social media posts are your opportunity to engage and entertain your audience, turning followers into loyal fans. For more practical tips on using social media to amplify your leadership voice, see Chapter 10.

What to Do

Use eye-catching visuals, such as photos from a recent company event, to draw attention. Write clear, compelling captions that encourage interaction. For instance, consider asking a question like, "What's your favorite productivity hack?" Incorporate relevant hashtags to increase reach, and consider the timing; for example, if your team is launching a new product, post during peak hours for maximum visibility.

Table 5.5 Data and Trends: Communication in the Workplace

To understand the importance of communication at work, consider these stats:

- 80% of professionals see clear communication as vital for career growth.[4]
- Poor written communication costs U.S. businesses an estimated $420 billion annually due to misunderstandings, errors, and delays.[5]
- 86% of employees and leaders cite ineffective communication as a top cause of workplace failures.[6]
- Organizations with strong internal communication are 3.5 times more likely to outperform their competitors financially.[7]
- 80% of professionals feel their written communication skills need improvement.[8]
- Digital communication skills are among the top leadership skills for the 21st century.[9]

These figures highlight that effective communication is crucial for individual success and organizational performance.

What NOT to Do

Avoid overly promotional language that feels salesy; instead, share stories of customer success or interesting insights from a recent project. Don't neglect to respond to comments or messages because ignoring your audience can crush engagement. Lastly, steer clear of excessive text; keep your posts short and snappy! Remember, social media thrives on authenticity, so show the human side of your workplace.

In today's workplace, effective communication is your secret weapon as a leader. Whether crafting a quick, informative email; delivering an engaging presentation; or designing a newsletter colleagues *actually* look forward to, each interaction is a chance to shine. For introverts or those who prefer written communication, these formats offer a space to express insights clearly and confidently. By honing these skills, you boost your influence (see Table 5.5).

ZOOM THIS: DIGITAL COMMUNICATION SKILLS

Welcome to the digital age, where effective communication can make or break your remote interactions. In our previous chapter, we honed the art of verbal and nonverbal communication, and now it's time to tackle the unique challenges of digital communication. From video calls on Zoom to instant chats on collaborative platforms, mastering these skills is essential for fostering connection and driving teamwork today.

We'll explore how to create inviting environments in virtual meetings, draw in even the quietest participants, and use tech tools to streamline discussions. With practical tips and a sprinkle of personality, you'll learn how to elevate your digital presence and make interactions impactful.

Nail That Video Call

In today's digital jungle, virtual meetings aren't just a trend; they're an essential skill for every modern professional. Think of video conferencing as your friendly, high-tech chat space where clarity, engagement, and connection matter most. In this section, you'll find practical tips to turn your virtual gatherings from snooze-fests into dynamic, productive conversations. We'll also explore how to create a welcoming atmosphere that makes everyone feel comfortable and gives quieter voices the space to shine.

1. **Welcoming Participants**
   - **Start with a warm greeting**: Kick off the meeting by personally welcoming everyone and using their names whenever possible. For example, "*Welcome, everyone! It's great to see you all today, especially [Name], who I haven't caught up with in a while.*" A little personal touch goes a long way in setting a warm tone.
   - **Break the ice**: Consider a simple icebreaker to create a friendly atmosphere. For example, ask everyone to share their current favorite book or drop an emoji in the chat that reflects how they're feeling today. Small gestures like these foster connection and set a positive tone right from the start.
   - **Set clear expectations**: Take a moment to briefly share the meeting agenda so everyone feels informed and prepared. If there will be breakout sessions, round-robin sharing, or individual reports, mention those ahead of time. This small step helps participants understand their role, stay engaged, and feel more at ease contributing to the conversation.

2. **Engaging Quiet Participants**
   - **Ask direct questions**: Gently invite quieter team members to share their thoughts by asking open-ended questions directly. For example, "*[Name], I'd love to hear your perspective on this topic.*" Personal invitations can help others feel valued and more comfortable speaking up.
   - **Use breakout groups**: Divide the larger meeting into smaller groups or pairs. People often feel more comfortable sharing ideas in a more intimate setting, which can encourage contributions from those who might be hesitant to speak up in a big group.
   - **Encourage written input**: Utilize the chat feature or shared documents to give participants a space to type their ideas. Some people find it easier to express themselves in writing first, which can lead to more thoughtful contributions and enrich the overall conversation.

- **Pay attention to nonverbal cues**: Utilize reactions like thumbs up, claps, or other emojis to promote engagement and show encouragement without interrupting the flow. These small gestures can make everyone feel seen and included.

3. **Using Polls Effectively**
   - **Start with a quick poll**: Kick off your meeting by inviting participants to share their thoughts or preferences, such as whether they prefer a virtual or in-person meeting next time. This simple, interactive step helps set a positive tone, makes everyone feel involved, and fosters a sense of connection right from the start. You can also do ice-breaker polls such as "what's your go-to weekend activity?" or "how are you feeling today in three words?"
   - **Real-time opinions**: During discussions, use polls to quickly check where everyone stands on a topic or to prioritize agenda items. For instance, a quick poll can help identify what the team feels is most urgent or important.
   - **Share live results**: Display poll responses as they come in, so everyone can see the feedback instantly. This transparency can spark further discussion and help clarify team priorities.
   - **Follow-up**: After polling, discuss the results and ask for additional input. This keeps the conversation flowing and makes participants feel their opinions truly matter.

4. **Discouraging Interruptions**
   - **Set ground rules**: Begin by gently setting expectations, such as raising hands—either virtually or physically—when someone wants to speak. This helps create a respectful atmosphere where everyone feels comfortable sharing their ideas without interruptions.
   - **Implement a "pause" strategy**: If interruptions happen, politely but firmly remind the team to let others finish their thoughts. For example, you might say, "*Let's give [Name] a moment to finish before we jump in.*"
   - **Encourage mute when not speaking**: Suggest that participants mute themselves when they're not talking. This simple step helps reduce background noise and keeps the focus on the speaker.

5. **Wrapping Up Meetings**
   - **Summarize key points**: End with a brief recap of the main takeaways and decisions made. This reinforces understanding, helps everyone stay on the same page, and ensures clear next steps as everyone leaves the meeting.
   - **Clarify action items**: Clearly state any next steps, assign responsibilities, and include deadlines. For example, "*Just to recap, [Name] will follow up with the report by next Tuesday.*" This keeps everyone accountable.
   - **Invite final comments**: Before closing, open the floor for any

last-minute questions or thoughts. It's a great way to ensure nothing is overlooked and everyone feels heard.
- **Thank participants**: Thank everyone for their time and input. A simple acknowledgment helps foster a positive, respectful team environment.

Additional Video Meeting Tips

To make your virtual meetings more effective, consider these additional suggestions

- **Encourage a proper setup**: Remind participants to check their audio and video before the meeting starts. Sharing quick tips or a help desk contact in advance can prevent technical hiccups and save time. For important calls like interviews, providing a phone number as a backup option ensures the conversation continues smoothly if technical issues arise.
- **Maintain eye contact**: Position the camera at eye level to foster better virtual rapport. Looking into the camera makes it feel like you're directly engaging with participants, creating a more personal connection.
- **Utilize breaks wisely**: For longer meetings, schedule short breaks to help everyone recharge and stay focused. Let participants know when these breaks will happen so they can plan accordingly, making the meeting more productive and comfortable.

By implementing these simple tips, you will foster more effective and engaging virtual meetings that support collaboration and effective communication.

MASTERING UBIQUITOUS DIGITAL COMMUNICATION SKILLS

Strong digital communication skills are now essential. We'll explore instant messaging, project management, collaboration, and feedback tools. Gone are the days of slow decision-making; now, being organized, clear, and agile is key to effective workplace communication.

1. Instant Messaging Tools (e.g., Slack, Microsoft Teams)

These platforms enable real-time conversations, making it easy to ask quick questions, share updates, and collaborate informally. They help reduce email overload and keep team members connected throughout the day.

Leadership Tip

Encourage your team to use instant messaging for quick check-ins and informal communication. Cultivate a culture where everyone feels comfortable reaching out, knowing it promotes openness and faster problem-solving.

2. Project Management Tools (e.g., Asana, Trello)

These tools help teams organize tasks, set deadlines, and track progress, ensuring everyone stays aligned with project goals. They also promote accountability and transparency within teams.

Leadership Tip

Lead by example. Keep your own tasks up-to-date and use these tools to communicate expectations and timelines. When leaders model effective use, it sets a standard for the entire team.

3. Document Collaboration Platforms (e.g., Google Workspace, Microsoft 365)

Real-time collaboration on documents, presentations, and spreadsheets fosters teamwork and allows for immediate feedback and improvements. It makes the process of creating and refining work more dynamic and inclusive.

Leadership Tip

Promote collaborative work sessions or document reviews. Empower employees to contribute ideas and edits, which builds ownership and encourages a team-oriented mindset.

4. Feedback and Signup Tools (e.g., SurveyMonkey, Signup Genius, Qualtrics)

These platforms are essential for gathering input, organizing events, and coordinating efforts. They help leaders make informed decisions and increase engagement by making participation easy and accessible.

Leadership Tip

Use feedback tools to listen actively and show that employee voices matter. Share the results transparently and explain how input influences decisions, fostering trust, inclusiveness, and a sense of community.

Creating an effective digital communication workflow is a journey that requires intentional effort and continuous improvement. By providing regular training, nurturing a flexible and open organizational culture, and encouraging team members to embrace these tools, you'll empower your team to work more smoothly and confidently. This, in turn, will strengthen collaboration, enhance decision-making, and boost overall productivity.

To help bring this process to life, Table 5.6 offers a clear, step-by-step view of how these tools come together in everyday teamwork. It highlights the typical

Table 5.6 Digital Communication Workflow Overview

Step	Activity and Description	Digital Tools	Notes
1.	Identify communication need	N/A	Is this a quick update or is more formal work needed?
2.	Use instant messaging for quick updates	Slack, Teams	For informal, real-time communication
3.	Decide if task requires formal planning	N/A	For more in-depth, formal work or complex tasks skip instant messaging
4.	Use project management tools for planning	Trello, Asana	Assign responsibilities, set deadlines
5.	Collaborate on documents	Google Workspace, MS 365	Real-time editing, feedback
6.	Gather feedback or organize input	SurveyMonkey, Signup Genius	Collect input for decision-making
7.	Make decisions and adjust plans	N/A	Incorporate feedback into planning
8.	Repeat process as needed	N/A	Continuous cycle of communication

sequence of activities and the key tools used at each stage, serving as a practical guide to integrating digital solutions for more efficient, connected, and dynamic work.

In addition to these core tools, there are other digital solutions that can enhance your communication process, such as automation platforms, knowledge bases, and scheduling tools. See Table 5.7 for an overview of these options.

As we've seen, strong written and digital communication is key to leading effectively today. Developing these skills takes ongoing effort and reflection, but the impact is powerful, helping you lead with clarity, confidence, and authenticity. Keep honing that leadership voice!

Table 5.7 Expanded Toolkit for Digital Communication

Tool Category	Examples	Purpose/Use	Notes
Video Conferencing	Zoom, Google Meet, Microsoft Teams	Conduct virtual meetings, webinars, and remote team check-ins	Essential for remote collaboration and face-to-face interaction
Automation and Workflow Integration	Zapier, Microsoft Power Automate	Automate repetitive tasks, connect different apps and workflows	Saves time and reduces manual effort

(Continued)

Table 5.7 Continued

Tool Category	Examples	Purpose/Use	Notes
Knowledge Base and Documentation	Confluence, Notion, SharePoint	Centralize team knowledge, documentation, and best practices	Facilitates easy access and sharing of information
Scheduling and Calendar	Outlook Calendar, Calendly	Coordinate meetings, manage availability, and automate scheduling	Ensures efficient time management
Internal Social and Engagement Platforms	Yammer, Workplace by Facebook	Foster community, share updates, and promote informal interaction	Builds organizational culture and engagement
Customer/ Stakeholder Communication	Intercom, Drift, Zendesk	Engage with external audiences, provide support, and gather feedback	Extends communication beyond internal teams

KEY TAKEAWAYS

1. **Your Virtual Presence Counts**: In the digital realm, first impressions matter, just like they do in person. Bring your A-game by ensuring you are camera-ready and have minimized possible distractions (i.e., phone silenced, tidy background, etc.). Whether it's a virtual meeting or a message, projecting confidence and professionalism makes a world of difference, and let's be honest, your audience will pay more attention when you do!
2. **Connect with Empathy**: Build bridges in virtual spaces by fostering connections that matter. Use warm welcomes, engage all voices, and sprinkle in some icebreakers to break the digital ice. Remember, creating an inclusive atmosphere can empower quieter participants to share their thoughts and ideas. Everyone deserves to be heard, so make it your mission to help draw them out.
3. **Simplify Your Message**: Clarity is key, especially when you're communicating across screens. Ditch the jargon and opt for straightforward language that resonates with your audience. Focus on the essentials. By distilling your thoughts into clear, digestible nuggets, you respect your audience's time and increase the chances of your message landing with impact.
4. **Leverage the Power of Technology**: Mastering digital tools is crucial in today's work environment. Whether you're using instant messaging,

video conferencing, or project management platforms, harness these technologies to streamline communication and efficiency. Keep those lines of dialogue open and ensure that everyone feels comfortable participating. Technology should serve as an enabler, not a barrier.

5. **Wrap Up with Purpose**: Every interaction should have a strong finish. Clear action items, recaps, and calls to action ensure everyone knows what's expected after the meeting ends. A well-structured conclusion reinforces accountability and demonstrates your leadership, inviting collaboration for the next steps.

NOTES

1 Omilion-Hodges, L. (Host). (2024, February 26). Writing as problem-solving & leadership: A conversation with Pam Hurley [Audio podcast episode]. *The Communicative Leader Podcast.* https://www.thecommunicativeleader.com/podcast/episode/7acb15ab/writing-as-problem-solving-and-leadership-a-conversation-with-pam-hurley
2 Radicati Group. (2021). *Email statistics report, 2021–2025.* The Radicati Group, Inc. https://www.radicati.com/wp/wp-content/uploads/2021/Email_Statistics_Report,_2021-2025_Executive_Summary.pdf
3 Salesforce. (2022). State of sales report. *Salesforce.* https://www.salesforce.com/resources/research-reports/state-of-sales/
4 PMI. (2022). *Pulse of the profession: The high cost of low performance.* Project Management Institute.
5 PMI. (2018). *Pulse of the profession: The high cost of low performance.* Project Management Institute.
6 Salesforce. (2019). *State of the connected customer.* https://www.salesforce.com/news/stories/state-of-the-connected-customer-report-outlines-changing-standards-for-customer-engagement/
7 Willis Towers Watson. (2009). Capitalizing on effective communication. In *Communication ROI: The business impact of effective communication.* 2009/2010 Communication ROI Study Report.
8 Grammarly. (2020). *The state of Business Communication.* https://www.grammarly.com/business/Grammarly_The_State_Of_Business_Communication.pdf
9 World Economic Forum. (2020). *The future of jobs report.* https://www.weforum.org/publications/the-future-of-jobs-report-2020/

Chapter 6

Breaking Barriers
Overcoming Obstacles to Your Leadership Voice

**Level 2.
Refine Your
Leadership Voice**

Even with strong communication skills, external and internal barriers can hinder your ability to speak freely. This chapter will help you identify common obstacles such as fear, self-doubt, or imposter syndrome and provide practical strategies to overcome them, empowering you to express your authentic leadership voice without hesitation.

Let's be honest, speaking up at work can sometimes feel like climbing Everest without supplies: daunting and intimidating. Even the most polished communicators occasionally face imposter syndrome and fear of rocking the boat. But mastering this isn't about eliminating those fears; it's about managing them with resilience and strategy. In this chapter, we'll explore the ten biggest barriers, like groupthink and fear of rejection, and show how to turn them into opportunities for growth. Learning to speak with clarity takes time and practice, and mistakes are part of the process. I'll share practical strategies, from setting goals to turning setbacks into lessons, to assist you whether you're new or experienced. It's about finding your voice, sharing ideas confidently, and contributing to richer conversations that make a real difference.

To help you better understand the path from identifying internal barriers to cultivating a confident and resilient leadership voice, check out Figure 6.1: Roadmap to Your Leadership Voice. The figure outlines the key steps along your journey and highlights the ongoing cycle of growth. It reminds us that resilience isn't built overnight, but rather is developed over time through intention, reflection, and consistent practice.

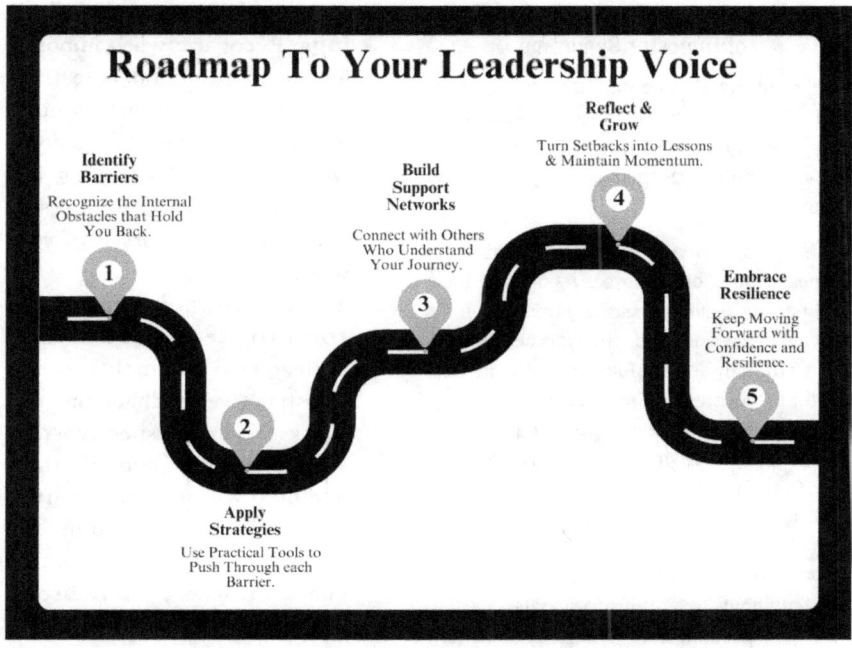

Figure 6.1 This roadmap outlines key steps—identifying barriers, applying strategies, building support, reflecting, and cultivating resilience—to develop and strengthen your leadership voice.

IDENTIFYING TEN COMMON BARRIERS TO SPEAKING UP AND STRATEGIES FOR OVERCOMING THEM

Barrier 1: Imposter Syndrome

Imposter syndrome is the lingering belief that you're not as capable as others see you, often fueling self-doubt despite clear evidence of your achievements. A project manager might finish a successful project yet feel they didn't contribute enough, worrying colleagues will soon see through their "luck." Even Maya Angelou, celebrated author and recipient of the Presidential Medal of Freedom, admitted, "I have written eleven books, but each time I think, 'Uh-oh, they're going to find out now. I've run a game on everybody, and they're going to find me out." If someone as accomplished as Angelou experiences these feelings, it shows how common imposter syndrome truly is. So, how can you quiet your inner critic?

Table 6.1 **Data and Trends: The Prevalence of Impostor Syndrome**

We've all experienced that nagging feeling of being less capable than others or worry that our luck might suddenly dry up. Let's explore how common these feelings really are among adults:

- *Harvard Business Review* found that nearly 60% of employees report that their imposter feelings negatively affect their confidence and productivity at work.[1]
- A study by *Psychology Today*[2] indicates that imposter feelings are not limited to early career stages but are prevalent across all age groups, with around 50–60% of adults experiencing them during career transitions or leadership roles.
- A survey conducted by *BetterUp*[3] found that about 70% of professionals have experienced imposter syndrome at some point in their careers.
- A survey by *Accenture*[4] revealed that nearly 75% of high-achieving women report feeling like frauds at some point.

These statistics show that imposter syndrome is a widespread experience affecting people across all stages of their careers, reminding us that we're not alone in these feelings and that many others have faced and overcome similar challenges.

1. **Acknowledge your feelings**: Recognize when imposter feelings pop up and note them in a dedicated journal or notes file on your phone. Write down what triggered the feeling and list specific instances of your success to remind yourself of your wins.
2. **Seek feedback and mentorship**: Reach out to trusted colleagues or mentors for constructive feedback on your work. Their perspectives can validate your contributions and help you see your abilities more clearly. I recommend setting up a standing monthly check-in where you discuss accomplishments and areas for growth. This can help to ensure steady progress.
3. **Celebrate successes**: Make it a habit to acknowledge and celebrate your achievements, no matter how small. Use techniques like a weekly review where you list at least three achievements or positive outcomes from your work. This practice can help change your mindset from focusing on self-doubt to recognizing your progress.

Barrier 2: Lack of Confidence

A lack of confidence can leave you feeling hesitant to share your ideas or take on new challenges, even when you have valuable insights to contribute. In the workplace, this might look like staying silent during meetings or avoiding leadership roles simply because you question your abilities. For instance, a software developer might have a great idea for improving a feature but chooses to stay quiet during a brainstorming session, feeling that their input isn't worthwhile. Here are some tips to help you build your confidence:

1. **Start small**: Begin your journey by sharing your ideas in smaller, more intimate settings, like one-on-one chats or small group discussions, to gently build confidence. Seek out safe spaces where you feel at ease, such as discussions with colleagues you trust or informal gatherings where you feel supported.
   - **Prepare a few topics that excite you**; this preparation can make it easier to contribute and share your unique perspective.
   - **Set manageable micro-goals** like sharing one idea each week or raising your hand in a meeting and taking pride in tracking your progress; it's all about celebrating those small victories!
   - **Practicing your ideas in low-stakes situations**, like with a friend, can help you find your voice. As confidence grows, gradually share in larger settings, appreciating each small win. Think of Oprah; she began with a local TV segment in Nashville before launching her own show and becoming a global icon.
2. **Confidence comes from competence**: Podcast guest Sairan Aqwar shared that confidence comes from competence, and I love this perspective! The more you invest in developing your skills, the more confident you'll feel when sharing ideas. This enhances your influence, as colleagues will turn to you for help or advice. Self-doubt is normal, even for experienced professionals, but focusing on building competence naturally boosts confidence.[5]
3. **Review your resume**: In academia, confidently expressing your ideas can be daunting, especially when presenting to field experts. One helpful tip I found was to regularly revisit my resume. Seeing my accomplishments provided tangible proof that I belonged at the table.

   If you're building your resume, keep a "Wins Document" on your phone or computer. At the end of each day or week, jot down your successes, big or small. Did you finally make that difficult call? Submit a proposal? Reflecting on wins can remind you of your capabilities and give you the courage to embrace new challenges.

> **READY TO PUT THIS INTO PRACTICE?**
>
> **Amplify Your Leadership Voice Further**
>
> For a more personalized exploration of strategies to overcome imposter syndrome, visit the Leadership Blueprint at TheCommunicativeLeader.com. There, you'll find activities, reflections, and expert guidance to support your growth and confidence as a leader.

Barrier 3: Fear of Rejection or Criticism

The fear of rejection or criticism can be paralyzing and may prevent you from expressing your thoughts or proposing new ideas. This fear might show up in the workplace when you're reluctant to speak your mind during team discussions or worry excessively about how your opinions will be received. For example, a marketing specialist might hesitate to suggest a bold campaign idea for fear that colleagues will think it's impractical or poorly thought out, missing the opportunity to innovate. Here are some concrete ways to overcome this obstacle:

1. **Reframe rejection**: View feedback or criticism as an opportunity to learn, not a reflection of your worth. Research[6] shows that adopting a growth mindset—seeing challenges as opportunities—boosts performance and resilience. Take Michael Jordan as a compelling example: after being cut from his high school basketball team, he used rejection as motivation to train harder, eventually becoming one of the greats. Journaling negative experiences and reflecting on lessons learned can also help transform setbacks into growth opportunities.
2. **Prepare for conversations**: Practice how you'll present your ideas. Role-playing can reduce anxiety, and seeking feedback from trusted colleagues before sharing can boost confidence and clarity. Being well-prepared helps you communicate more effectively and feel more assured.
3. **Engage in active listening**: Focus on truly understanding others' viewpoints. Active listening fosters support and innovation by creating psychological safety.[7] Techniques like summarizing points or asking open-ended questions help everyone feel valued, reducing fear of judgment and enabling you to contribute meaningfully to meetings.

Barrier 4: Fear of Misinterpretation

Worrying that others might misunderstand your words or intentions can cause hesitation to speak up. In the workplace, this may lead to over-clarifying or holding back altogether, which can stifle creativity and collaboration. For example, a team member might avoid giving feedback, fearing it will be taken personally rather than as an opportunity to improve.

1. **Clarify Intentions**: When communicating, be clear about your purpose and message to prevent misunderstandings. Here's how:
    - **State your purpose explicitly**: Before sharing ideas or feedback, start with a clear statement like "*I'm sharing this to help us improve the project*," to show your goal is constructive, not critical.
    - **Outline key points**: Prepare a brief outline or notes beforehand. This mental checklist can help you stay on track and avoid rambling. Sharing

this outline in advance via email or meeting notes can also help clarify your main ideas.
- **Use simple, direct language**: Avoid jargon or complex phrasing. Clear, straightforward language reduces the risk of misinterpretation.

2. **Encourage Feedback**: Invite colleagues to ask questions or share their interpretations after you speak, creating an open environment where clarification is welcomed. Ending with open-ended questions like *"What are your thoughts?"* or *"How does this align with your thinking?"* encourages dialogue and clarifies any misunderstandings. You might also consider:
   - **Establishing a feedback loop**: Dedicate time in meetings for Q&A and encourage everyone to rephrase key points in their own words to confirm understanding.
   - **Sharing summaries:** At the end of the discussion, briefly review the main takeaways and ask for confirmation, such as, *"Here is what I heard—please let me know if I've missed anything."*

3. **Leverage Written Communication:** If speaking up feels difficult, communicating your thoughts in writing can reduce the chances of misinterpretation.
   - **Draft and revise**. When you are unsure about verbally conveying a message, write it out first. Reviewing and refining it ensures your thoughts are clear before sharing.
   - **Use structured formats**. Lists, bullet points, and short paragraphs make complex or sensitive information easier to understand.
   - **Combine written and verbal communication**. For important discussions, follow up with an email summarizing the takeaways and next steps. This reinforces your message and offers colleagues a chance to review and ask questions.

Barrier 5: Fear of Rocking the Boat

The fear of rocking the boat reflects a concern that voicing your opinions might disrupt harmony or cause conflict. In the workplace, this often manifests as avoiding difficult conversations or holding back constructive criticism. For example, an employee might notice inefficiencies in a process but hesitate to speak up, fearing upsetting team dynamics and backlash. Here are some positive steps to tame this fear.

1. **Build a support network:** Connect with colleagues who share your concerns. Discuss ideas with them first to create a safe space for brainstorming and mutual support.
2. **Frame ideas positively:** Present suggestions as improvements rather than criticisms.

- **Focus on future benefits:** Emphasize how your suggestion could lead to growth or efficiency rather than simply criticizing the current practice.
- **Use collaborative language:** Say *"What can we do as a team to improve this process?"* instead of *"I think we're doing this wrong."*
- **Support with data:** Back up suggestions with examples or metrics to emphasize shared success rather than personal opinions.

3. **Start with informal discussions:** Casually bring up ideas over coffee or during team lunches to get a sense of reactions before diving into more formal discussions. This can yield insight into how the idea is likely to be received.

Barrier 6: Fear of Being Seen as Confrontational

Worrying that speaking up might make you seem aggressive or difficult to work with can hold you back from addressing important issues. For example, a finance team member might avoid questioning budget decisions, fearing it will appear confrontational, even though they believe it could improve resource management.

1. **Focus on active listening and mutual goals:** Frame conversations around finding solutions, not just pointing out problems.
   - **Active listening.** Show you value others' perspectives. You might say, *"I'd like to understand your view. What do you think about this idea?"* This encourages dialogue rather than confrontation.
   - **Highlight common objectives.** Highlighting shared benefits can go a long way in cultivating goodwill. Express your intention to improve the project. For example, *"I believe these changes could enhance our team's efficiency and help meet our shared targets."*
2. **Be Assertive, Not Aggressive:** This suggestion embodies the adage: it's not what you say, but how you say it. Here are some tips to assert your ideas in a way that will allow you to be heard *and* maintain relationships:
   - **Mind your tone.** Keep a neutral, calm voice, especially if you're frustrated. Focusing on the message rather than your feelings helps you assert yourself without seeming aggressive—a crucial first step!
   - **Address behaviors, not personalities.** Identify and describe the specific behavior or situation that needs addressing. It can be easy to generalize (e.g., *"You never meet deadlines!"*) when we're upset. Instead, mention the exact concern and its impact. For example, *"I noticed that the report was delivered two hours late yesterday, which impacted our meeting schedule."*
   - **Invite dialogue.** After sharing your observation, ask open-ended questions like, *"What are your thoughts on this?"* or *"Can you help us to understand what contributed to this situation?"*

3. **Embrace your conflict management skills:** Let's be real: not every idea will be met with a standing ovation, and that's a good thing. It means you have a team that's engaged and thinking critically. Fear of rocking the boat or facing pushback should never stop you from sharing your ideas.
    - **Prepare for resistance**. Anticipate potential pushback, especially from team members wary of change, and develop responses that keep the conversation constructive.
    - **Use "I" statements**. This should sound familiar by now, but framing your feedback this way can avoid sounding accusatory. Statements like "*I feel that . . .*" or "*I have noticed . . .*" can make your input feel more personal and lead to a constructive conversation.

Barrier 7: Cultural Context

Cultural norms can greatly influence how comfortable you feel speaking up. Chapter 7 is fully dedicated to navigating cultural communication, highlighting how unspoken rules about hierarchy, gender, or age can silence voices. For example, junior employees may hold back ideas to defer to senior staff in some organizations. Recognizing and adapting to these nuances is essential for making your voice heard and fostering an inclusive environment. Here are some practical steps you can take:

1. **Learn the Culture:** Take time to understand the unspoken rules and dynamics of your workplace. Observing successful communicators can help you adapt your style to align with the cultural context.
    - **Observe practices**: Notice how successful communicators express themselves in meetings, emails, or casual chats. If colleagues tend to be indirect to show deference, try doing the same. Let's look at the example below.
    - **Adapt your language**: Instead of saying, "*We need to change our timelines,*" try, "*I wonder if there's an opportunity to review our timelines—perhaps a slight adjustment could help us meet our goals.*" This respectful, dialogue-friendly phrasing respects cultural norms and increases receptivity.
2. **Encourage Inclusivity:** Building an inclusive environment is a leadership goal that benefits everyone. When diverse viewpoints are welcomed, innovative ideas and critical thinking flourish.
    - **Start conversations.** Whether it's during a team meeting or informal gatherings, pose questions like, "*How can we ensure that everyone feels comfortable sharing new ideas, regardless of their position or background?*" This signals that inclusivity is valued and creates space for all voices.
    - **Model inclusive communication.** When you share or seek ideas, explicitly encourage a broad range of responses. For instance, "*Incorpo-*

rating different perspectives can strengthen our strategy and impress clients. I'd love to hear everyone's thoughts."
3. **Seek Mentors:** Find mentors who have successfully navigated similar cultural contexts and challenges.
    - **Identify experienced mentors.** Seek out leaders or peers known for their effective communication, especially those who have navigated similar barriers, such as individuals from diverse backgrounds or leaders recognized for championing inclusivity.
    - **Schedule informational meetings.** When reaching out to potential mentors, be clear about your purpose. For example, say, "*I admire how you navigate our company's communication style and would appreciate any guidance on sharing my ideas more effectively. Could we find some time to discuss your approach?*" Being specific helps the mentor understand your needs and how they can best support you.

        Additionally, suggest informal settings like a coffee shop or a lunch walk. These relaxed environments can create a safe space for people to share openly and get advice outside of a work setting.

Barrier 8: Lack of Role Models and Support

Not having role models or support can make you feel isolated, especially when facing workplace challenges. Without examples of people who have successfully spoken up, it can be hard to see how to do it yourself. For example, an entry-level employee in tech might hesitate to suggest new ideas if they rarely see other women doing so, which can lead to self-doubt about their potential to make a difference.

1. **Network with peers:** Join or form employee resource groups or mentorship networks to connect with colleagues with similar backgrounds or interests. For example, if you're one of the few women in tech at your company, consider creating a Women in Technology group to share experiences, practice presenting ideas, and organize informal meetups. Such groups offer safe spaces to discuss challenges and strategies, reminding you you're not alone.
2. **Identify role models:** Seek out role models within your organization and industry by following their journeys and learning from their experiences to inspire and empower yourself. Since senior executives may not always come from diverse backgrounds, explore industry conferences or online communities. Seeing others successfully speak up and advance can boost your confidence and provide practical communication strategies to adopt.
3. **Create safe spaces:** Create or participate in forums where employees can openly share experiences and challenges, fostering a culture of support.

For example, a monthly "Innovation Hour" or "Voice Your Vision" session provides a judgment-free environment for idea exchange and improvement. Regularly holding these sessions promotes open dialogue and collective growth.

Barrier 9: Emotional Drain and Burnout

Emotional exhaustion and burnout often happen when ongoing pressures and barriers to speaking up become overwhelming. This can show up as fatigue, disengagement, or difficulty concentrating, making it feel almost impossible to find the energy to advocate for your ideas. For example, a healthcare worker might feel drained after long shifts and hesitate to raise safety concerns out of fear it will add to their workload.

1. **Prioritize self-care:** Make self-care a regular part of your routine. Engage in activities that recharge you outside of work, like exercise, hobbies, or spending time with loved ones. A quick 5-minute walk or a simple trigger meditation like taking a deep breath each time you touch a doorknob can help you reduce stress during the workday. Over time, these small practices can lower stress levels and prevent burnout. Chapter 11 focuses on leadership resilience and self-care, offering strategies to support your well-being.
2. **Set boundaries:** Establish clear boundaries around your work hours and commitments to ensure you have time to disconnect and recharge. You might also need to set limits on how much you take on at work.
   - **Leave work at work.** Clearly separate work time from personal time. For example, if you're prone to checking emails late at night, set a rule like: After 6 p.m., I won't respond to work emails until the next day. Depending on your organization, communicating these boundaries to your team can help manage expectations and model healthy behavior.
   - **Just say no.** Remember, "no" is a complete sentence. If your workload is already full, don't feel obligated to accept more projects. If saying "no" directly feels difficult or isn't culturally accepted in your organization, you can say, "*I've been advised not to take on additional tasks at this time,*" or "*I'd love to help, but I need to prioritize the Smith project to meet the deadline.*"
3. **Seek support:** If you're feeling overwhelmed, don't hesitate to reach out to colleagues, supervisors, or HR. Sharing your feelings can open the door to adjustments that improve your work experience. For example, you might say to your manager, "*I've been feeling overwhelmed lately. Can we brainstorm ways to adjust my workload or find strategies to better manage the pressure?*" Asking for support helps find solutions and promotes a workplace culture that values employee well-being.

Barrier 10: Groupthink

Groupthink happens when a team's desire for harmony or conformity suppresses diverse opinions, leading to poor decisions and stifled innovation. In the workplace, this often looks like everyone tacitly agreeing to avoid conflict, even if some team members have concerns or different ideas. For example, a team might support a new initiative without critically examining its risks, simply to keep the peace or avoid questioning a leader, ultimately missing out on better alternatives.

1. **Encourage open dialogue:** Foster an environment where team members feel comfortable sharing different opinions. When diverse perspectives are valued, decision-making improves. You might say, "*I appreciate everyone's input. Let's explore some alternative ideas to spot potential issues early. What are some thoughts that challenge our current plan?*" This invites honest discussion and shows that disagreement is a healthy part of finding the best solution.
2. **Utilize decision-making techniques:** Incorporate tools like brainstorming sessions or the "devil's advocate" method to deliberately surface differing views and avoid rushing consensus. For example, taking time to create "pros and cons" lists can help critically evaluate options and flag possible unintended consequences.
3. **Gather anonymous feedback:** Use surveys or anonymous suggestion boxes to collect honest input without putting anyone on the spot. After meetings, consider sending a brief anonymous survey asking, "*Were there any ideas or perspectives that weren't shared or that we might have overlooked?*" This approach ensures that all voices are heard, especially those hesitant to speak up openly.

BEST COMMUNICATION PRACTICES TO GET YOU STARTED

We've explored many common obstacles to speaking up and practical strategies to overcome them. If you're feeling overwhelmed or unsure where to begin, I recommend focusing on these five proven communication techniques. They're simple to implement and can make a meaningful difference as you build your confidence and voice.

"I" Statements and "We" Language

You may have noticed "I" statements appearing multiple times in this book, and there's a good reason for that—they are incredibly powerful! Using "I" statements helps you express your thoughts clearly and respectfully, reducing defensiveness and making it easier to navigate conflicts with confidence and grace.

Frame your feedback around your own observations rather than assigning blame. For example:

"I noticed that we tend to run through the agenda with very little space for discussion or brainstorming. I'm wondering if there's a way we could adjust our meeting structure to create more space for input in the future." This approach keeps the conversation focused on facts and your perspective, helping to foster a constructive conversation without personal judgments. For a step-by-step guide on crafting effective "I" statements, check out Table 6.2.

Table 6.2 Actionable Insights: "I" Statements in Action

"I" statements are a powerful leadership communication tool that helps you communicate honestly and effectively while reducing defensiveness. Let's explore the structure and check out some workplace examples.

- **Step 1. Start with how you feel**
  Express your emotions honestly. Example: "*I feel overwhelmed . . .*"

- **Step 2. Describe the behavior**
  Focus on specific actions without blame. Example: "*. . . when I receive last-minute changes . . .*"

- **Step 3. Explain why it matters**
  Share how it impacts you or the team. Example: "*. . . because it makes planning difficult and affects our efficiency.*"

- **Step 4. Express a need or request**
  State what you want moving forward. Example: "*I'd appreciate more timely updates.*"

More Workplace Examples:

- **Lack of Communication:** "*I feel frustrated when I find out about changes through informal channels instead of official announcements. It makes me feel out of the loop. I'd like to request more regular updates from management.*"
- **Workload Concerns:** "*I feel overwhelmed with the additional responsibilities during this transition because it's a lot to manage alongside my current tasks. I would appreciate discussing ways to balance our workloads more effectively.*"
- **Addressing Team Dynamics:** "*I feel disconnected when tensions rise in team discussions about upcoming changes. It impacts our ability to collaborate. I'd like to set up a meeting to openly share our feelings and ideas for supporting each other.*"
- **Uncertainty about Skills:** "*I feel concerned that my current skills may not align with the company's new direction, and I am unsure of how to adapt. I would appreciate guidance on training or development opportunities.*"

(Continued)

Table 6.2 Continued

> Using "I" statements fosters honest, respectful communication that builds understanding and promotes a positive workplace culture. As a bonus, these skills work in your personal life too. For example, use "I" statements by saying, "I'm having a hard time managing the laundry, dishes, and cooking," rather than "I do EVERYTHING around here!"

We language is another powerful way to express ideas, such as dissent, in a productive way. Let's look at an example: *"I've been thinking about our project timeline and how we can make sure we meet our deadlines with as little stress as possible. I wonder if we might explore ways to streamline our workflow. It seems like if we adjust how we're currently reporting progress, we could reduce overlap and free up some time for everyone? What do you all think? Could we brainstorm some approaches that might work for us?"* We language fosters collaboration and shows you're aligned with team goals, often leading to a positive reception from both peers and leaders.

Prepare for Resistance

They say the best offense is a good defense, and that's especially true when speaking up. Before your next meeting, take a moment to identify colleagues who might be hesitant about change. Think about their possible concerns and plan responses that acknowledge their perspectives while also guiding the conversation toward collaborative solutions.

For example, if you know a teammate tends to react negatively to change, you might start with:

> *"I realize this is a departure from our usual way of doing things, but I'd like to explore how we can adapt this change to better fit our current workload."*

Preparing for potential resistance helps you address concerns proactively and refine your proposal. It encourages more thoughtful, nuanced ideas and demonstrates that you've considered different viewpoints. When you present your suggestions, they'll be more compelling and better positioned for success.

Mind Your Tone and Body Language

Remember, your tone and body language often communicate just as much, if not more, than your words. A sharp tone combined with aggressive gestures, like pursed lips or lowered eyebrows, can obscure your message and make others feel defensive. We all have bad days, but if your tone and body language are tense, it can make others feel uneasy or avoid involving you altogether. To foster open and respectful communication, try these strategies:

- **Practice:** Rehearse your message in advance or record yourself to observe your tone. Pay attention to whether your voice remains calm and steady, especially when discussing sensitive topics like layoffs or salary changes.
- **Nonverbal cues:** Maintain open body language such as uncrossed arms, a relaxed posture, and steady eye contact to project approachability and respect. These cues reinforce that you're sharing ideas and seeking collaboration, not issuing commands or causing conflict.

Use Precise Language and Have Examples Ready

Misunderstandings often happen simply because our message isn't clear or articulated carefully. Even when speaking with experts, using simple, precise language helps ensure your ideas are understood, especially on sensitive topics or when expecting resistance.

Clear language, paired with concrete examples, is also the most effective way to deliver constructive feedback. Instead of saying, *"You're always dismissive of everyone's ideas,"* try:

> *"In our last team meeting, I noticed that you responded to Olivia and Christine's suggestions quite quickly, without asking for more details or clarification. It seemed to shut down their ideas early, which might have limited our discussion. How do you think we could approach these conversations to encourage more open dialogue next time?"*

This approach focuses on specific behaviors rather than personal criticism, making it easier to address the issue productively and collaboratively.

Create Opportunities for Dialogue

One of the most effective ways to share your ideas is by inviting input from others. After sharing your idea (while incorporating the earlier best practices), you should open the floor for dialogue. This can be as simple as saying, *"What are your thoughts?"* or *"Is there a way we can collaborate to adjust this process, so it benefits everyone?"* These statements signal that you're interested in solving the problem together rather than imposing a solution unilaterally (see Table 6.3).

AMPLIFYING YOUR LEADERSHIP VOICE

Table 6.3 Instant Impact: Leadership Takeaway from Mountaineer and Business Expert, Jenn Drummond

Conversations with Leaders: Keep a Failure Story on Speed Dial	Internationally acclaimed mountaineer and business expert Jenn Drummond shared some powerful insights on resilience and success during her visit to The Communicative Leader. Jenn revealed one of her secret tools: keeping a failure story ready to go. At first glance, this might sound surprising—after all, who wants to focus on failure? But Jenn explains that having a specific story of a setback on hand can be a game-changer when facing current obstacles. Her story? On Jenn's first attempt to climb K2, tragedy struck when an avalanche killed one of her teammates. Despite being close to the summit, Jenn chose to turn back and stay with her team. Later, during her second attempt, Jenn teamed up with a Pakistani climber she met after that tragedy, and together, they successfully reached K2's summit—an achievement made even sweeter by overcoming her past failure. Jenn's lesson? Having stories of setbacks, especially those that turned into triumphs, on "speed dial" makes setbacks feel less overwhelming when they happen again. They remind us that failure is often a stepping stone to success. Learn more in Episode 1 of Season 7 of *The Communicative Leader* podcast.[8]

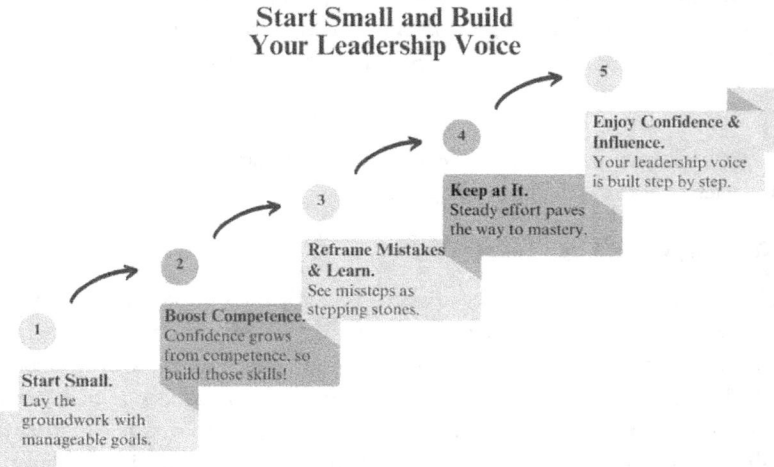

Figure 6.2 This step-by-step guide illustrates how starting small and building your leadership voice through steady effort and reflection leads to confidence and influence.

Remember, mastery doesn't happen overnight. Think of developing your leadership voice as building a staircase where each small step brings you closer to your goal. Figure 6.2 shows how focusing on manageable actions can lead to significant confidence and influence over time.

THE CHALLENGES OF LEARNING A NEW SKILL

Let's face it, learning or sharpening a skill can feel both exciting and a little intimidating. Remember, every expert was once a beginner, stumbling through mistakes and figuring things out as they went. The key isn't perfection; it's progress. Growth happens gradually, through steady effort and a willingness to learn from missteps. Start small and trust that those small steps add up to big change over time. Embracing the journey, finding joy in your growth, and turning challenges into opportunities is how you build a lifelong learning mindset.

Learning or Honing a Skill Takes Time and Practice

Think of mastering leadership communication like learning a new language; you won't be fluent overnight. It takes patience, consistent practice, and a bit of grace for the moments when you stumble. Approach each conversation as an opportunity to improve one thing, such as active listening or expressing your ideas more clearly. Incorporate these habits gradually into your day-to-day interactions. Over time, you'll find your confidence growing and your leadership voice becoming stronger.

Table 6.4 Recommended Resources to Support Your Leadership Voice Development

To enhance your journey in overcoming internal barriers and strengthening your leadership voice, consider exploring the following resources:

Habit and Goal Tracking

- **Coach.me:** Build daily communication habits with support
- **Streaks:** Maintain consistency in your practice
- **Habitica:** Gamify your progress to stay motivated

Mindfulness and Stress Management

- **Headspace:** Guided meditation to cultivate calmness
- **Calm:** Sleep stories and breathing exercises

Reflection and Journaling

- **Day One:** Record lessons learned and successes
- **Penzu:** Keep a private, online reflection journal

Networking and Community

- **LinkedIn Groups:** Connect with and learn from like-minded professionals
- **Reddit's r/communication:** Share experiences and advice

Learning and Development

- **Coursera:** Leadership and communication courses
- **LinkedIn Learning:** Short skill-building classes
- **Udemy:** Affordable soft skills courses

Practice and Presentation

- **Zoom/Teams/Google Meet:** Role-play and coaching sessions
- **Loom:** Record practice videos for review

To stay motivated, consider using habit-tracking apps (see Table 6.4) or subscribe to LinkedIn newsletters to keep your skills sharp. Remember, small, consistent efforts are what turn learning into lasting change.

Mistakes Are Part of the Process

Think of mistakes as teachers. Instead of dreading slip-ups, see them as signs you're stretching beyond your comfort zone. After a tough conversation, pause—what can you learn? What might you do next time? These reflections deepen your understanding and help you grow more resilient. Adopting a growth mindset where failure is just part of success encourages you to experiment with new techniques, styles, or approaches without fear. Keep a journal or use online apps to track your wins and lessons learned. And don't forget, asking colleagues or mentors for feedback can provide fresh perspectives and encouragement.

Start Small and Build

Think of building your communication skills like constructing a house: lay a solid foundation first. Focus on one small thing at a time, maybe making eye contact or telling a quick story, so it doesn't feel overwhelming. As those habits become second nature, gradually take on more complex skills like leading tough conversations or persuading others. Celebrating each milestone reinforces your confidence and keeps you moving forward. Use tools like Trello or Asana to break down your goals into manageable steps and review recordings of your meetings to observe your body language and delivery. Brick by brick, you're creating a leadership communication style that's adaptable, confident, and ready for anything.

Focus on Progress—Because Perfection Is a Myth

Perfection? It's a myth; don't fall for it. Instead, focus on steady progress. Every small step—whether it's speaking more clearly, listening more attentively, or handling a tricky situation skillfully—is proof of your growth. That momentum keeps you motivated. Remember, learning is an ongoing journey, not a destination. Be kind to yourself, embrace the process, and take pride in how far you've come.

You can find coaching tools to help you set reminders, reflect on your progress, and adjust your goals in Table 6.4.

STRATEGIES FOR MAINTAINING MOMENTUM AND RESILIENCE

Maintaining momentum and building resilience in your communication journey require ongoing focus and strategic practices. Here are some actionable tips and tools to support your growth.

Celebrate Your Wins

I've emphasized this before, and we'll revisit it because recognizing wins is crucial for building momentum. Whether big or small, every success deserves acknowledgment. Consider maintaining a "Success Board" or a "Wins Document"—whether it's a Trello board, a sticky note on your desk, or a journal—to track moments like handling a tough conversation well or sharing a great idea. Sharing these wins with colleagues or mentors can boost your confidence and motivate others around you.

Prioritize Self-Care and Well-Being

Your ability to communicate effectively hinges on taking care of yourself. Incorporate daily habits like quick walks, mindfulness exercises, or breathing breaks. Apps like Headspace or Calm can help you stay grounded. Schedule wellness reminders in your calendar to ensure these moments become part of your routine. When you nurture your mind and body, you'll have the clarity and calmness needed to respond thoughtfully, not impulsively.

Build Support Networks

Resilience grows when you have a strong support system. Join LinkedIn Groups, local meetups, or online communities like Reddit's r/communication to share experiences and advice. Consider establishing a "communication buddy system" at work with regular check-ins with a colleague for feedback and encouragement. Remember, connecting with others who understand your challenges reminds you that you're not alone on this journey.

Reframe Mistakes as Growth Opportunities

View mistakes and setbacks as opportunities to learn. Adopt a growth mindset by reframing failures as stepping stones to improvement. Use a journal to reflect on setbacks, what you learned, and how to approach similar situations differently. Seeking feedback from mentors or peers can yield new insights and strategies. If this feels too challenging to do face-to-face, then set up a phone or video call. This mindset fosters resilience and continuous development.

Keep Moving Forward

By applying these strategies, you'll sustain your momentum and develop a resilient communication style that adapts with grace to whatever comes your way. Each small step builds confidence, sharpens your leadership skills, and reinforces your communication capacity.

KEY TAKEAWAYS

1. **Embrace Fear**: Let's be honest, fears like imposter syndrome, rejection, and confrontation love to tag along on our journeys. But here's the secret: it's not about kicking them to the curb for good; it's about learning to walk with them confidently and strategically. By embracing techniques that tame these anxieties, you can confidently speak up and let your ideas take center stage.
2. **Take Small Steps in Skill Development**: Think of developing your communication prowess as a marathon, not a sprint. It takes time, practice, and yes, a bit of patience. Consider each conversation a stepping stone to improving areas like active listening or message clarity. Embrace tools like habit trackers or online courses to keep you on track and motivated. Remember, those small steps add up to big leaps over time!
3. **Progress Is Your North Star, Not Perfection**: Perfection is an elusive myth, and chasing it can leave you feeling worn out. Instead, turn your attention to progress, a far more rewarding journey. Each stumble is a valuable lesson, and every small victory fuels your motivation tank. This adaptable mindset encourages you to experiment and grow, building resilience in your communication skills.
4. **Build a Circle of Support**: No one is an island, especially not when growing into a confident communicator. Identify peers, join professional groups, or seek mentors who understand the challenges you face. This collective support not only offers a sense of belonging but also bolsters accountability and provides a fresh perspective on growing your skills.
5. **Reflect and Adapt for Resilience**: Think of every misstep as a chapter in your leadership voice journey, where each holds a lesson. Capture your experiences in journals or digital tools and seek out feedback from trusted sounding boards. By reflecting thoughtfully, you transform setbacks into springboards for future success, fortifying your resilience.

NOTES

1 Harvard Business Review. (2020). *Imposter syndrome is more common than you think.* https://hbr.org/2020/03/imposter-syndrome-is-more-common-than-you-think
2 Psychology Today. (2019). *Imposter syndrome: Who experiences it and why.* https://www.psychologytoday.com/us/blog/the-main-ingredient/201903/imposter-syndrome-who-experiences-it-and-why
3 BetterUp. (2021). *The imposter syndrome study.* https://www.betterup.com/blog/imposter-syndrome
4 Shook, E., & Sweet, J. (2019). Getting to equal 2019: Creating a culture that drive innovation. *Accenture.* www.accenture.com/content/dam/accenture/final/a-com-migration/thought-leadership-assets/accenture-equality-equals-innovation-gender-equality-research-report-iwd-2019.pdf

5 Omilion-Hodges, L. (Host). (2025, March 17). Redefining the path: Empowering midlife women through communication—a conversation with Sairan Aqrawi [Audio podcast episode]. *The Communicative Leader Podcast*. https://www.thecommunicativeleader.com/podcast/episode/7c184278/redefining-the-path-empowering-midlife-women-through-communication-a-conversation-with-sairan-aqrawi
6 Dweck, C. S. (2006). *Mindset: The new psychology of success*. Ballantine Books.
7 Castro, D. R., Anseel, F., Kluger, A. N., Lloyd, K. J., & Turjeman-Levi, Y. (2018). Mere listening effect on creativity and the mediating role of psychological safety. *Psychology of Aesthetics, Creativity, and the Arts, 12*(4), 489.
8 Omilion-Hodges, L. (Host). (2025, May 12). From catastrophe to K2—breaking boundaries, resilience, and leadership: A conversation with Jenn Drummond [Audio podcast episode]. *The Communicative Leader Podcast*. https://www.thecommunicativeleader.com/podcast/episode/7ae0fdf3/from-catastrophe-to-k2-breaking-boundaries-resilience-and-leadership-a-conversation-with-jenn-drummond

Chapter 7

Communicating across Boundaries

Navigating Cultural Spaces with Confidence

Level 2. Refine Your Leadership Voice

Effective leadership often involves communicating across diverse cultural contexts. Here, you will learn how to navigate cultural differences with confidence, respect, and adaptability, ensuring your voice is both inclusive and impactful in any environment.

Buckle up; this chapter dives into a landscape more vital than ever for modern leaders: culture. We've talked about finding your voice, building confidence, and connecting with others, but in today's world where borders are smaller, understanding how culture shapes communication isn't just nice-to-have, it's essential. If you want your leadership voice to truly resonate, you need to navigate these diverse spaces with awareness and skill.

Globalization isn't just a buzzword; it's shaping how we work and relate every day. Teams are more diverse than ever, bringing a wealth of perspectives and different ways of communicating and advocating. As a leader, you can't rely on your default cultural settings and expect to connect and build trust effectively. What feels natural to you might be interpreted completely differently by someone with a different background.

So, how do we bridge these gaps? How do we ensure our voice is heard across diverse groups? That's what this chapter is all about. We'll explore why culture impacts communication, how it plays out in real leadership scenarios, and address the unique challenges faced by minorities and underrepresented groups.

This isn't about mastering every culture on the planet—that's impossible. It's about building cultural competence by boosting self-awareness, adapting your communication, and creating inclusive spaces where every voice is amplified.

FOUNDATIONAL CONCEPTS IN CULTURAL LEADERSHIP

To understand how leadership and communication vary across cultures, we'll start with three foundational approaches: Hofstede's cultural dimensions, Trompenaars' cultural dimensions, and Hall's high-context versus low-context insights. Keep in mind that while these dimensions are often tied to geography, companies and teams develop their own unique cultures as well. We'll then look at another useful framework—Meyer's Cultural Map—in the next section. As you'll see in Table 7.3, these different frameworks work together to provide a deeper understanding of communicating across cultural divides.

Hofstede's Cultural Dimensions

Let's talk about Geert Hofstede. His work gives us a powerful lens for understanding how different cultures tick. These core dimensions reveal how societies are wired, helping you avoid headaches and communicate more effectively.

Power Distance

This is about how societies handle unequal power. Do people accept a clear hierarchy, or do they push for equality? While power distance sounds like a literal space or gap, this is a metaphorical divide.

- **High-power distance**: In these places, there's a clear pecking order, and everyone pretty much knows their place. You respect authority, follow the boss's lead, and generally don't question the folks higher up the chain. Think of countries where hierarchy is just the way things are. Countries like Malaysia and Mexico often score high here. In a high-power-distance company environment, you might see very formal communication, less direct challenges of superiors, and decisions flowing strictly from the top down.
- **Low-power distance**: Here, people are more about flattening the hierarchy. They expect power to be distributed more equally and are more likely to speak up, challenge the boss (respectfully, hopefully!), and expect to be involved in decisions. Think of places that value a more egalitarian feel, such as countries like Austria and Denmark. In a low-power distance company environment, you might see more informal communication across levels, open-door policies, and leaders who encourage input from their teams.
- **How this impacts your leadership communication**: It shapes how you speak to your team, how they respond, and how feedback flows—whether freely or with hesitation. It also influences who feels comfortable participating in decisions. For example, in high-power distance cultures, team members might hesitate to approach their boss with concerns. An

"open door" policy alone may not be enough. Instead, try group brainstorming or regular check-ins to build trust, identify issues, and gradually create shared norms that encourage open dialogue.

Individualism Versus Collectivism

This dimension gets at where society puts its focus: on the individual or the group.

- **Individualism:** This is the "every person for themselves" end of the spectrum where each person looks out for themselves and their immediate circle. It's not about being harsh but about valuing independence, personal achievement, and standing out. Think of cultures that celebrate the solo star, like the USA, where success is often measured by individual effort and rewards go to those who shine brightest.
- **Collectivism:** On the other hand, collectivism is about being part of a strong, loyal group, whether family, team, or community. The group's harmony and well-being come first, with loyalty offering protection and support. Countries like Guatemala and many in East Asia tend to score high here, where decisions often happen by consensus, and group harmony is more important than confrontation.
- **How this impacts your leadership communication:** It shapes everything from how you handle conflict (direct or by preserving harmony), to how decisions are made (by an individual or a group), to how you praise or give feedback (focused on the individual or the team). It also influences what motivates your team: individual goals or collective success. Understanding these differences helps you connect more authentically and motivate effectively.

Masculinity Versus Femininity

Now, this isn't just about gender roles; it's about what a society values most. While it's often linked to how men and women are socialized, it's really about the priorities a culture places on achievement and competition or care and relationships.

- **Masculinity**: These cultures prize assertiveness, ambition, and material success. They celebrate the competitive spirit and tend to reward achievement. Think of Japan and Hungary, where performance, winning, and clear goals are emphasized. In these environments, conversations are often direct and goal-focused, and motivation comes from striving for success and recognition.
- **Femininity**: These cultures value cooperation, humility, and caring for others. They focus on building strong relationships, work–life balance,

and consensus. Countries like the Netherlands and Sweden exemplify this, where teamwork, employee well-being, and harmony are central. Communication here tends to be more collaborative and empathetic, with success measured by everyone feeling valued and supported.
- **How this impacts your leadership communication**: It influences whether you're direct and competitive or supportive and relationship-focused. It also guides how you motivate your team and define success. Recognizing these differences helps you create a culture that aligns with your team's values.

Uncertainty Avoidance

This describes how comfortable societies are with the unknown, ambiguity, and change.

- **High uncertainty avoidance**: These cultures prefer things to be clear, structured, and predictable. They like rules, guidelines, and avoiding ambiguity. Contracts tend to be prized over a "handshake" deal, and new or different ideas can feel threatening. Greece and Portugal have cultures that value stability and clear instructions. In high uncertainty avoidance company environments, there might be a strong preference for clear processes, detailed plans, and less tolerance for ambiguity and risk-taking. Communication is likely to be very precise and detailed.
- **Low uncertainty avoidance**: These societies are more relaxed about ambiguity. They're comfortable with change, open to new ideas, and willing to take calculated risks. Singapore and Denmark are good examples, where flexibility and innovation thrive. Here, deal-making might be based on a handshake rather than a detailed contract, and communication tends to be more fluid and adaptable.
- **How this impacts your leadership communication**: It affects how much detail your team needs, how they respond to change, and how openly they discuss risks. For example, teams from high uncertainty avoidance cultures might want detailed plans and reassurance, while those from low uncertainty cultures might prefer agility and trust in the process.

Understanding these dimensions offers a valuable foundation for connecting across cultures, revealing the unseen forces behind reactions and interactions. This awareness enables you to communicate, lead, and build relationships with greater empathy, confidence, and success. Table 7.3 summarizes frameworks and workplace examples to support your journey and Table 7.1 offers key stats on cross-cultural communication.

Trompenaars' Cultural Dimensions

While Hofstede's framework is a great starting point, Trompenaars' dimensions give us a relationship-focused view of culture. Think of these insights into how societies approach rules, relationships, and identity—all key to connecting across borders.

Universalism Versus Particularism

This describes how societies decide what's right and fair. Do they follow rules that apply equally to everyone, or do they adjust based on relationships and circumstances?

- **Universalism:** These cultures see rules, laws, and standards as applying to all equally. Fairness and consistency matter most. Think of the USA or Germany, where policies are clear, and everyone is held to the same standards, like the idea of "universal human rights." In workplaces with a universalism culture, rules are often firm, and fairness is straightforward.
- **Particularism**: Here, relationships and context take center stage. Rules might bend or change depending on who you're dealing with or the situation. Countries like China and Venezuela often operate this way, valuing trust, personal connections, and flexibility over strict adherence. It's a way of saying, "That's just how they do things over there," and understanding that different situations call for different approaches.
- **How this impacts your leadership communication**: Knowing whether your team prefers a rule-based or relationship-based approach helps you set expectations, give feedback, and build trust in ways that feel natural to them. For example, in a particularist culture, investing time in personal relationships can go a long way, while in a universalist culture, clarity and fairness in policies will earn respect.

Individualism Versus Communitarianism

This dimension looks at how cultures balance the needs of the individual versus the group.

- **Individualism**: Cultures that lean this way emphasize personal freedom, independence, and self-expression. People are encouraged to stand out, pursue their goals, and be recognized for their achievements. Think of the UK or Australia, where personal success is often celebrated.
- **Communitarianism**: In these cultures, the group, whether family, community, or organization, is the priority. Loyalty, harmony, and collective

well-being are what matter most. Countries like Japan and Colombia often emphasize strong bonds and shared goals.
- **How this impacts your leadership communication**: Knowing whether your team values individual achievement or group harmony helps you motivate and connect more authentically. For example, in cultures that prize individual success, recognizing personal accomplishments can be a powerful motivator. In contrast, in cultures that prioritize group harmony, emphasizing team achievements and collective goals resonates more.

Specific Versus Diffuse

This one's about how much of a person's life they're willing to share at work.

- **Specific**: Cultures that are more specific keep their personal and professional lives separate. Relationships are often transactional: you do your job, and that's it. The USA and the Netherlands are good examples of this approach.
- **Diffuse**: Here, personal relationships, values, and social ties are woven into work life. Trust is built over time, and people often bring their whole selves to the table. Countries like China or Spain tend to be more diffuse.
- **How this impacts your leadership communication**: Recognizing whether your team prefers a more transactional or relational style helps you foster trust and build thoughtful connections.

Table 7.1 Data and Trends: Key Stats on Cross Cultural Communication

In today's diverse workplaces, these stats highlight why developing strong cross-cultural communication skills is essential:
• By 2030, approximately 30% of the workforce in many countries will be multicultural and multigenerational.[1]
• Over 70% of minority employees face microaggressions or subtle biases undermining confidence and inclusion.[2]
• Up to 60% of international business failures are linked to miscommunication across cultures.[3]
• Companies with inclusive leadership are 35% more likely to financially outperform their peers and enjoy higher employee engagement.[4]
These numbers show how prevalent and impactful microaggressions and miscommunication are. Cultivating cultural awareness, empathy, and inclusion is essential for success today, helping you navigate boundaries and foster a more engaged, high-performing team.

Neutral Versus Affective

This dimension explores how openly cultures express emotions.

- **Neutral**: Cultures leaning neutral tend to keep their feelings in check. Think: polite, composed, and restrained. Think Japan or the UK, where emotional control is valued.
- **Affective**: In these cultures, emotions are expressed openly and naturally. People are comfortable showing enthusiasm, frustration, or joy. Countries like Italy or Brazil often fall into this category.
- **How this impacts your leadership communication**: Knowing how people express feelings helps you interpret their reactions more accurately and respond in a way that feels respectful and genuine.

Achievement Versus Ascription

Finally, this dimension looks at how societies bestow respect and status.

- **Achievement**: Respect is earned through accomplishments, skills, and performance. Leaders and team members are valued based on what they've achieved. The USA and Australia often favor this approach.
- **Ascription**: Respect and status are given based on age, gender, social connections, or titles. Tradition, hierarchy, and social roles matter more here. Countries like Japan or Egypt tend to lean this way.
- **How this impacts your leadership communication**: Understanding how respect is conferred helps you navigate recognition and authority in ways that resonate with your team's cultural expectations.

HOW CULTURE SHAPES COMMUNICATION

Understanding how culture influences communication is like having a secret decoder; once you get it, conversations across diverse workplaces become smoother. From the words we choose to how we give feedback or express disagreement, culture subtly but powerfully shapes every interaction.

Hall's High Versus Low Context

Hall offers a simple and useful way to understand culture: high-context versus low-context. Think of it as how much is left unsaid versus explicitly stated (see Table 7.2).

- **High-context cultures**: These rely heavily on shared understanding, nonverbal cues, and relationships. People expect you to read

between the lines. Examples include Japan, Arab countries, and many Latin American cultures. Imagine a leader who assumes their team understands unspoken norms or subtle cues, sometimes without saying anything outright.
- **Low-context cultures**: In places like the USA, Germany, or Scandinavia, clear, direct communication is the norm. Words are taken at face value, and clarity is key. Leaders are comfortable giving straightforward feedback and instructions.
- **Context in action**: A high-context leader might say, *"You did okay,"* expecting the team member to understand that's praise. A low-context leader might say, *"Great job on that project—your presentation was clear and well organized."* Both work, but knowing the difference helps you adapt your style to different cultural expectations.

Table 7.2 **Actionable Insights: Cultural Norms and Leadership Communication**

Let's bring these ideas to life with some real-world examples so you can see how cultural norms shape everyday interactions at work.
Giving Feedback: A German manager might say, "Your last project lacked thorough analysis," directly pointing out issues. Meanwhile, a Japanese manager might say, "The report is well-done. I wonder if it would be even more impactful with tables and graphics included," starting with praise and softening the critique.
Handling Disagreement: During a strategy session, a French leader might openly challenge a plan, encouraging debate. A Chinese leader, on the other hand, might listen politely, take notes, and discuss reservations privately, valuing harmony and face-saving.
Expressing Emotion: An Italian manager may show enthusiasm with expressive gestures and vocal warmth, conveying passion. A Scandinavian leader might stay calm and composed, projecting steadiness—even under pressure.
Self-Promotion: An American employee might confidently highlight their achievements, expecting recognition. A Japanese colleague might downplay successes, valuing humility and group harmony.
Pro Tip: When working across cultures, don't assume your style will automatically fit. Instead, observe and listen—notice how colleagues express themselves and respond. If you sense hesitation, ask open-ended questions like, "*How do you prefer to receive feedback?*" or "*Would you like me to be more direct?*" Showing genuine curiosity and adaptability builds trust and keeps communication flowing smoothly.

Building on Hall: Erin Meyer's Cultural Map

While Hall's framework offers a broad view, Erin Meyer's Cultural Map provides a practical, detailed guide to how cultures communicate at work. Developed by interculturalist Erin Meyer, it helps leaders navigate real-world scenarios, like giving feedback, persuading, or handling disagreements, by showing how cultural norms influence these interactions.

Think of Meyer's map as a set of scales revealing how different cultures approach key communication habits. These aren't stereotypes but tools for awareness and adaptability. Let's explore some of the most relevant ones for effective cross-border communication.

Communicating: Explicit Versus Implicit

Building on Hall's high- and low-context idea, Meyer's Communicating scale asks: do people prefer to say things directly or leave some things unsaid?

- **Explicit cultures** (like the Netherlands or the USA) say what they mean. Leaders are straightforward, and clarity is valued.
- **Implicit cultures** (like Japan or Saudi Arabia) prefer subtlety and reading between the lines. Leaders might imply rather than state directly.
- **Communication in action**: A US leader might say, "*Your report needs more data,*" directly. A Japanese leader could say, "*Your report is good, but adding a few details could strengthen it,*" softer and more nuanced.
- **Leadership insight:** Recognizing these cues and knowing when to be direct or subtle can significantly impact your influence and how your message is received across cultures.

Evaluating: Direct Negative Feedback Versus Indirect

How comfortable are cultures with giving and receiving negative feedback?

- **Direct feedback cultures** (like Scandinavia or the USA) see honesty as the best policy. Leaders are clear and direct, even if it's tough.
- **Indirect feedback cultures** (like Japan or Thailand) value harmony and often soften criticism or give it privately to avoid embarrassment, and face-saving is very important.
- **Evaluating in action**: Giving critical feedback in a direct culture might involve straightforward comments like "*This needs improvement,*" whereas in an indirect culture, it might be framed as "*There are some areas we could develop further,*" delivered privately and delicately.
- **Leadership insight**: When leading diverse teams, adapt your feedback style. Be clear and honest with some, gentle and private with others.

Persuading: Principles First versus Applications First

Persuading reveals whether cultures prefer to start with principles and theories or jump straight to practical results.

- **Principles-first cultures** (like Germany or Sweden) want to understand the underlying logic before acting. This might look like providing the reasoning behind the process, helping to illustrate why it is done in a specific way.
- **Applications-first cultures** (like the USA or Australia) prefer quick results and practical steps. In this culture, you will want to show the end results before explaining the process that took place to get there.
- **Persuading in action**: When pitching a new idea, a principle-first culture might ask "What's the rationale behind this?" while an application-first culture might focus on "Show me how this will work in practice."
- **Leadership insight**: Tailor your presentations and proposals based on your audience's preference: detailed and logical, or practical and results-oriented.

Disagreeing: Confrontational versus Avoids Confrontation

How do different cultures handle disagreement?

- **Confrontational cultures** (like France or the USA) see debate as healthy and necessary for progress. Leaders and team members are comfortable challenging ideas openly.
- **Avoidance confrontation cultures** (like Japan or Korea) prioritize harmony, often avoiding direct disagreement to prevent conflict.
- **Disagreeing in action**: A French team might openly critique a proposal in a meeting, while a Japanese team might nod politely but later share their reservations in private.
- **Leadership insight**: Recognize when disagreements are a sign of engagement versus conflict avoidance and create safe spaces for open dialogue when needed.

Leading: Egalitarian versus Hierarchical

While Hofstede's power distance already touches on hierarchy, Meyer's leading scale zeroes in on how leaders interact with their teams.

- **Egalitarian cultures** (like Denmark or the Netherlands) encourage open dialogue with leaders, who see themselves as facilitators rather than authority figures.

- **Hierarchical cultures** (like China or India) expect clear authority, with leaders making decisions and team members following.
- **Leading in action**: An egalitarian leader might ask for input before making decisions, while a hierarchical one might issue directives with little consultation.
- **Leadership insight**: Adjust your leadership style to match cultural expectations, foster participation in some contexts, and provide clear directives in others.

Trusting: Task-Based versus Relationship-Based

Finally, how do cultures build trust?

- **Task-based cultures** (like the USA or Germany) are based on performance and competence.
- **Relationship-based cultures** (like China or Brazil) develop trust over time through personal connections.
- **Trusting in action**: In a task-based culture, a leader might focus on project milestones to evaluate trust. In a relationship-based culture, trust is built through social interactions and personal rapport.
- **Leadership insight**: Effective leadership requires understanding whether your culture builds trust through performance and competence or through personal relationships and social bonds.

Understanding these dimensions is a great start, but seeing how they interconnect can deepen your insights. Here's a concise comparison of key cultural dimensions and frameworks:

Table 7.3 Key Cultural Dimensions and Practical Leadership Tips: Navigating Differences with Confidence

Dimension	High-Scenario	Low-Scenario	Leadership Communication Tip
Power Distance	Formal hierarchy, top-down decisions	Flat structure, open dialogue	Build trust gradually with inclusive practices, especially in high power distance cultures. Encourage participation through group activities.
Individualism versus Collectivism	Rewards individual achievement, personal recognition	Emphasizes group harmony and consensus	Tailor motivation: recognize individual efforts in individualist cultures, foster team success in collectivist contexts.

(Continued)

Table 7.3 Continued

Dimension	High-Scenario	Low-Scenario	Leadership Communication Tip
Masculinity versus Femininity	Competitive, goal-oriented, direct communication	Cooperative, caring, empathetic	Adjust your messaging: be goal-driven in masculine cultures, supportive and relationship-focused in feminine cultures.
Uncertainty Avoidance	Clear rules, detailed plans, risk-averse	Flexible, adaptable, open to change	Provide detailed guidance when working with high uncertainty avoidance cultures; stay agile and open-minded with low uncertainty cultures.
Long-Term versus Short-Term Orientation	Focus on tradition, stability, delayed gratification	Emphasis on quick results, adaptability	Align goals: emphasize tradition and planning with long-term thinkers, highlight immediate benefits with short-term-oriented teams.
Indulgence versus Restraint	Emphasizes leisure, freedom of expression	Restricts gratification; social norms limit personal enjoyment	Respect cultural attitudes toward leisure and expression; foster motivation accordingly.
Universalism versus Particularism	Strict adherence to rules, fairness	Relationships and context influence decisions	Build trust through fairness in universalist cultures; prioritize personal relationships in particularist cultures.
Individualism versus Communitarianism	Personal achievement celebrated	Group loyalty and harmony prioritized	Recognize individual contributions where valued; emphasize team and collective success in communitarian cultures.
Specific versus Diffuse	Clear boundaries between work and personal life	Overlapping personal and professional spheres	Respect boundaries: keep work relationships transactional in specific cultures, and build trust over time in diffuse cultures.
Neutral versus Affective	Controlled emotional expression	Open display of emotions, expressive communication	Adapt your emotional expression: be composed in neutral cultures, show genuine emotion in affective cultures.
Achievement versus Ascription	Respect earned through performance	Status based on age, gender, or social connections	Recognize achievements in achievement-based cultures; honor social roles and hierarchy in ascriptive cultures.

(Continued)

Table 7.3 Continued

Dimension	High-Scenario	Low-Scenario	Leadership Communication Tip
Hall's High versus Low Context	Reliance on shared understanding, nonverbal cues	Explicit, direct verbal communication	Be aware of cues: interpret subtle signals in high-context cultures; communicate clearly and directly in low-context cultures.
Meyer's Communication Scales	Explicit communication: say what you mean	Implicit communication: read between the lines	Adjust your style: direct in explicit cultures, nuanced and polite in implicit cultures.
Meyer's Feedback Styles	Honest, straightforward feedback	Gentle, private, face-saving criticism	Tailor your feedback: be forthright in direct cultures; be soft and private in indirect cultures.
Meyer's Persuasion	Logic and principles first	Results and practical application first	Present your ideas according to cultural preferences: rationale for principle-driven cultures, results for application-focused ones.
Meyer's Disagreement	Open debate, challenge ideas	Harmony, avoiding conflict	Create safe spaces for disagreement: be direct in confrontational cultures, tactful and private in harmony-oriented cultures.
Meyer's Leadership and Trust	Leader as facilitator, open dialogue	Leader as authority, hierarchy respected	Adjust your leadership style: participative in egalitarian cultures, directive in hierarchical ones. Trust through performance versus relationships.

IMPACT ON VERBAL AND NONVERBAL COMMUNICATION STYLES

What you say is just the tip of the iceberg, especially when communicating across cultures. Communication is also about tone, gestures, facial expressions, and unspoken cues. Understanding these differences helps prevent misunderstandings and foster a respectful, collaborative environment. Table 7.4 offers some cautionary tales of communicating across cultures without a thorough understanding.

Verbal Styles

In places like Germany, the Netherlands, or the USA, direct, clear communication is valued. Expectations, instructions, and feedback are expressed openly, promoting trust and transparency.

Table 7.4 Cultural Blunders: Brands Gone Wrong

A powerful way to understand how culture shapes communication is to examine organizational missteps in expanding into new markets, which are often caused by a lack of cultural awareness.
Mike Fromowitz,[5] former partner and chief creative officer of Ethnicity Multicultural Marketing + Advertising in Toronto, compiled some examples of such faux pas:
Gerber. When Gerber began selling baby food in Africa, they used the same packaging as in the USA, featuring a cute baby on the label. However, they later discovered that many African consumers relied on pictures to identify products because literacy rates were low. The familiar USA packaging didn't communicate effectively, leading to confusion. Yikes!
Parker Pen. When Parker launched a ballpoint pen in Mexico, their advertisement claimed, "It won't leak in your pocket and make you pregnant." A translation error changed the message from the original tagline: "It won't leak in your pocket and embarrass you."
Pepsi. Pepsi faced a significant setback in Southeast Asia when they changed the color of their vending machines and colors from a deep blue to a light blue. Unbeknownst to them, in that region, light blue is associated with death and mourning, which adversely impacted their brand image.
These examples serve as an important reminder of how deeply cultural values and interpretations can differ and how crucial it is to understand local customs, symbols, and language nuances.

Meanwhile, many Asian, Middle Eastern, and Latin American cultures prefer a softer approach to maintain harmony and respect relationships. They might use gentle suggestions such as *"it's a good start, but there is room for growth,"* to deliver feedback without causing defensiveness. Recognizing these styles shows you care about harmony and trust.

- **Practical insight:** When working across cultures, observe how colleagues phrase things. If unsure, ask thoughtfully, such as *"Would you prefer I be more direct or is this tone comfortable?"* Showing openness and adaptability builds warmth and stronger trust.

Nonverbal Cues

Nonverbal communication is a powerful way people express themselves—and it varies across cultures:

- **Eye contact:** In the USA or Europe, steady eye contact signals confidence and honesty. However, in some Asian cultures, prolonged eye contact can be seen as confrontational, so subtler cues are better.

- **Gestures:** Hand signals and gestures are rich with cultural meanings. A thumbs-up or an open palm is generally positive in the West, but in some cultures, these can be misunderstood or even offensive. The "OK" sign, for example, can be harmless in the USA but considered rude elsewhere.
- **Facial expressions and posture:** A warm, relaxed posture might be seen as friendliness in one culture but inattentiveness in another. Similarly, expressions of enthusiasm or disagreement can be misinterpreted based on cultural norms for emotional display.
- **Practical insight:** Pay close attention to nonverbal cues such as eye contact, gestures, and facial expressions. When unsure, ask: *"Would you prefer I be more formal or relaxed?"* Showing curiosity and respect for others' style helps foster trust and connection.

SELF-ADVOCACY AND APPROACHES TO DISSENT

Knowing how people voice their opinions, advocate for themselves, or challenge ideas is key to cross-cultural communication. These behaviors are rooted in culture and can impact teamwork, collaboration, and decision-making.

Self-Advocacy

In individualistic cultures like the USA, Australia, or the UK, speaking up is encouraged and seen as a sign of confidence and initiative. Employees and leaders openly share ideas, ask for what they need, and highlight wins, which tends to foster innovation and quick decision-making.

In contrast, collectivist cultures like Japan and South Korea prioritize harmony and face-saving. Disagreements are often kept private, expressed indirectly, or softened with respectful language to avoid confrontation.

- **Practical insight:** When leading diverse teams, it's important to understand these norms. Create safe spaces such as anonymous feedback and reassure everyone that all opinions, whether shared openly or privately, are valued.

Approaches to Dissent

Dissent, the act of expressing disagreement or challenging ideas, is vital for innovation. But how openly it's expressed varies:

- **Direct dissent**: Common in many Western cultures, where frank debates are welcomed. Team members may openly question decisions, seeing disagreement as constructive.

- **Indirect dissent**: More typical elsewhere, where people nod in agreement but hold reservations. They may communicate disagreement privately or through subtle cues to protect relationships.
- **Practical insight:** Foster an environment where all forms of dissent are valued. Encourage open debate for cultures that favor directness and create confidential channels for those who prefer indirect feedback. Reassure everyone that honest input, in any form, helps the team grow.

By tuning into these norms and cues, we can create safe, trusting environments where everyone feels heard. When we adapt our communication styles to these cultural nuances, we build stronger, more authentic connections and cohesive teams across borders. In the next section, we'll explore how these differences influence team dynamics, decision-making, and trust in our increasingly connected world.

> **READY TO PUT THIS INTO PRACTICE?**
>
> **Amplify Your Leadership Voice Further**
>
> For deeper insights into cross-cultural communication, including case studies, explore the Leadership Blueprint at TheCommunicativeLeader.com.

IMPACT ON LEADERSHIP AND TEAM DYNAMICS

Understanding and developing cultural intelligence not only enhances individual communication skills but also profoundly influences leadership effectiveness and team cohesion across diverse environments.

Up Your Cultural Intelligence (CQ)

Imagine having a superpower to connect, influence, and lead across all cultures. CQ isn't fixed; it's a skill you can develop, a way of thinking and acting that builds confidence in diverse environments. It has four key parts:

1. **CQ drive**: Your motivation to learn about and engage with other cultures. Are you curious and open-minded? Willing to step outside your comfort zone? Embracing mistakes and misunderstandings is part of the journey.
2. **CQ knowledge**: Your understanding of cultural differences like gestures, tone, and decision-making. Knowing these nuances helps you interpret behaviors accurately.

3. **CQ strategy**: Your ability to plan, anticipate, and adapt before and during intercultural interactions. How do you prepare? How do you interpret unfamiliar behaviors? Strategic thinking keeps you flexible and thoughtful.
4. **CQ action**: Your ability to adjust your communication, verbal and nonverbal, in real time. Can you soften your tone or rephrase your message when needed? Authentic connection depends on your ability to adapt smoothly.

Adapting Leadership Communication Across Cultures

Developing your CQ isn't just about accumulating knowledge; it's about translating that understanding into action. Here are some strategies to adapt your communication style effectively:

- **Observe and listen**: Pay close attention to how colleagues from different cultures communicate: what they emphasize, how they give feedback, and their nonverbal cues.
- **Ask clarifying questions**: When unsure, ask respectful questions like, *"Could you help me understand how you prefer to receive feedback or suggestions?"*
- **Be flexible**: Adjust your style based on your observations. If your team values harmony, soften your language and tone. If they appreciate directness, be clear but respectful.
- **Respect cultural norms**: For example, in cultures that value indirectness, framing feedback as suggestions rather than directives can be more effective.
- **Workplace example**: Leading a multinational team, a manager might notice some members avoid disagreeing openly. To encourage honest input, they could hold private chats or create a safe space for dissent, respecting cultural preferences.

When leaders recognize and adapt to these differences, trust grows, and diverse perspectives lead to more innovative solutions.

Creating Inclusive Group Communication Practices

Inclusive communication isn't just about individual adaptation; it's about designing practices that respect and leverage cultural diversity (see Table 7.5). Here are methods to make meetings, presentations, and feedback sessions more culturally sensitive and inclusive:

- **Set ground rules for respect and tact**: Encourage everyone to listen actively, avoid interrupting, and be mindful of different communication styles.

- **Balance directness with tact**: In multicultural settings, aim for clarity without sacrificing respect. For instance, frame critical feedback with positive language and private discussions.
- **Use multiple communication channels**: Combine verbal discussions with written summaries or visual aids to cater to different preferences.
- **Facilitate equitable participation**: Use round robin techniques or anonymous input tools to ensure all voices are heard, especially those who may be less comfortable speaking up openly.
- **Be mindful of timing and context**: Recognize that some cultures prefer formal, scheduled interactions, while others value spontaneity and flexibility.
- **Practical insight**: When conducting virtual meetings with an international team, consider cultural differences in time zones, formality, and decision-making styles. For example, some cultures may prefer consensus building, while others expect clear directives.

By intentionally designing inclusive communication practices, you foster a team environment where diversity is a strength and where everyone feels valued, heard, and motivated to contribute their best.

Table 7.5 Instant Impact: Leadership Takeaway from Global Communication Leader, Heather Hansen

Conversations with Leaders: Supporting ESL Colleagues	Heather Hansen, a leader in global communication, shares practical tips in her book *Unmuted: How to Show Up, Speak Up, and Inspire Action* for staying confident and connected across cultures.
	She reminds us that, while English may be your first language, it's not for everyone, and in multinational workplaces, this can pose challenges.
	Her top tips for being a better teammate to those whose first language is not English: 1. Withhold judgment 2. Be present 3. Put yourself in their shoes 4. Stay curious
	I loved my chat with Heather—listen on *The Communicative Leader*, Season 2, Episode 9.[6]

CHALLENGES FOR MINORITIES AND UNDERREPRESENTED GROUPS

Leadership is about more than titles. It's about creating space for every voice to be heard and valued. For many minorities and underrepresented professionals, ongoing barriers rooted in workplace culture, bias, and tradition can make this journey tough. Recognizing these challenges and knowing how to navigate them helps build an environment where everyone feels empowered to step up and lead.

Barriers in Traditional Leadership Settings

In many workplaces, subtle but impactful behaviors like stereotyping, microaggressions, and tokenism can quietly chip away at confidence and limit opportunities for underrepresented colleagues. For example, you might observe a talented team member being overlooked during key meetings or hear dismissive comments like, "That's just how they are," which reinforce stereotypes instead of addressing root issues (see Table 7.6 for spotting and addressing biases).

Table 7.6 Spotting and Addressing Workplace Biases

Understanding how biases manifest in the workplace is essential for creating a inclusive environment. Here's how to recognize and address some of the most common forms: stereotypes, microaggressions, and tokenism.

Stereotyping

Stereotyping happens when we make assumptions about someone based solely on their membership in a group—like race, gender, age, or ethnicity—without knowing who they truly are.

Workplace Example: Assuming that an older employee is less tech-savvy and therefore not suitable for a digital leadership role, simply because of their age, rather than evaluating their skills or experience.

Microaggressions

Microaggressions are subtle, often unintentional comments or actions that convey bias, insult, or dismissiveness based on someone's identity. They can be verbal, nonverbal, or environmental, and often happen repeatedly.

Workplace Example: A colleague repeatedly mispronounces a coworker's name despite being corrected, signaling a lack of respect or acknowledgment of their cultural identity. Or, asking a person of color, "Where are you really from?" implying they don't belong or aren't 'truly' part of the team.

Table 7.6 Continued

Tokenism

Tokenism occurs when an organization makes a superficial effort to appear inclusive—like hiring a single person from a marginalized group—without genuinely valuing their contributions.

Workplace Example: A company hires a single woman of color for a leadership role to fulfill diversity quotas but doesn't provide her with meaningful opportunities or authority, and her opinions are consistently overlooked during decision-making.

Common Workplace Scenario #1: Marginalized Voices Overlooked

A highly capable woman of color shares an innovative idea during a team meeting, only to have it dismissed or attributed to someone else. Later, she hesitates to speak up again, fearing her contributions won't be valued.

What NOT to do

- Ignore or dismiss microaggressions when they happen.
- Assume that silence means agreement or disinterest.
- Overlook the importance of diversity in decision-making roles.

Tips for navigating this situation

- Be vigilant about microaggressions, whether intentional or unintentional, and address them respectfully when they occur.
- Create opportunities for diverse voices to be heard, like round-robin sharing or anonymous input tools.
- Actively seek out and elevate underrepresented voices, especially in meetings where they might be overshadowed.

How to be an ally

- When you see someone being overlooked or dismissed, speak up by redirecting the conversation or privately checking in afterward.
- Offer mentorship or sponsorship to colleagues from underrepresented backgrounds, helping them navigate subtle barriers.
- Educate yourself on the biases that exist and reflect on how your behaviors or assumptions might unintentionally perpetuate them.

Common Workplace Scenario #2: Fear of Being Seen in a Negative Light

A talented Black employee hesitates to voice concerns about team processes, fearing it might be seen as complaining or causing tension. This employee is also hesitant to express contrary opinions for fear of perpetuating the "angry Black woman" stereotype. Meanwhile, colleagues continue with the status quo, unaware of the missed opportunities for improvement.

What NOT to do

- Dismiss or ignore cues that someone might be uncomfortable sharing feedback.
- Rely solely on formal channels for feedback, missing out on other ways to learn of nuanced concerns.

Tips for navigating this situation

- Foster a culture of psychological safety where everyone feels comfortable sharing candid feedback, whether in meetings, one-on-one check-ins, or anonymous surveys.
- Model vulnerability yourself by admitting mistakes and asking for honest input.
- Regularly check in with underrepresented colleagues privately to understand their experiences and gather insights that might not surface publicly.

How to be an ally

- Amplify underrepresented voices by echoing their ideas and giving credit where it's due.
- When someone shares a concern, listen actively and follow through with action. Don't dismiss or delay responses.
- Educate your team about bias and microaggressions, creating shared language and understanding to address issues proactively.
- Take turns assuming a devil's advocate role in meetings so questioning a plan or raising concerns becomes the team's norm, and the stigma of raising potential concerns is not attached to one employee.

Remember, identities don't exist in isolation; they overlap and influence experiences profoundly. A Black woman, for instance, might face different challenges than a Latino man, but both are navigating a landscape shaped by intersecting biases.

Common Workplace Scenario #3: Intersectionality

A young, gay man in a traditional, conservative industry, like manufacturing, faces a unique set of challenges. His youth may lead older colleagues to question his experience, while his sexual orientation may make him feel like an outsider in a predominantly heteronormative environment. This can influence how his ideas are received in meetings, and how his leadership potential is perceived by senior management.

What NOT to do

- Assume all underrepresented individuals face the same challenges.
- Overlook the complexity of overlapping identities when designing inclusion strategies.
- Tokenize or single out individuals based on their identities, rather than seeing them as a whole person.

Tips for navigating this

- Recognize and celebrate the diverse experiences within your team.
- Create mentorship and development programs that address specific intersectional needs.
- Encourage open dialogue about identity, bias, and inclusion to create safe spaces for sharing and learning.

How to be an ally

- Educate yourself about intersectionality and its impact.
- Use your privilege to advocate for policies and practices that recognize and support diverse identities.
- Listen without judgment and amplify underrepresented voices in your organization.

Creating an inclusive leadership culture means actively recognizing barriers, challenging biases, and supporting every individual's voice. It's about asking yourself, "Am I doing enough to lift others up? Am I creating a safe space where everyone can lead?" When you lead with awareness, empathy, and action, you're not just breaking down barriers; you're building a stronger, more innovative organization.

STRATEGIES AND BEST PRACTICES FOR INCLUSIVE LEADERSHIP AND ADVOCACY

Being an inclusive leader isn't just a goal; it's a journey that requires intention, curiosity, and a willingness to grow. The good news is that every step you take toward understanding and embracing diversity makes a real difference. Let's explore some practical strategies and best practices to help you lead with empathy, authenticity, and impact.

Developing Cultural Competence

Think of cultural competence as your leadership superpower. It helps you connect across differences and create a workplace where everyone feels valued. Here are some practical tips to get you started:

- **Reflecting on your biases**: Regularly ask yourself, "What assumptions might I be making about others?" Journaling or mindfulness exercises can help uncover unconscious biases.
- **Seeking out education**: Attend workshops, webinars, or read books on intercultural communication. Books like *The Culture Map* or *Blindspot* can open your eyes to hidden biases and cultural nuances.
- **Using assessments**: Tools like the Intercultural Development Inventory (IDI) or the Harvard Implicit Bias Test can provide insight into your cultural awareness and areas for growth.

Every conversation, reading, or reflection is a step toward becoming a more culturally competent leader.

Bridging Cultural Gaps in the Workplace

Creating a truly inclusive environment means fostering open dialogue and encouraging respectful dissent where everyone feels safe sharing their perspectives. Effective techniques include:

- **Encouraging curiosity and listening**: When someone shares a different view, ask, *"Can you tell me more about how your background influences your perspective?"* Remember, background can mean their previous work or education experiences; it doesn't have to relate to a demographic difference.
- **Creating safe spaces**: Hold regular team check-ins focused on diversity and inclusion topics.
- **Modeling respectful disagreement**: Show that disagreement isn't about confrontation but about collective growth. For example, *"That's an interesting point. Let's explore it further together."*

Promoting Underrepresented Voices

Every leader has the power to amplify voices that might otherwise go unheard. It starts with creating platforms where diverse perspectives can shine. Strategies that can help include:

- **Establishing inclusive forums**: Use roundtables, mentorship programs, or employee resource groups that give minorities and underrepresented employees dedicated space to share ideas and concerns.

- **Being intentional about visibility**: When recognizing achievements, make sure diverse team members are highlighted and celebrated.
- **Mentor and sponsor**: Invest time in mentoring promising talent from underrepresented groups, and advocate for their growth opportunities. Help them navigate organizational pathways and champion their leadership potential.

Make mentorship a two-way street and learn from their experiences too. These insights can help shape better policies and enhance organizational culture.

KEY TAKEAWAYS

1. **Understand Culture as a Leadership Tool**: Recognizing how cultural values shape communication helps you lead more effectively across diverse teams. By learning key frameworks, like Hofstede's dimensions and Hall's high-versus low-context cultures, you can tailor your approach to build trust, foster inclusion, and prevent misunderstandings.
2. **Adapt Your Communication Style**: Flexibility is key. Pay attention to verbal and nonverbal cues and modify your tone, gestures, and feedback to align with your team's cultural expectations. This sensitivity creates a safe space where everyone feels valued and understood.
3. **Foster Inclusive Dialogue:** Create environments that encourage respectful dissent and curiosity. Use strategies like anonymous feedback and clear ground rules to ensure all voices, regardless of background, are heard and respected.
4. **Lead with Empathy and Awareness:** Be proactive in understanding the intersectional identities within your team. Recognize that challenges faced by minority or underrepresented colleagues are complex and advocate for policies and practices that promote equity and belonging.
5. **Cultivate Your Cultural Intelligence (CQ):** Developing CQ involves curiosity, self-reflection, and ongoing learning. Regularly reflect on biases, seek educational resources, and practice real-time adaptation. Building your CQ empowers you to connect authentically and lead confidently across borders.

NOTES

1 McKinsey & Company. (2020). *Diversity wins: How inclusion matters.* https://www.mckinsey.com/business-functions/organization/our-insights/diversity-wins-how-inclusion-matters

2 Harvard Business Review. (2019). *The harm of microaggressions in the workplace.* https://hbr.org/2019/07/the-harm-of-microaggressions-in-the-workplace
3 Harvard Business Review. (2018). *The secrets of successful global teams.* https://hbr.org/2018/03/the-secrets-of-successful-global-teams
4 Deloitte. (2019). *The diversity and inclusion revolution: Eight powerful truths.* https://www2.deloitte.com/us/en/insights/topics/talent/diversity-and-inclusion-revolution.html
5 Fromowitz, M. (2013, October 7). Cultural blunders: Brands gone wrong. *Campaign.* https://www.campaignasia.com/article/cultural-blunders-brands-gone-wrong/426043
6 Omilion-Hodges, L. (Host). (2023, March 20). Language as belonging: An interview with TED speaker & author, Heather Hansen [Audio podcast episode]. *The Communicative Leader Podcast.* https://www.thecommunicativeleader.com/podcast/episode/7b884c0c/language-as-belonging-an-interview-with-ted-speaker-and-author-heather-hansen

Level 3

Amplify Your Leadership Voice

Chapter 8

Authentic and Confident
Crafting Your Unique Leadership Voice

WELCOME TO LEVEL 3: AMPLIFYING YOUR LEADERSHIP VOICE

Congratulations on refining your skills! You're now ready to amplify your influence by shaping a leadership voice that is authentically yours. This chapter will focus on cultivating confidence and authenticity, enabling you to create a compelling presence that resonates deeply with others.

Think of this as tuning your instrument to your unique sound. When aligned with your true self, your voice becomes a powerful and inspiring reflection of your leadership style.

- In this chapter, "Authentic and Confident," you'll explore how to build conviction, authenticity, and confidence—qualities that make your leadership voice truly compelling.
- Next, Chapter 9, "Command Attention," will show you how to elevate your leadership presence and build a brand that amplifies your influence.
- Finally, Chapter 10, "Amplify with Tech," will teach you to harness digital tools to extend your reach and impact in a connected world.

AUTHENTIC CONFIDENCE: THE HEART OF YOUR LEADERSHIP VOICE

Leadership communication isn't about volume; it's about resonance. It's not about being the loudest voice in the room, but the one that truly resonates. This chapter will show you how to transform your leadership by building a voice that is authentically yours. You'll learn to move past generic styles and unlock a presence that builds trust, inspires action, and leaves a lasting impression.

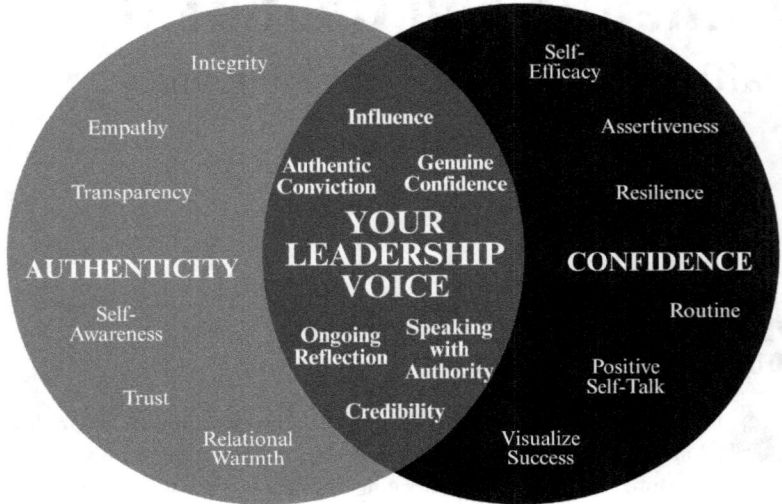

Figure 8.1 This Venn diagram illustrates how the most powerful leadership voice resides at the center of authentic and confident communication, combining qualities like integrity, empathy, self-efficacy, and resilience.

In a world saturated with information, trust is currency. The market is flooded with voices, but few are truly credible. As you see in Figure 8.1, your authentic confidence—supported by reflection and core values—forms the foundation of this credibility. Qualities like integrity, self-awareness, and resilience aren't just buzzwords; they're the bedrock of genuine communication.

The alternative is costly. Just 30% of employees feel engaged at work,[1] a sobering statistic that highlights the disconnect between leaders and their teams. Inauthenticity erodes trust, damages relationships, and fuels burnout. We will explore practical strategies to transform self-doubt into confidence and communicate with clarity and purpose. By leading with authenticity, you will not only strengthen your relationships but also elevate your influence for long-term success.

THE ROLE OF AUTHENTICITY IN LEADERSHIP

Forget trying on different leadership styles. The most impactful leaders aren't wearing a costume; they're tuning their instrument. They don't just adopt a voice, they cultivate one that's authentically theirs, built on their core values and strengths. This is how you stop reflecting on a type of leader and start becoming one. Take Steve Jobs, for example. Known for his innovation, he also led with an autocratic style—making unilateral decisions and setting exacting standards.

The problem with copying leadership styles is that we often imitate famous figures, but our values and communication strengths may differ. The key is to lean into your own unique gifts. When you do, you lead authentically and with integrity, making your influence genuine and sustainable.

Below is a summary (see Figure 8.2) highlighting the key benefits of authentic leadership and the potential risks of inauthenticity. Use it as a quick reference guide to understand how genuine leadership fosters trust and engagement, while inauthenticity can lead to disengagement and burnout.

By embracing authenticity and being mindful of the risks of inauthenticity, you can create a healthier, more trusting environment that drives sustainable success. Now that we understand why authenticity is vital, let's explore how to discover and embody your own authentic, values-driven leadership style.

BENEFITS OF AUTHENTICITY VS **RISKS OF INAUTHENTICITY**

Build Trust & Psychological Safety

Authentic leaders create a secure environment where employees feel valued and confident.

Enhance Credibility

Authentic leaders follow through on promises and communicate openly to strengthen trust and influence.

Foster Open Communication

Authentic leaders create safe spaces for honest dialogue, fueling innovation and collaboration.

Poor Work Outcomes

Inauthenticity leads to inconsistent messages which causes confusion, misalignment, and lower performance.

Emotional Labor & Burnout

Inauthenticity means concealing true feelings, which drains energy and leads to exhaustion and stress.

Disengagement & Skepticism

Lack of sincerity breeds distrust, detachment, and decreased morale.

Figure 8.2 This comparison highlights how authenticity fosters trust, credibility, and open communication, while inauthenticity risks confusion, burnout, and disengagement.

DISCOVERING YOUR AUTHENTIC SELF

It's time to discover the leader you already are. By identifying and prioritizing your core values like integrity, empathy, and creativity, you'll forge a foundation of authentic leadership. We'll also help you set meaningful, value-aligned goals to guide your journey. Through reflection, you'll uncover and leverage your natural strengths, whether it's problem-solving, communication, or adaptability, and learn how to use them with unwavering confidence (see Table 8.1).

Identify Core and Complementary Values

Your leadership is defined by two types of values. First, the core values—like integrity and empathy—that are your non-negotiables. They are the consistent drivers of your decisions. Second, are your complementary values—like creativity and resilience—that activate when you need them most. Identifying both allows you to lead with an authenticity that is both stable and adaptable. The tables below (Tables 8.2 and 8.3) are designed to help you pinpoint your core and complementary values and guide your leadership journey.

Table 8.1 Instant Impact: Leadership Takeaway from President and CEO, Dr. David Schreiner

Conversations with Leaders: Values-Driven Leadership	Dr. David Schreiner is the President and CEO of a hospital and author of *Be the Best Part of Their Day: Supercharging Communication with Values-Driven Leadership*. David discussed the ins and outs of values-driven leadership when he stopped by *The Communicative Leader*. But here are some pillars to get you started in thinking about how to enact values-driven leadership: • Be intentional in word and deed • Listen deeply • Reflect before responding • Use multiple channels to communicate and connect In short, values-driven leadership means that you show up as your authentic self and give your full attention to your team, work, and community. David expands on this idea and offers thoughtful suggestions for engaging in values-driven leadership in the workplace in season 4, episode 3 of *The Communicative Leader* podcast.[2]

Core Values: Your North Star

Table 8.2 Core Values

Category	Values	Description	In Action
Principled Foundations	Integrity, Honesty, Trustworthiness	Values emphasizing honesty, transparency, and building reliable relationships.	A leader admits to a mistake in a report, corrects it openly, and shares lessons learned with the team, strengthening trust and credibility.
People-Centric Values	Empathy, Compassion	Values highlighting understanding, care, and emotional support for others.	A team member notices a colleague is overwhelmed and offers to help with their workload, fostering a supportive environment.
Responsibility and Support	Accountability, Loyalty	Values related to responsibility, commitment, and steadfast support.	An employee takes ownership of a project's setbacks, communicates transparently with the team, and works extra hours to help meet deadlines.
Bold Leadership	Vision, Courage	Values driving forward-looking leadership, bold decision-making, and inspiring change.	A team member proposes a new idea during a brainstorming session, encouraging the group to think creatively and embrace innovation.
Equity and Dignity	Respect, Justice	Values centered on fairness, equity, dignity, and inclusive treatment.	A manager ensures all voices are heard during meetings, valuing diverse perspectives and fostering inclusion.

In addition to our core values, we all have complementary values that we lean into to help us flex across different situations and contexts.

Complementary Values: Helping You Shine

When you embody these values intentionally, they become guiding stars, strengthening your authentic leadership. Knowing your core and complementary values provides clarity as you work to expand your influence and amplify your leadership voice. Figure 8.3 helps you reflect and uncover your guiding principles.

AMPLIFYING YOUR LEADERSHIP VOICE

Table 8.3 Complementary Values

Category	Values	Description	In Action
Adaptive Thinking	Creativity, Innovation, Resourcefulness, Open-Mindedness	Values that foster new ideas, flexibility, and problem-solving.	A team member suggests a fresh approach during a project standstill, inspiring creative solutions that adapt to changing circumstances.
Steadfast Attitude	Resilience, Optimism, Patience	Emphasize mental toughness, hope, and ongoing progress.	An employee maintains a positive outlook after setbacks, encouraging colleagues to stay motivated and focused.
Inclusive Engagement	Collaboration, Humility	Focus on teamwork, openness to feedback, and approachability.	A leader actively seeks input from quieter team members, valuing diverse perspectives and promoting a collaborative environment.
Foundation of Trust	Fairness, Dependability	Cultivate reliability, justice, and consistency to strengthen trust.	A manager consistently follows through on commitments and ensures all team members are treated equitably, fostering loyalty.

With your core values and strengths identified, here are concrete ways to communicate authentically and confidently.

Prioritize Your Values

1	2	3	4	5
REVIEW THE LISTS	**SELECT 10**	**SORT INTO 2 CATEGORIES**	**RANK & NARROW**	**REFLECT**
Take time to review and think about the core and complementary values.	Select 10 total values across the core and complementary values.	Take your list of 10 and sort them into Core (*Your North Star*) and Complementary (*Supporting*) values.	Rank each category from most to least important, selecting your top 3 values for each.	Consider how to incorporate these values into your communication and decisions.

Figure 8.3 A step-by-step process to identify, categorize, and reflect on your values, helping you integrate them into your communication and decision-making.

TIPS FOR PRIORITIZING YOUR VALUES IN DECISION-MAKING AND COMMUNICATION

Knowing your values is only half the battle—the real impact comes from embodying them consistently in your daily interactions and choices. Research shows that leaders who demonstrate authenticity and integrity don't just build trust; they ignite employee motivation and strengthen team cohesion. So, how can you put your values into practice every day? Here are some practical strategies:

1. **Clarify your values**: We can't infuse our values into our actions until we are clear on them. Identify your values and understand how you want them to influence your decisions and interactions.
2. **Use your values as a decision compass**: When facing tough or uncertain situations, ask yourself if your choices align with your values. This reflection keeps your actions grounded in your principles.
3. **Ensure consistency**. Strive to align your words and actions with your values. This builds trust and reinforces what you stand for. What's more? When your words and actions align with your values, you eliminate the mental drain of reconciling inconsistencies.
4. **Balance and adapt.** Adjust the emphasis on different values based on the situation, allowing flexibility without compromising your core values. For example, during a tight deadline, you might focus on resilience and collaboration, encouraging your team to work together and stay motivated, while still upholding integrity and respect.
5. **Develop a personal values statement**. Develop a concise statement that captures your core and complementary values. For example:

   "I act with honesty and kindness, aiming to be reliable, open to feedback, and supportive of my colleagues."

6. **Communicate your values**. Clearly articulate your values in conversations and writing, especially when explaining decisions, to show how they align with your core beliefs. See Table 8.4 for an example of what this might look like in an organization.
7. **Seek feedback and reflect**. Regularly ask peers or mentors for input on how well your actions embody your values and use their insights to grow.
8. **Learn from role models**. Observe and learn from leaders who exemplify the values you wish to exemplify or from those who embody a value-driven approach to leadership. This can provide insight into effectively integrating values into your leadership, communication, and decision-making.
9. **Reflect and reassess regularly**. Make it a habit to evaluate how well your actions align with your values. Review your values statement and consider how you've embodied your principles. For example, Peggy Sullivan, CEO and author, grades herself weekly across areas like family, work, and personal life to ensure she stays true to her priorities.

Table 8.4 Actionable Insights: Integrating Values into Your Communication and Decision-Making

Let's consider a company facing the decision of whether to implement a new policy on remote work to provide employees with more flexibility. Example: The leader, Bryan, prioritizes values such as *trust, transparency,* and *work–life balance.* In a company-wide email and subsequent town hall meeting, he communicates his decision about the new remote work policy. **Email to Staff:** **Subject:** New Remote Work Policy Aligned with Our Core Values Dear Team, I am excited to announce that, effective next month, we will be implementing a new remote work policy that allows greater flexibility for all employees. This decision was not made lightly, and it reflects our core values of trust, transparency, and work–life balance. **Trust** is central to our workplace culture. By offering flexible remote work options, we are reaffirming our trust in each of you to manage your workload effectively. We believe that when you are trusted with the freedom to choose how and where you work best, it fosters a more engaged and productive environment. **Transparency** guided us through every stage of this decision-making process. We conducted surveys and hosted focus groups to ensure your voices were heard, and we are committed to an open dialogue as we move forward with this policy. Finally, valuing **work–life balance** is essential to maintaining a healthy and motivated team. We recognize the diverse needs of our employees and aim to support your well-being, believing it will enhance both personal and professional satisfaction. I look forward to discussing this further in our town hall meeting tomorrow, where we can address any questions or concerns you might have. Together, we continue to build a workplace that respects and promotes our shared values. Best regards, Bryan

With your core and complementary values clear, the next step is to build confidence and presence so your leadership voice is both authentic and compelling.

UNCOVERING YOUR STRENGTHS

Confidence isn't something you find; it's something you build. It starts with appreciating the unique strengths you already possess. This section will guide you to uncover your natural abilities and even find hidden talents in your hobbies, whether it's the resilience of a runner or the patience of a gardener. We'll also revisit core leadership skills and foundational qualities to ground you in your growth journey.

Reflecting on Your Natural Strengths

Discovering your strengths can be an inspiring journey and one that extends beyond your work environment. Tools like CliftonStrengths or VIA Strengths, reflecting on peak moments, and seeking honest feedback from trusted friends and family can illuminate qualities you might not have fully recognized.

As you explore these areas, pay attention to the strengths that resonate most with you. Notice how your natural talents show up in everyday activities, relationships, and challenges. Recognizing these can help you intentionally leverage your abilities as you grow personally and professionally. Now let's move from what you do well to who you are at your core.

The following sections are designed to help you pinpoint the unique qualities that are already a part of who you are. A powerful leadership voice is a blend of your natural talents and character. By reflecting on your core attributes, relational abilities, and strategic skills, you'll discover the unique blend that defines your leadership.

Your Personal Attributes

While strengths are what you do, your personal attributes define who you are. Your personal attributes are the core qualities that shape how you face life's challenges and grow into your best self. Think of them as your character compass.

- **Adaptability**: The ability to adjust smoothly to new environments and situations.
- **Flexibility**: Willingness to change or compromise in response to new situations.
- **Resilience**: The capacity to recover quickly from setbacks and keep moving forward.
- **Patience**: Staying calm and tolerant, even in stressful or difficult moments.
- **Self-Discipline**: Controlling impulses and staying focused on your goals.

- **Dependability**: Being reliable and trustworthy, so others can count on you.
- **Integrity**: Upholding strong moral principles and honesty.
- **Perseverance**: Staying committed and persistent despite obstacles or delays.
- **Positivity**: Maintaining an optimistic outlook, even during tough times.
- **Confidence**: Trusting in your abilities and judgments.
- **Vision**: The ability to imagine future possibilities and plan accordingly.

So, which of these attributes do you rely on most? The next step is to explore how to apply them in your communication and daily interactions.

Your Relational Skills

These skills are the bridge to authentic connection, helping you build trust with colleagues, clients, and stakeholders. They create a foundation for collaboration, influence, and positive work environments.

- **Empathy**: Truly understanding and sharing others' feelings.
- **Emotional Intelligence**: Understanding and managing your own emotions and those of others.
- **Social Intelligence**: Navigating social dynamics with awareness and tact.
- **Communication**: Clearly expressing ideas and actively listening.
- **Empowerment**: Supporting others to develop and succeed.
- **Teamwork**: Collaborating effectively toward shared goals.
- **Persuasiveness**: Influencing others in a positive, genuine way.
- **Initiative**: Proactively taking action and leading without waiting to be asked.

Beyond how you connect, your leadership is also defined by how you think. Let's now explore your analytical and strategic skills.

Your Analytical and Strategic Thinking

Your leadership isn't just about how you connect with others; it's about how you think as well. These mental tools enable you to approach complex challenges with clarity and purpose, helping you make informed decisions, innovate solutions, and envision future opportunities.

- **Analytical Thinking**: Breaking down complex information logically.
- **Critical Thinking**: Evaluating options objectively and thoughtfully.
- **Strategic Thinking**: Seeing the big picture and planning long-term.
- **Problem-Solving**: Finding effective solutions to tough issues.

- **Attention to Detail**: Ensuring accuracy and thoroughness.
- **Resourcefulness**: Making the most of available resources and adapting quickly.
- **Creativity**: Generating innovative ideas and approaches.
- **Vision**: Anticipating future trends and preparing for them.

While these traits are essential, true leadership and influence happen when you combine them all. The next section will show you how to leverage your unique blend of strengths, attributes, and skills to guide others and make a lasting impact.

Your Leadership and Influence

These qualities are the engine of your influence, empowering you to motivate, guide, and inspire others.

- **Leadership**: Inspiring and guiding others toward shared goals.
- **Persuasiveness**: Influencing others to see your perspective.
- **Initiative**: Taking proactive steps to move forward.
- **Accountability**: Owning your actions and their outcomes.
- **Empowerment**: Enabling others to reach their potential.

With a clear understanding of how you lead and influence others, let's now look at the organizational skills that turn vision into reality.

Your Organizational Skills

Your organizational skills are the foundation for turning vision into action. From planning and prioritizing to managing resources and deadlines, these skills help you stay focused, productive, and resilient amidst busy schedules and competing demands.

- **Organization**: Structuring tasks and resources for efficiency.
- **Time Management**: Prioritizing and using time wisely.
- **Resourcefulness**: Finding solutions quickly and effectively.
- **Perseverance**: Staying committed despite obstacles.

Finally, let's explore the last component of your authentic voice: your outlook and personal growth.

Your Outlook and Personal Growth

The optimistic and growth-minded attitude that fuels your professional journey. Embracing hope, confidence, and a commitment to continuous learning, as this perspective helps you adapt to change, overcome setbacks, and evolve into a more effective, fulfilled professional.

- **Positivity**: Maintaining optimism, even in challenging times.
- **Confidence**: Believing in your abilities and worth.
- **Optimism**: Expecting good outcomes and embracing growth opportunities.

Your unique strengths are the building blocks of your leadership, shaping not just your career but every aspect of your life. By identifying the qualities that resonate most, you can begin to intentionally leverage them for greater impact.

Consider how your talents show up beyond the office. The attention to detail and time management that make a family gathering a success are powerful skills for leading a project. The strategic thinking and perseverance you apply on the basketball court are the same traits that help you overcome challenges at work.

The key is to connect these dots. Take a moment to reflect on your daily life: Where do you see your strengths in action? How can you nurture and apply them more intentionally to elevate your leadership journey?

Putting Your Strengths To Work

Once you've identified your key strengths, the real impact comes from using them intentionally to drive results. Here's how to align your strengths with your work and your team's needs:

- **Align with opportunities**. Understand your project's goals and challenges: review plans, reflect on lessons learned, or chat with colleagues. Then, match your strengths to those needs. For example, if problem-solving is your forte, volunteer to lead innovation efforts.
- **Grow your strengths**. Find ways to develop them further. If communication is your strength, consider speaking at events or leading client meetings. Seek workshops, podcasts, or courses to refine these skills.
- **Lead by example**. Demonstrate your strengths daily. If empathy is one, foster an inclusive, supportive environment. Your modeling can inspire others and set new norms. Don't hesitate to share your strengths and express interest in responsibilities that match them, as this shows confidence and enhances the work you enjoy.

Ultimately, this isn't just about professional growth; it's about finding fulfillment by aligning who you are with what you do. When you lead with your strengths, you not only elevate your own effectiveness and confidence, but you also inspire a higher level of performance from everyone around you. With a clearer understanding of your strengths and how to apply them, you're now ready to translate that insight into action by setting intentional goals.

Set Personal and Professional Goals

Aspirations without a plan are just wishful thinking. By setting SMART goals — Specific, Measurable, Achievable, Relevant, and Time-bound—you can align your actions with your values and confidently and powerfully guide your own growth.

- **Specific**. Be clear about what you want. Instead of "improve professionally," try "complete three professional development courses in the next six months."
- **Measurable**. Your goals must be measurable. This allows you to track progress with concrete criteria and celebrate every win along the way.
- **Achievable**. Set challenging yet realistic goals. Reflect on your resources and capacity and adjust goals if they feel too far out of reach.
- **Relevant**. Ensure your goals align with your core values and long-term vision. Ask if they reflect who you want to become.
- **Time-bound**. Add deadlines to keep focus. Set start and end dates and hold yourself accountable to maintain momentum.

Applying these principles creates a purposeful path toward growth. Each step brings you closer to your authentic self. Let's explore some examples:

SMART Goal Example #1: Leading Quarterly Presentations

- **Specific**: Develop and deliver a presentation on key project updates.
- **Measurable**: Deliver a 15-minute presentation and gather feedback from at least two colleagues.
- **Achievable**: Prepare over four weeks, using organizational data and peer input.
- **Relevant**: Improves communication skills vital for leadership.
- **Time-bound:** Complete and deliver the presentation by the end of each quarter.

SMART Goal Example #2: Improve Active Listening Skills

- **Specific:** Enhance active listening skills during team meetings to increase engagement and understanding.
- **Measurable:** Practice active listening techniques in at least two meetings weekly and accurately summarize key feedback.
- **Achievable:** Incorporate these techniques in regular team updates and one-on-ones and at home for practice!

- **Relevant:** Strong listening builds trust and collaboration, key qualities for effective leadership.
- **Time-bound:** Focus on applying these skills over the next three months, with regular reflection and feedback from trusted colleagues.

By aligning your strengths and goals, you're not just planning for the future; you're actively shaping the leader you're meant to become. Now, let's bring all these pieces together and discover your unique leadership voice.

YOUR UNIQUE LEADERSHIP VOICE

Leadership isn't just about giving orders or charisma; it's about discovering and owning your authentic communication style—a unique blend of your values and strengths that commands attention, builds trust, and inspires others. Think of your leadership voice as having three key elements: task-focused clarity, relational warmth, and visionary storytelling. The most effective leaders don't just choose one; they learn to flex between all three to achieve goals, strengthen relationships, and motivate those around them.

In this section, you'll also learn to own the room by cultivating self-awareness, using impactful language, reframing negative scripts, and celebrating your wins. With these tools, your leadership voice will be as unique as your fingerprint.

Leadership Communication Needs

Many leadership communication books miss the mark by framing tasks and relationships as if they're in an epic duel.[3] The texts imply that leaders must be either task-focused or relationship-focused and that being visionary is only necessary from time to time. But the truth is that the most effective leaders don't just juggle three different styles—they seamlessly blend them. Your role requires you to *share ideas*, *manage projects*, and *nurture relationships* simultaneously. Below, we'll explore how to blend these elements effectively in the workplace.

Your Task-Focused Voice

Your task-focused voice is all about driving results with clarity and efficiency. For example, in a meeting about a tight deadline, you define milestones, assign responsibilities, and set clear timelines. Simple actions like asking team members to share their next steps ensure everyone knows what to do and by when. While focusing on tasks is critical, neglecting relationships can hamper long-term success.

Your Relationship-Focused Voice

Your relationship-focused voice is all about building trust and camaraderie to fuel engagement and innovation. Imagine noticing low morale after a tough project, so you host a casual coffee chat. Listening with empathy and showing genuine care can lift spirits and create a culture of openness. Strong relationships turn teams into supportive communities that thrive together.

Your Visionary Voice

Your visionary voice inspires a compelling story about the future. Instead of overwhelming your team with data, share a story about how a new initiative aligns with your organization's future. When you connect the vision to your team's aspirations, it sparks buy-in and energizes everyone to move forward together.

Bringing It All Together

Real power lies in integrating these elements. Picture leading a cross-departmental product launch: start by sharing the inspiring vision, then clearly outline responsibilities, and invite input from quieter voices. This balanced approach, which combines vision, clarity, and connection, ensures goals are achieved, relationships are strengthened, and your team is motivated to succeed. Remember, these elements aren't separate; they work together to drive sustainable, meaningful leadership.

BUILDING CONFIDENCE AND PRESENCE

Confidence and conviction are the cornerstones of truly effective leadership. It's not about being the most dominant voice, but about owning your unique style and playing to your strengths. By cultivating self-awareness, understanding your emotions, and gaining insight into how others perceive you, you can banish self-doubt. Practice positive self-talk, reframe challenges as growth opportunities, and communicate with assertiveness and purpose. When you lead with authenticity and self-assurance, you not only command attention but also inspire others to act.

Confidence-Building Strategies

Cultivating Internal and External Self-Awareness

In a *Harvard Business Review* article,[4] Jennifer Porter highlighted foundational skills that are valuable across all industries, setting the stage for success. Among them are internal and external self-awareness. When combined with your natural strengths, these skills help you to stand out.

Internal self-awareness is the ability to understand your emotions, beliefs, and values. It's about recognizing how your inner narrative influences your reactions, and, in turn, how you show up for others. Leaders with high self-awareness often pause to reflect and ask questions like:

- What emotions am I feeling right now?
- What assumptions am I making?
- What are the facts, and what are my personal interpretations?
- How do my core values influence my reactions?

This kind of reflection helps you respond thoughtfully rather than react impulsively.

External self-awareness is the ability to understand how your words and actions affect others. It's about paying attention to cues—like tone, body language, and silences—to gain insight into your impact. You can gain valuable insight by asking specific questions like:

- What am I doing in meetings that's helpful?
- What might I be doing that's not helpful?
- If you could change one aspect of how I interact with the team, what would it be?

Timing is important too. Approaching someone one-on-one often leads to more honest feedback than asking in a group setting. Regular reflection and seeking feedback strengthen your impact and help build stronger relationships. Now that you have the tools to understand yourself and your impact on others, let's learn how to leverage that self-awareness to build confidence through positive self-talk.

Positive Self-Talk

The conversations you have with yourself are the most important ones you'll ever have. Would you tell a loved one they're a failure? Probably not. Yet, we're often quick to use that harsh voice with ourselves. Ouch!

Healthline[5] identifies four categories of negative self-talk:

- **Personalizing**: Believing you are to blame for everything.
- **Magnifying**: You overlook any positives of the situation and focus only on the negative outcomes.
- **Catastrophizing**: You tend to set logic or reason to the side and expect the worst.
- **Polarizing**: You tend to see things as either good or bad, rarely seeking to see the middle ground.

We all fall prey to negative thinking traps from time to time. However, problems arise when these tendencies become our default, causing us to see everything as personal or to catastrophize. This way of thinking can hold you back from communicating with confidence and conviction. Here are some steps to strengthen your positive self-talk:

- **Catch the inner critic**: Notice when your mind turns negative. Instead of saying, "*I always mess up presentations*," try, "*I'm improving my presentation skills.*" That small shift makes a big difference.
- **Check in with your feelings**: When negative thoughts creep in, pause. Challenge yourself to find at least one positive aspect of the situation. Interrupting negativity is key to changing your mindset.
- **Practice gratitude**: Spend a moment each day identifying at least one thing you're grateful for. If work is extra challenging at the moment, focus on professional wins like a compliment or recognition for a project. This helps shift focus from problems to appreciation.

With a new perspective on how to manage your inner voice, you are ready to build a deeper sense of conviction. The next section will explore how to build self-efficacy and prove to yourself that you can tackle any challenge.

Building Self-Efficacy

Self-efficacy is the belief in your ability to succeed, and it's the fuel that allows you to take risks, learn from setbacks, and ultimately achieve your goals.

- **Dive right in**: Action is one of the quickest ways to boost confidence. Whether it's taking a professional course, reading that book, or trying a new activity, taking steps forward builds belief in yourself.
- **Social persuasion**: As Henry Ford said, "Whether you think you can, or you think you can't—you're right." Surround yourself with support and remind yourself: you've prepared, you know your stuff, and you're ready to shine.
- **Watch role models**: Seeing others succeed, like a colleague nailing a presentation, can boost your own belief in your abilities.
- **Butterflies into boosters**: Turn those pre-challenge jitters into your secret weapon. What starts as nervousness can transform into excitement and focus with practice and positive self-talk. It's not about conquering nerves overnight but about slowly training yourself to see them as an extra burst of energy that can enhance your performance.

Building self-efficacy gives you the confidence to speak up. Now, let's explore how to choose the right words to make your authentic voice heard.

> **READY TO PUT THIS INTO PRACTICE?**
>
> **Amplify Your Leadership Voice Further**
>
> Visit TheCommunicativeLeader.com to access the Amplifying Your Leadership Voice: Leadership Blueprint. You'll find guidance on tapping into your self-efficacy, making it easier to see obstacles as opportunities for growth. Start transforming challenges into your leadership strengths today!

Using Powerful Language

Your words are a direct reflection of your confidence. Another step in building your leadership voice is to use powerful language—words that project authority and conviction. By eliminating powerless language like disclaimers ("You probably won't like this idea, but. . ."), hedges ("kind of" or "sort of"), and tag questions ("Don't you think?"), you can communicate with greater clarity and assertiveness. Here are more proven tips for asserting yourself with confidence:

- **Nix the negatives**: Instead of saying "*I think we should do this project differently,*" try "*I'm confident that adjusting our approach will deliver better results.*"
- **Assert your ideas**: Tackle meetings head-on with clear language. Instead of saying "*I might have an idea,*" assert yourself instead, "*Here's a suggestion that could streamline this process.*"
- **Ditch noncommittal language**: Instead of saying, "*Maybe we can discuss this later,*" say, "*Let's connect this week to finalize this plan—what day works best for you?*"
- **Action-oriented approach**: Use verbs that signal action. Instead of "*I'll try to get that done,*" say "*I will have this to you by Thursday.*"
- **Ask empowering questions**: Pose questions that inspire action and avoid playing the blame game. Try questions like, "*What steps can we take to solve this?*" instead of getting stuck in pointing fingers.
- **Acknowledge others**: Powerful language is not just about you and your achievements; it's about others too. While you need to own your successes, it is also important to use collaborative language like "*We can,*" "*Let's,*" and "*Together,*" when appropriate.

Reframe Negative Thoughts

Confidence can't grow in a bed of negativity. If you're prone to negative thoughts, it's time to take control of that conversation. Consider these tricks for transforming your inner critic:

- **Adjust your assumptions**: Notice yourself thinking *"Nobody values my input?"* Change this thought to *"How can I communicate my ideas more clearly to ensure they're heard?"*
- **Focus on solutions, not problems**: Skip *"This project is failing"* and instead go for, *"What steps can we take to turn this project around?"*
- **Emphasize growth, not perfection**: When critiquing your work, change *"I messed up,"* to *"What can I learn from this experience?"* By concentrating on growth, you'll be more open to feedback and less likely to take mistakes personally.
- **Reframe criticism as feedback**: Replace thoughts like, *"My manager is always criticizing me,"* with *"My manager is giving me feedback that will help me grow."*

Building a powerful, authentic voice is a journey that starts from within. By mastering self-awareness, you understand your impact on others. Through reframing negative thoughts and positive self-talk, you can silence your inner critic and build confidence. By developing self-efficacy and using powerful language, you're not just speaking with authority; you're leading with conviction. These strategies are the foundation of a leadership presence that's uniquely yours.

ENHANCING CONVICTION, SETTING BOUNDARIES, AND MANAGING STRESS

It's easy to get lost in the daily grind, losing sight of what truly matters. This section is about finding your anchor. Cultivating a strong sense of conviction and purpose gives you the clarity and direction you need to lead authentically. When you connect with what genuinely drives you, your actions become more intentional and impactful. Here are some practical ways to deepen your purpose and stand confidently in your convictions.

Revisit Your Values and Goals

- **Reflect on what matters most,** such as your core values like innovation, integrity, teamwork, or creativity. Write down your core values and think about how they shape your actions. For example, if integrity is a key value, commit to honest communication and ask yourself, *"Does this decision align with my value of integrity?"* This practice will ensure that your decisions align with your goals.
- **Set values-driven goals**. Create goals that reflect your core values. If family is a priority, aim to protect your evenings and weekends for personal time, making your goals both successful and meaningful.

Adopt a Growth Mindset

A growth mindset helps you see challenges not as insurmountable barriers, but as opportunities to grow. Here's how to cultivate this perspective at work:

- **Embrace challenges**. I know this sounds counterintuitive, but leaning into a "can-do" attitude can make difficult tasks a bit more approachable. For instance, when tasked with leading a complex project, instead of getting bogged down in feeling overwhelmed, view it as an opportunity to enhance your leadership skills and showcase your abilities.
- **Feedback as fuel**. Welcome constructive criticism as a tool for growth rather than a critique of your abilities. This means actively seeking feedback from peers after a presentation to enhance your skills for the next time.

Boundary Setting

Setting clear boundaries is essential for maintaining balance and avoiding burnout (Table 8.5). Here are some practical tips:

- **Define non-negotiables**: Identify what your non-negotiables are at work and at home. For many, this means setting specific times for when you'll end your workday to prioritize personal time.
- **Prioritize**: It's easy to get sidetracked by less important tasks. To stay focused, identify your most urgent and important tasks first, so that you can focus on what truly matters. This way, you won't be left worrying about unfinished priorities at the end of the day.
- **Say no**: Politely but firmly decline additional work that exceeds your capacity or infringes on your personal time. When I became a new Assistant Professor, I learned to say, *"I've been advised not to take on any new projects or commitments at this time."* No one ever asked me who did the advising, and if someone had, we all would have had a good laugh when I responded with "me!" You can also say *"I'd love to help, but I'm currently focusing on a high-priority project, and I don't want to compromise on quality."*
- **Monitor burnout signals**: Be vigilant about signs of burnout, such as chronic exhaustion, irritability, consistently feeling overwhelmed, and loss of interest in activities. Recognize when it's time to recalibrate and reinforce your boundaries. Engaging the help of a partner or close friends can also help to shed some light on your mental and physical state.

Table 8.5 Data and Trends: The Benefits and Challenges of Boundary Setting

Many adults struggle with saying no and establishing healthy boundaries, but knowing how common this challenge is can be empowering.

- Only 50% of employees feel comfortable saying no at work,[6] often fearing damaged relationships or appearing uncooperative.
- 70% of workers report feeling overwhelmed by their workload, increasing the risk of burnout.[7]
- Research shows that assertively communicating needs correlates with higher job satisfaction and better mental health.[8]
- Less than 40% of managers feel confident in enforcing boundaries with their teams.[9]
- A *Harvard Business Review*[10] study links boundary-setting to greater psychological safety and trust for team engagement and growth.

Remember, you're not alone. Building confidence in setting boundaries is a skill that improves with practice. Recognizing these shared experiences can inspire you to prioritize your well-being, communicate effectively, and lead with purpose and conviction.

- **Regular boundary review**: Periodically revisit your boundaries to ensure they still meet your needs. I recommend setting aside time to assess your workload, commitments, and stress levels, as adjustments may be needed. I do this twice a year, and it has helped me reconnect with my work and reset my boundaries.

Preparing Mentally

Your performance starts before you even step into the room. Creating a pre-engagement routine can reduce nerves and help you perform at your best.

- **Develop a routine.** Develop a routine. Before key meetings or presentations, do a mental "pre-game" ritual like a quick breathing exercise, a power pose, or jotting down your main objectives. Just 5 to 10 minutes of review can boost your confidence and clarity.
- **Deep breaths.** Use deep breaths to calm nerves. Inhale through your nose for 4 seconds, hold for 4, then exhale through your mouth for 6. This simple exercise centers your focus and relaxes your body.
- **Set clear intentions**. Before you begin, define what you want to accomplish. For example, aim to listen actively and contribute meaningfully to a meeting. Clear goals keep you focused and confident.

KEY TAKEAWAYS

1. **Anchor in Authenticity:** Authenticity is the bedrock of effective leadership. By aligning your communication with your core values, you build trust and credibility, fostering an environment where open dialogue thrives. Remember, it's not just about portraying an image of authority but about genuinely connecting with those around you.
2. **Embrace Your Unique Leadership Style:** Avoid the pitfalls of trying to mimic others. Instead, blend your core values and natural strengths to carve out a distinct leadership voice. This genuine style not only represents your true self but also resonates with those around you, making you more influential.
3. **Foster Open Communication:** Lead with sincerity to nurture a culture where ideas can be shared without fear of judgment. Authentic communication breaks down barriers and sets the stage for collaboration and innovation.
4. **Leverage Strengths for Authentic Influence:** Identify and utilize your unique strengths to reinforce your leadership style. When you lead from a place of authenticity, your influence grows, and your communication becomes more persuasive and impactful.
5. **Inauthenticity Comes With Risks:** Recognize that inauthentic leadership can lead to emotional labor, burnout, and disengagement. Prioritize being genuine in your interactions to prevent these pitfalls and cultivate a workplace environment that supports well-being and productivity.

NOTES

1 Gallup. (2017). *State of the American manager: Analytics and advice for leaders.* https://www.gallup.com/services/182138/state-american-manager.aspx
2 Omilion-Hodges, L. (Host). (2024, January 22). Values-driven leadership: A conversation with Dr. David Schreiner [Audio podcast episode]. *The Communicative Leader Podcast.* https://www.thecommunicativeleader.com/podcast/episode/7b81520b/values-driven-leadership-a-conversation-with-dr-david-schreiner
3 Omilion-Hodges, L. M., & Wieland, S. M. (2016). Unraveling the leadership dichotomy in the classroom and beyond. *Journal of Leadership Education, 15*(1), 110–128.
4 Porter, J. (2019, January 29). *To improve your team, first work on yourself.* https://hbr.org/2019/01/to-improve-your-team-first-work-on-yourself
5 https://www.healthline.com/health/positive-self-talk#identify-the-negative
6 Gallup. (2017). *State of the American manager: Analytics and advice for leaders.* https://www.gallup.com/services/182138/state-american-manager.aspx

7 Healthline. (2021). *The impact of burnout and how to prevent it*. https://www.healthline.com/health/mental-health/burnout#statistics
8 Maximo, N., Stander, M. W., & Coxen, L. (2019). Authentic leadership and work engagement: The indirect effects of psychological safety and trust in supervisors. *SA Journal of Industrial Psychology*, *45*(1), 1–11.
9 Gallup. (2017). *State of the American manager: Analytics and advice for leaders*. https://www.gallup.com/services/182138/state-american-manager.aspx
10 Petriglieri, J., & Petriglieri, G. (2017). The talent curse: Why high potentials struggle—and how they can grow through it. *Harvard Business Review*. https://hbr.org/2017/05/the-talent-curse

Chapter 9

Command Attention
Elevate Your Presence and
Build Your Platform

**Level 3.
Amplify Your
Leadership Voice**

With your authentic voice established, the next step is to develop a commanding presence that captures attention and inspires trust. In this chapter, you will learn how to elevate your visibility and build a personal platform that amplifies your influence across your organization and beyond.

WE WANT TO HEAR YOU

In a world where every voice competes for attention, effective communication becomes your greatest tool. It's not just about speaking up; it's about connecting authentically and sharing your perspective in ways that land. Whether presenting ideas in a meeting, captivating an audience, or sharing insights personally, this chapter offers guidance to make those moments meaningful. You'll discover how to make every interaction resonate.

We'll start with the fundamentals: preparation and storytelling. By clarifying your core message and weaving in compelling anecdotes, you'll approach conversations with confidence and purpose.

But communication is a two-way street. I'll show you how to nurture dialogue by asking open-ended questions and genuinely valuing others' perspectives. Finally, we'll build a personal brand rooted in your values and authenticity, ensuring that your voice is not just heard, but truly felt.

These strategies will help you leave a lasting impression and elevate your presence. As we'll see in Figure 9.1, developing a strong leadership presence starts with core skills, grows through authentic connection, and leads to strategic impact.

How to Make Your Messages Stick

Effective communication isn't just a skill—it's the very heartbeat of leadership. It's more than sharing information; it's about connecting genuinely, understanding

COMMAND ATTENTION

```
                    Strategic Impact
                  Visibility & Influence
                Confidence & Self-Assurance
            ELEVATED LEADERSHIP PRESENCE

                  Clarity & Conciseness
                  Engagement & Dialogue
                Consistency & Authenticity
                  BUILDING COMPETENCE

                  Preparing & Planning
                  Authentic Storytelling
                  Emotional Intelligence
                       FOUNDATIONS
```

Figure 9.1 The Building Blocks of Elevated Leadership Presence: From Foundations to Strategic Impact.

others' needs, and cultivating an environment where everyone feels valued. When you communicate with clarity and purpose, you build trust and foster a thriving team. In this section, we'll explore strategies to ensure that your messages don't just reach your audience; they stick, inspire engagement, and spark action. Whether speaking to a small group or a larger audience, these insights will help you forge meaningful, lasting connections (see Table 9.1).

Step 1: Prepare with Purpose
Clarify Your Core Messages

Instead of just being clear, be memorable. Your audience will connect with a few powerful ideas, much more than a lengthy monologue. When presenting a project plan, focus on just three main elements: goals, timelines, and responsibilities.

- **Structure your delivery**. Arrange your points logically, whether chronologically or by priority. This isn't just about order; it's about creating a natural flow that makes your message easy to follow and impossible to forget.

Table 9.1 Data and Trends: The Power of Effective Communication

Understanding the impact and importance of communication can boost your confidence and help you approach interactions with intention and clarity.

- A survey by *Harvard Business Review* found that 69% of managers believe poor communication is a leading cause of workplace failures.[1]
- Over 60% of employees experience some level of communication apprehension at work.[2]
- Well-prepared speakers are perceived as 50% more trustworthy.[3]
- Even experienced speakers report feeling nervous before presentations.[4]

By leveraging these insights and focusing on preparation, storytelling, and authenticity, you can transform communication from a source of anxiety into a powerful tool that enhances your confidence and professional impact.

- **Refine your delivery.** Don't just wrap it up; nail the landing. Use visuals to reinforce your key takeaways and practice your delivery until it feels effortless and confident. Most importantly, tailor your message to your audience's needs and interests for maximum impact.

Anticipate and Prepare

Don't just impress your audience; earn their trust by preparing thoughtful, data-driven answers. This demonstrates you understand not only your content but also your audience's concerns. For example, backing up budget questions with data on ROI doesn't just show readiness—it builds undeniable credibility. So how can you anticipate questions?

- **Step into their shoes**: Go beyond just "understanding your audience." Empathize with their interests and concerns. By considering what your stakeholders might prioritize or worry about, you can address their fears before they even ask.
- **Learn from your past**: Instead of just reviewing feedback, learn from common concerns or objections you've faced before. Every past question is an opportunity to strengthen your future answers.
- **Strategize your answers**: Create a FAQ list for your topic. This isn't just about having answers; it's about being prepared to address any emotional reactions or objections proactively, so you can lead the conversation with confidence.

The "So What?" Framework: Make Your Messages Stick

Instead of just sharing information, show why it matters. By using the 'So What?' framework, you'll clarify the purpose of your message and ensure it's both relevant and actionable. For example, don't just say the team needs better communication; explain that "*Weekly check-ins will help identify issues early and reduce delays by up to 20%.*" Here are a few more tips to help you focus on key takeaways:

- **Give clear directives:** Make your takeaways actionable. Rather than offering vague suggestions, give specific directives. For instance, say, "*By Tuesday, finalize your project updates and share them in the project folder.*" This clarifies everyone's role and promotes accountability.
- **Focus on priorities**: Don't just share what's important—highlight the most critical points. By focusing on the top priorities, like, "*The three metrics to track are X, Y, and Z,*" you help your audience remember what truly matters and where to direct their efforts.
- **Reinforce key takeaways**. Don't be afraid to repeat yourself. Revisit your key takeaways throughout the conversation and offer a brief recap of the main action items before you end. This ensures clarity and commitment from your team, making it easier for everyone to follow through.

Step 2: The Power of Storytelling

Build Connection

Stories aren't just for entertainment; they are one of the most powerful communication tools you have. Why?

- **Stories are memorable**. While lists and lectures have their place, they don't create the lasting connection and impact you're aiming for. Stories stick with your audience long after the conversation ends, making them an essential tool for creating true engagement.
- **Stories enhance comprehension.** As storytelling expert Karen Eber notes, stories engage more of the brain than simple lectures. By using storytelling, you activate more of your audience's brain, leading to enhanced comprehension and retention.
- **Stories foster trust**. When we listen to a story, our brains mirror the activity of the storyteller, creating a shared experience. This mirroring effect builds empathy and trust, helping you forge a deeper connection with your audience.

The Power of Personal Stories

Storytelling is personal, but that doesn't mean you have to share private details. Instead, share anecdotes about your experiences, failures, or victories to build connection and foster psychological safety. In my classes, I often share my own public speaking journey—from shaking hands and a quivering voice to uncomfortable silences. Being authentic and sharing how I improved creates rapport and sets a supportive, empathetic tone.

Know Your Audience

Before you share a story, take a moment to consider who you're speaking to. Whether it's a quick check-in or a keynote, ask yourself:

- **Who am I talking to?** A story about wrestling probably won't resonate in a finance meeting. Make sure your story connects by tailoring it to your audience's interests so that it feels relevant and engaging.
- **What's the goal?** Think about what you want them to feel or do. Do you want them to feel inspired, motivated, or ready to act? Frame your story to guide them toward that next step or call to action.
- **What's their mindset now?** Use empathy to gauge whether they're overwhelmed, energized, or somewhere in between. This awareness allows you to tailor your message so that it resonates just right.
- **What are the potential obstacles?** Anticipate challenges and offer ways to navigate them. By showing you've considered potential roadblocks, you demonstrate thoughtfulness and set your audience up for success.

Use Concrete Examples

Storytelling works best with specifics and a clear structure. Here's how:

- **Create a narrative arc.** Every compelling story has a beginning, middle, and end. Use this structure to guide your audience through your message, making it easier to follow and harder to forget.
- **Choose relatable experiences**. Share anecdotes that reflect common challenges or situations your audience can connect with. For instance, we all understand pressure, obstacles, and teamwork. You can relate to colleagues by describing the shared chaos of "crunch time" with details like long hours, back pain, and stacks of empty coffee cups.
- **Be specific.** Don't just state facts; paint a picture with your words. Use sensory details and vivid descriptions to engage emotions. Instead of just saying *"learning a new system takes time,"* say, *"It might be uncomfortable at first, but I believe it will boost our client leads by 30% next quarter."* This kind of specificity makes your stories more memorable and impactful.

Make Connections Crystal Clear

Remember: Don't just share your story—link it directly to your audience's experiences to make it relatable. For example, sharing a story about your team navigating a demanding project, from overcoming communication hurdles to celebrating a major milestone, helps your audience see their own challenges and successes reflected in your story. These connections are what make your messages truly impactful.

Step 3: Communicate with Intention
Speak Clearly, Ditch Jargon

Don't just speak; be understood. Avoid confusing jargon and choose simple, clear language. Instead of *"conversion funnel optimization,"* say, *"turning interested customers into buyers."* This makes your message accessible to everyone.

Take Your Time

Pacing is power. Slow your speech to help your audience absorb and remember your key points. During a project kickoff, for example, pause after outlining each goal: "Increase market share by 15%" [pause], "improve customer satisfaction" [pause], and "enhance team collaboration" [pause]. These deliberate pauses give listeners time to understand and remember your message.

Make Eye Contact

Establishing eye contact builds a sense of connection and sincerity. During a presentation, make an effort to look at each person. This simple act of engagement fosters genuine connection and shows you're speaking with, not just at, your audience.

Vary Your Tone

A steady, professional delivery builds trust, but varying your delivery keeps your audience engaged. For example, you might start with a professional tone: *"We are launching a new customer service platform that will revolutionize how we interact with clients."* Then brighten your tone: *"Imagine—24/7 support and truly personalized experiences for our customers!"* Then, return to a reassuring tone: *"This change will boost efficiency and help reduce your workload, too."* By varying your tone, you make your message both engaging and memorable.

Step 4: Engage with Your Audience
Practice Emotional Intelligence

Tune into your audience's feelings. When delivering tough news, like layoffs, acknowledge the emotional weight directly: *"I know this is incredibly difficult for all of us, and I appreciate how much you've invested."* Invite sharing: *"Please feel free to reach out or share your thoughts afterward."* Showing empathy builds trust and demonstrates that you care.

Ask Open-Ended Questions

Instead of yes or no questions, encourage meaningful conversations. Use questions like, *"What are your thoughts on the new policy?"* or *"How do you think this change will affect your work?"* This invites others to share their perspectives and makes them feel valued, creating a dialogue rather than a monologue.

Show Genuine Interest

Invest in your colleague's experiences and interests. During a meeting, for example, if a colleague shares their struggles with a current project, respond with empathy. You might say, *"I appreciate you sharing that. It sounds like you're facing some real challenges. How can we support you?"* This not only validates their feelings but also cultivates a supportive workplace culture where everyone feels valued and understood.

Step 5: Be Proactive

Start the Conversation

Take the initiative to discuss important topics before issues arise. For example, if you notice a colleague looks overwhelmed, say, *"I see you've got a lot on your plate. Want to chat about how I can help?"* This shows immediate support and strengthens your team's connection.

Ask Questions

Foster dialogue by asking open-ended questions. This isn't just about gathering information; it demonstrates you value others' input, which helps build a culture of openness and leads to enhanced decision-making.

Follow-Up

Proactivity doesn't stop after the initial conversation. Check back later with a specific question like, *"Following up on our last meeting about the timeline—do you have any new thoughts?"* This simple act demonstrates that you care, reinforces trust, and keeps communication flowing.

Step 6: Create a Feedback Loop

Establish a Way to Receive Feedback

Create channels for honest input, like anonymous surveys after meetings or dedicated feedback sessions. Emphasize confidentiality and a nonjudgmental environment, saying, *"Your insights are valuable, and we want to hear from you. Your honest feedback helps us grow."* Regularly scheduling these opportunities shows that you're committed to continuous improvement.

Use Feedback to Improve

Don't just listen; act on what you hear. If feedback indicates meetings are too long, respond, "*That's helpful. Let's adjust our agenda to stay on track and respect everyone's time.*" When you implement changes, share how feedback influenced your decisions, saying, "*Based on your suggestions, we're shortening meetings and focusing on key topics.*" This reinforces that their input drives real change and helps build a culture where everyone feels invested in collective success.

In Summary: The Six-Step Approach to Effective Communication

Effective communication isn't just a skill—it's the engine that drives successful leadership. By embracing these six key strategies, you can truly make a difference:

- **Prepare and plan:** Clarify your core points to feel confident and show your audience that you value their time.
- **Use storytelling:** Transform your message from dry facts into engaging narratives that connect with your audience.
- **Communicate with intention:** Speak clearly, vary your pace and tone, and make eye contact to keep your audience's attention.
- **Engage with your audience:** Practice emotional intelligence, ask open-ended questions, and show genuine interest in their thoughts.
- **Be proactive:** Initiate important conversations and follow up afterward to show that you care and to foster a sense of teamwork.
- **Create a feedback loop:** Welcome input to continuously refine your messaging and improve together.

MAKING YOUR MARK: IMPACTFUL IN-PERSON COMMUNICATION

Every interaction is a chance to leave a lasting impression. By combining thoughtful preparation with authentic engagement, you can make your presence memorable. This guide provides key communication strategies and examples to help you succeed in any setting.

Presentations

Your audience wants to connect with you. Hook them immediately by starting with a personal story or a relatable anecdote. Remember, your slides are signposts, not scripts—keep them simple and visual to support your message.
To build confidence, practice your delivery and master your body language. Stand tall, make eye contact, and use deliberate gestures. Enhance your impact

by using strategic pauses to emphasize key points, weaving in powerful stories, and asking questions to encourage engagement.

In action: Brené Brown masterfully uses personal stories and minimal visuals to foster empathy and trust, showing how a story told well can be more impactful than any data point.

Meetings and Conferences

Successful meetings hinge on clarity and genuine engagement. Start by warmly greeting everyone and expressing appreciation for their contributions. You can enrich the discussion by actively inviting input from quieter members, ensuring a truly inclusive environment. Build trust and rapport by practicing active listening—nodding, paraphrasing, and summarizing to show you value others' insights. Before the meeting, set a clear agenda to maintain focus and always conclude by summarizing key action items. This ensures that everyone leaves with a shared understanding of the next steps.

In action: Microsoft's Satya Nadella consistently promotes a growth mindset by asking team members what they've learned from challenges. This practice builds psychological safety, allowing for greater innovation and a stronger team. It demonstrates how a leader can turn a simple question into a powerful catalyst.

Networking Events

Networking can feel daunting, but it doesn't have to be! Start conversations with genuine questions about the other person's work or interests. Prepare a few conversation starters and personal anecdotes to keep the dialogue flowing. To build on these connections, follow up with a friendly email or message within 48 hours.

In action: Richard Branson often asks about others' passions, not just their professions, which invites deeper conversations and builds rapport. For instance, instead of asking, *"What do you do?"* try, *"What drives you to come to events like this?"*

Pitches

When pitching an idea, passion is key. Articulate your value proposition while clearly tying it back to the audience's interests and remember to answer the question, "What's in it for me?" Use storytelling to creatively present data, adding a human element to the numbers. Rehearse your pitch multiple times and seek feedback to come across as confident and prepared. Finally, remember to pause for impact, giving your audience time to absorb key points.

In action: Steve Jobs famously opened Apple product pitches with compelling stories about user experiences, not just technical specifications, which made the audience feel the excitement firsthand.

Mentorship and Coaching

Effective mentoring involves active listening and empathy. Begin sessions by checking in with your mentee and asking open-ended questions to encourage reflection on their challenges and successes. Share relevant resources or personal experiences to foster a supportive environment. Collaboratively create a plan with actionable steps and remember to celebrate wins to build momentum.

In action: Sheryl Sandberg's mentoring style involves vulnerability, as she shares her own challenges to create a trusting atmosphere where both parties feel comfortable sharing.

Community or Professional Organizations

When you participate in community or professional organizations, remain open to diverse perspectives and embrace the power of inclusion. Take the time to learn members' names and backgrounds to create a sense of belonging. Don't hesitate to share your own insights, but be mindful to balance speaking with active listening. Invite quieter members to contribute by directly asking for their thoughts.

In action: Howard Schultz, the former CEO of Starbucks, exemplified this approach by consistently advocating for community involvement, which created a strong sense of loyalty and shared identity.

Panel Discussions and Roundtables

Participating in panel discussions and roundtables provides a platform to share insights and learn from others. Preparation is vital, so familiarize yourself with other panelists' work and perspectives. When responding, reference their points while adding your unique contribution to promote a collaborative dialogue. To keep the conversational gears turning smoothly, speak confidently while also listening attentively. Using examples or stories will make your contributions more memorable, and acknowledging other panelists' ideas enriches the overall discussion.

In action: Michelle Obama nods to fellow speakers' points, showing respect for their ideas while seamlessly weaving her perspective into the dialogue.

Lunch and Learn Sessions

Lunch and learns are great informal opportunities for sharing knowledge. Keep the session interactive by asking participants to share their insights or experiences and break up your presentation with discussion points. Engage attendees with hands-on activities or case studies that are relevant to the material, making it easier for them to absorb the information.

In action: At Google, employees often present projects during lunch, inviting feedback and discussing lessons learned, which fosters camaraderie and a continuous growth mindset.

Volunteer Engagements

Engaging in volunteer activities can profoundly impact your in-person communication skills. Approach these opportunities with enthusiasm and encourage others to share their motivations. Creating opportunities for everyone to participate and celebrating small successes helps maintain high spirits. Volunteering also provides a platform to practice leadership, teamwork, and active listening. Sharing stories of impact can inspire others and deepen personal connections.

In action: Oprah Winfrey often highlights how volunteering allows people to connect on a more personal level. She actively engages with volunteers, listening to their stories and inspiring them to make a lasting impact together.

With your communication skills honed, you are ready for the next crucial step: building trust-based relationships with key stakeholders. This is where your efforts transform into lasting influence and powerful collaboration.

READY TO PUT THIS INTO PRACTICE?

Amplify Your Leadership Voice Further

For more on making your messages stick, explore the Amplifying Your Leadership Voice: Leadership Blueprint available at TheCommunicativeLeader.com.

BUILDING RELATIONSHIPS WITH KEY STAKEHOLDERS

Effective communication with stakeholders begins with knowing who they are. Identify the individuals or groups who have a vested interest in your work—from team members to clients. A quick glance at LinkedIn profiles or a casual coffee chat can reveal shared interests and values. Leverage these commonalities to build rapport from the start.

When communicating, tailor your message to what matters most to your audience. Use language that aligns with their priorities and avoid jargon. For example, emphasize data for engineers and creativity for marketing teams. Starting with the "why" can inspire and make your message more compelling.

Trust is the foundation of strong relationships. Be reliable, transparent, and consistent. If you commit to a deadline, meet it. Respond promptly to questions and concerns to demonstrate respect. As your colleagues see you as trustworthy, they will be more open to sharing insights and feedback, strengthening your partnership.

Remember, building these relationships requires ongoing attention. Schedule regular check-ins to share updates and celebrate successes. Small gestures, like a thank-you message or recognizing someone's support, can deepen the connection. As Stewart Butterfield, CEO of Slack, says, "We don't just want to hear what people think; we want to build a relationship."

Building these relationships also lays the groundwork for a personal brand that is authentic and consistent, reinforcing your reputation and influence (see Table 9.2). In this chapter, we focus on cultivating your face-to-face brand; in the next, we'll explore how to translate that into the digital space.

Table 9.2 **Actionable Insights: Crafting a Personal Mission Statement**

Understanding your purpose and values is a powerful step toward building a strong personal brand and making intentional career choices. A personal mission statement acts as a guiding star—helping you stay aligned with what truly matters. It's a brief declaration of your core purpose, passions, and the impact you want to make.
For example, you might say: "*I strive to empower others by fostering collaboration and creativity within my team.*"
This offers clarity and focus, serving as a compass for your actions. When new opportunities come up, revisiting your mission helps you see if they align with your broader goals.
To create your own, reflect on your strengths, values, and what motivates you. Think about how you want to contribute to your organization or community. Keep it brief, authentic, and aspirational—something you can revisit often. **Your personal mission isn't fixed; it evolves as you grow.** Use it as a practical tool to turn insight into purposeful action and build a consistent, authentic personal brand—every day and in every interaction.

CREATING A PERSONAL BRAND IN FACE-TO-FACE SETTINGS

Building your personal brand in face-to-face interactions is key to expressing your authentic self and making a lasting, positive impression. Your brand isn't a mask but rather a reflection of your core values and how you want others to feel around you. Figure 9.2 outlines the steps to cultivate your personal brand.

Let's take a closer look at each step to explore how you can develop your personal brand.

Identify Your Core Values and Unique Traits

To begin building an authentic personal brand, you must first cultivate self-awareness. Begin by exploring what makes you truly unique. Reflect on your strengths, core values, and leadership style. Identify moments when you felt most authentic—whether mentoring, leading a project, or standing up for your beliefs—to reveal your true self. Write down the qualities and principles that define you, such as integrity, creativity, or resilience, and think about how these traits show up in your daily actions. This is the essential first step in building a compelling personal brand.

Figure 9.2 Key steps to cultivate an authentic and impactful leadership presence: defining core values, aligning words and actions, presenting yourself intentionally, engaging purposefully, and continuously evolving through feedback.

Consistent Messaging and Behavior

Consistency is key! Ensure that your words and actions align. If you value teamwork, demonstrate it by supporting your colleagues, collaborating regularly, and celebrating shared successes.

Create a brief, clear value statement you can easily share. For example, you might say, "*I focus on supporting my colleagues, fostering collaboration, and celebrating shared successes.*" This reinforces your personal brand and helps others understand what you stand for.

Setting personal and professional boundaries is also essential. If maintaining work–life balance is a core part of your brand, ensure your actions reflect that. Avoid being the person who responds to emails at all hours. Demonstrating that you value your time and respect others' boundaries builds credibility and trust.

Dress and Appearance

Your appearance plays a significant role in first impressions. Choose attire that aligns with your brand and suits the setting. Being well-groomed and thoughtful in your style shows respect for yourself and others. For example, if your brand embodies professionalism and innovation, opt for smart casual attire that strikes the right balance.

Understanding your audience's expectations is equally important. If you're attending a creative industry event, consider dressing in a way that showcases your personality while maintaining professionalism. Observing how industry leaders dress at conferences can also provide valuable insight. Your appearance should support and reinforce your authentic self. As a rule of thumb, it's better to be slightly overdressed than underdressed for any occasion.

Networking with Purpose

Be strategic about the events and opportunities you pursue. Choose those that align with your personal brand and professional goals. Before attending a networking event, define your purpose. Are you aiming to connect with potential mentors, customers, or peers?

As you interact, engage in thoughtful conversations that reflect your brand values. Instead of exchanging pleasantries about the weather, ask questions that showcase your interests, such as, "*What is the most rewarding project you've worked on lately?*" This approach not only deepens connections but also positions you as someone genuinely engaged and passionate about your field. For practical networking strategies, consider reading *Never Eat Alone* by Keith Ferrazzi, which offers valuable tips for building authentic relationships.

Authenticity and Transparency

Authenticity is a magnet for building lasting relationships. Be genuine by sharing stories and experiences that reflect your values, making your interactions more relatable. For example, talk about a mentor who influenced your growth or a challenge you overcame. Being open about areas for improvement, like *"I'm working on my public speaking skills,"* invites collaboration and builds trust. If you're looking for examples of authenticity in action, consider talks by leaders like Brené Brown or Michelle Obama, who share their personal stories in relatable and impactful ways.

Feedback and Adaptation

Seek honest feedback from trusted colleagues or mentors about how your brand is perceived. Use their insights to refine your approach, ensuring your actions remain aligned with your evolving goals. Remember to adapt your messaging to different contexts while staying true to your core values. For example, if feedback suggests you come off as too serious, find ways to incorporate warmth and humor to balance your communication.

Be flexible in how you present your brand across various settings, but always ensure that the essence of what makes you unique shines through. Your approach in a team meeting might differ from how you connect with peers at a casual event, but your core values should remain consistent. For further guidance on evolving your personal brand thoughtfully, consider reading *Reinventing You* by Dorie Clark.

Building a Legacy

While this might seem lofty, considering the long-term impact you want to have can shape and strengthen your personal brand. Engage in initiatives and mentorship opportunities that extend your influence and support the legacy you aspire to create. For instance, volunteering for community projects not only elevates your personal brand but also demonstrates your commitment to leadership, community building, and personal growth.

Document your milestones along the way, using them as reference points to reflect on your journey and articulate your evolving brand. This practice provides clarity about your path and grounds you in your vision. Reflecting on your experiences helps reinforce your identity and allows others to better understand and connect with your story. Journaling your insights or creating a portfolio of your work can be practical tools for tracking your growth and development.

As you cultivate your personal brand in face-to-face interactions, remember that authenticity is key. By consistently embodying your values and forging genuine connections, you'll express your true self. This is how you create a brand that stands out and leaves a lasting impact.

Turning your vision into reality requires deliberate planning. Table 9.3 presents a powerful framework to guide your journey.

Table 9.3 Instant Impact: Leadership Takeaway from Life Strategist, Nancy Ho

Conversations with Leaders: The PACT Framework	Nancy Ho, a top life strategist and executive coach, shares her powerful PACT approach to goal setting designed to help you turn ambitions into meaningful action. What is PACT? • **Purpose:** Start with your "why." Knowing what drives you and the impact you want to create fuels your motivation through challenges. • **Action:** Break your goal into clear, manageable steps. Map out your priorities to stay focused and steady. • **Commitment:** Success demands dedication. Use check-ins, accountability partners, or reflections to stay motivated and persevere through setbacks. • **Timeframe:** Set a specific deadline. For example, "Launch my website by June 2026." Smaller milestones and celebrating progress help keep you on track. Why use PACT? It roots your goals in purpose and connection, leading to more meaningful achievements and lasting fulfillment. Learn more about PACT and from Nancy on season 5, episode 1 of *The Communicative Leader*.[5]

KEY TAKEAWAYS

1. **Your Voice Matters:** In a bustling workplace, effective communication is your strongest ally. Whether speaking in meetings or engaging one-on-one, view every interaction as an opportunity to connect and inspire. By preparing key messages and practicing storytelling, you can make your message resonate with clarity and warmth, leaving a lasting impression on your audience.
2. **Plan with Intent:** Successful communication starts with solid preparation. Identify your core messages, organize your points logically, and anticipate questions to engage your audience confidently. Remember, clarity breeds trust—which can be cultivated through intentional messaging and visuals that reinforce your main ideas.
3. **Embrace the Power of Storytelling:** Utilize storytelling to create emotional connections. When you share relatable anecdotes, you make your messages more memorable and impactful. Tailor your stories to your audience, ensuring that they align with their values and interests, so that your points resonate and enhance comprehension.

4. **Foster Engagement and Dialogue:** Building relationships is essential for effective communication. Actively practice emotional intelligence by asking open-ended questions and demonstrating genuine interest in others' opinions. This not only validates their feelings but also fosters a culture of collaboration, making your interactions more meaningful and productive.
5. **Cultivate Your Personal Brand:** Your personal brand is how you are perceived by others. It's a reflection of your core values, and it must be built on a foundation of authenticity and consistency. By aligning your words and actions, and seeking feedback to adapt and grow, you create a lasting impact that resonates in every face-to-face encounter.

NOTES

1 Harvard Business Review. (2013). The impact of communication failures in the workplace. *Harvard Business Review*. https://hbr.org/2013/07/the-impact-of-communication-failures
2 Gallup. (2018). State of the American workplace: Communication and engagement. *Gallup*. https://www.gallup.com/workplace/236441/state-american-workplace.aspx
3 Forbes. (2019). How trustworthiness impacts leadership perception. *Forbes Magazine*. https://www.forbes.com/sites/forbescoachescouncil/2019/05/09/how-trustworthiness-impacts-leadership-perception
4 Toastmasters International. (2015). Overcoming anxiety: Tips from experienced speakers. *Toastmasters Magazine*. https://www.toastmasters.org/magazine/magazine-issues/2015/mar/overcoming-anxiety
5 Omilion-Hodges, L. (Host). (2024, September 9). The balancing act: Navigating the professional paradox and leading with communication with Nancy Ho [Audio podcast episode]. *The Communicative Leader Podcast*. https://www.thecommunicativeleader.com/podcast/episode/7c26b331/the-balancing-act-navigating-the-professional-paradox-and-leading-with-communication-with-nancy-ho

Chapter 10

Amplifying with Tech
Harnessing Digital Tools to Elevate Your Voice

**Level 3.
Amplify Your
Leadership Voice**

In today's connected world, technology provides powerful tools to extend your leadership influence. This chapter will guide you in leveraging digital platforms and tools effectively, ensuring your voice reaches a broader audience and creates meaningful impact.

YOUR IDEAS NEED TO BE SHARED

You have important ideas and insights that deserve to be heard. While in-person communication is valuable, the digital world offers powerful opportunities to amplify your voice and showcase your values to a wider audience. In this chapter, I'll guide you in using technology to elevate your leadership presence and turn your ideas into influential content.

We'll start by creating a professional online persona that reflects who you are and what you stand for. You'll learn to select the right social media platforms and engage meaningfully, allowing your unique perspective to shine.

Next, you'll learn to craft engaging content that sparks interest and inspires action. We'll cover practical tips for creating compelling headlines and insights that resonate with your audience, and you'll hear from Deevo Tindall, a branding expert who will share his wisdom on igniting your thought leadership brand.

Finally, we'll focus on building an authentic community. You'll discover how genuine engagement boosts your visibility and fosters growth. By reviewing analytics and refining your strategies, you can ensure that every interaction counts.

By the end of this chapter, you'll be inspired and equipped to harness technology as a powerful tool for your leadership voice. Let's unlock your digital potential and share ideas that truly matter.

Step 1: Choosing the Right Social Media Platforms for You

Before hitting "submit" on your first post, take a moment to consider what platform(s) will serve you best. Reflect on your target audience, the type of content you want to share, and how frequently you plan to post. As the saying goes, "failing to plan is planning to fail." While this might be a bit of an overstatement, those approaching their social media strategy thoughtfully often achieve greater success because they plan in advance.

Aligning Your Platform with Purpose

- **Find your audience**: Understand the demographics of each platform. For instance, LinkedIn is ideal for professional networking, while Instagram appeals to a younger, visually driven audience. Post where your target audience spends their time. For more guidance, check out Table 10.1.
- **Align with your goals**: Clarify what you want to achieve. Is it brand awareness, networking, or establishing yourself as a thought leader? If building authority is your goal, LinkedIn and X are great options. If you want to foster community engagement, Facebook might be a better choice.
- **Test and experiment**: Don't be afraid to test different platforms. By starting with just a couple of them and evaluating the engagement, you can make data-driven decisions on where to invest your time.

Now that you have a sense of where to post, let's bring it all together. Table 10.1 highlights how different channels serve different audiences and goals, helping you choose the right approach for each.

To help you get started, I've included some examples of what you might share on each platform. Think of these as suggestions to spark your creativity. Use these ideas as a starting point to craft authentic, engaging content that showcases your expertise and builds genuine connections.

- **LinkedIn**: Share detailed articles on leadership lessons learned from managing complex projects or post case studies on innovative problem-solving. This will establish your authority and showcase your expertise.
- **X/Twitter**: Live-tweet insights from industry events, share quick tips, or comment on trending news with your perspective to enhance your visibility and thought leadership in real time.
- **Instagram**: Post behind-the-scenes moments from speaking engagements, share short leadership advice videos, or showcase your workspace to humanize your personal brand and connect with your audience visually.
- **Facebook**: Host live Q&A sessions on career growth, share success stories, or promote local workshops through posts and events to foster a sense of community and engagement.

- **TikTok:** Create quick, engaging tip videos; share day-in-the-life clips; or offer bite-sized advice to resonate with a younger, trend-savvy audience.
- **YouTube:** Develop a series of in-depth videos on specific strategies, interview industry experts, or produce tutorials on professional development topics to establish yourself as a trusted authority.

Table 10.1 Platform overview with icon sources from Icons8.com showcasing ideal content strategies for building your thought leadership and personal brand

Platform	Audience	Content Style	Best For	Goals
LinkedIn	Professionals, B2B	Articles, Thought leadership, Industry networking	Networking, Branding, Industry leadership	Establish authority, Recruit, Share expertise
X/Twitter	Broad, News-focused	Short insights, Real-time updates	Quick engagement, Discourse, Trend participation	Building visibility, Thought leadership
Instagram	Younger audience, Visual learners	Photos, Stories, Short videos	Personal branding, Showcasing culture	Building community, Personal branding
Facebook	Community-focused, Broader age range	Groups, Events, Longer posts	Community building, Event promotion	Engagement, Local networking
TikTok	Younger, Trend-driven	Short-form videos	Creative storytelling, Viral content	Brand awareness, Personal branding
YouTube	Adults, Professionals, Learners	Long-form videos, Webinars, Interviews	Deep dives, Thought leadership, Education	Establish expertise, Build a loyal following, Educate

Get to Know Your Audience

To maximize your impact, you need to know who you are talking to.

- **Identify your target audience**: Develop a clear picture of who they are. Consider their professional backgrounds and the challenges they face. Creating audience personas can help you visualize your audience and tailor your messaging accordingly.
- **Engagement patterns**: Pay attention to where your audience interacts most. For example, if a career coach notices higher engagement on LinkedIn than on Facebook, it makes sense to focus efforts there.
- **Create feedback loops**: Encourage conversations through surveys or polls to learn what content your audience wants. Showing you value their input builds rapport and guides your content strategy.

Quality versus Quantity of Messages

When it comes to posting, focus on quality over quantity.

- **Prioritize meaningful engagement**: Focus on creating high-quality, authentic interactions rather than simply broadcasting messages. A thoughtful LinkedIn post that invites discussion will often yield better results than multiple generic posts.
- **Maintain a balanced approach**: While consistency is key, you don't need to flood your audience with content. A few well-crafted posts per week can be more effective and build greater trust than daily, lower-quality messages.
- **Develop evergreen content**: Create content that remains relevant over time. For example, a well-written article on leadership best practices can continue attracting engagement long after its initial posting, saving you time while still providing value.

Step 2: Establish a Professional Digital Presence

Now that you know which platforms suit your audience, it's time to build your digital footprint. A strong online presence showcases your expertise and builds credibility in your field (Table 10.2). Let's explore the practical steps to create an impactful digital identity.

Set Up Your Online Presence

- **Define and create your brand**: Reflect on your core values and unique expertise. Identify what makes you stand out. For instance, if you're a project manager known for innovative technology solutions, make that the focal point of your brand.
- **Craft a cohesive profile**: Develop strong profiles on platforms like LinkedIn, X, or industry-specific networks. Use a high-quality professional headshot and a clear banner that reflects your work. For instance, a marketing professional might showcase successful campaigns in their banner. Use tools like Canva to design eye-catching banners.

Table 10.2 Instant Impact: Leadership Takeaways from Branding Expert, Deevo Tindall

Conversations with Leaders: Ignite Your Thought Leadership Brand	When I asked Deevo Tindall, Chief Experience Officer and branding expert, for his top tips on sharing your leadership insights on LinkedIn, he didn't hold back, and his advice is gold. • **Bring Value:** Ask yourself, what's unique about what I offer? Think about what's been done before and what people expect, and then find fresh, innovative ways to improve or simplify things. That's how you stand out as a true leader. • **Disruption Alone Isn't Enough:** Deevo reminds us that just wanting to shake things up isn't enough. To really lead, you need to offer thoughtful ideas or new solutions to old problems because that's what makes a real impact. • **Go Beyond Just Informing:** Sharing what you know is great, but don't stop there. Challenge outdated ways of thinking, inspire your audience to see new possibilities, and aim to connect, motivate, AND educate. Learn more from Deevo in season 4, episode 6 of *The Communicative Leader* podcast.[1]

Use Strategic Keywords and Watch for Trends

- **Research relevant keywords**: Use tools like Google Keyword Planner or social media analytics to discover what potential employers or clients search for.
- **Incorporate keywords naturally**: Seamlessly include these keywords in your bio, summary, and job descriptions. For example, if you're a content strategist, use terms like "digital marketing," "SEO," and "content marketing" to boost your profile's visibility.
- **Focus on niche terms**: Highlight specific keywords that showcase your unique value. If you specialize in user experience design for healthcare apps, using terms like "healthtech UX" can attract the right audience.
- **Monitor trends**: Stay updated on trending keywords via Google Trends or social conversations. Adjust your content to reflect these trends, keeping your profile fresh and relevant.

Consistency Across Platforms

- **Unified messaging**: Ensure that your personal brand message is consistent across platforms. For example, if your LinkedIn highlights your

leadership in team building, make sure your X bio reflects a similar passion for mentorship. Each platform should serve a unique purpose, with your content complementing rather than duplicating what's shared elsewhere.
- **Profile alignment**: Use the same bio format and images across platforms. This makes it easier for people to recognize you. If you are a public speaker, keep your headshot and bio consistent in your profiles and promotional materials.
- **Standardized tone**: Maintain a consistent voice. If you're professional yet approachable, reflect that tone in your LinkedIn posts and casual Instagram shares.
- **Regular updates**: Set quarterly reminders to review and refresh your profiles. Add new skills, recent projects, or achievements like certifications or speaking engagements. Keeping your profiles current ensures they accurately represent your evolving expertise.

Step 3: Creating Engaging Content

With your online presence established, it's time to focus on the heart of your messaging: content creation. Crafting compelling content is key to capturing your audience's attention and fostering genuine engagement. In this section, I'll share actionable strategies for developing captivating headlines and valuable content.

Crafting Compelling Headlines and Captions

- **Use strong action words**: Start with action-oriented words that grab attention. Instead of "Tips for Presentations," try "Master Your Next Presentation with These Essential Tips!" This sparks curiosity and invites clicks.
- **Highlight value**: Clearly convey what the reader will gain. Headlines like "Boost Your Team's Productivity by 20% with These Proven Strategies" make readers eager to learn more.
- **Utilize numbers and lists**: Headlines with numbers like "5 Proven Ways to Enhance Your Leadership Skills" often perform better because they promise concise, digestible content.
- **Create a sense of urgency**: Use language that conveys time-sensitivity, such as "Don't Miss Out!" or "Act Now to Transform Your Leadership Skills," motivating quick engagement.
- **Appeal to emotions**: Incorporate words that resonate emotionally. For example, "Overcome Your Fear of Public Speaking with These Proven Techniques" addresses a common fear and offers reassurance.
- **Test and iterate**: Experiment with different headline formats and track their performance. Use A/B testing on social media or email to see which headlines generate more clicks and engagement.

Sharing Valuable Content

- **Focus on your audience's needs**: Share content tailored to your audience's interests and challenges. If you know your followers struggle with time management, posting tips on time-blocking techniques would be especially helpful.
- **Leverage visuals**: Incorporating images, infographics, or videos makes your content more engaging. For example, creating a visually appealing infographic summarizing key communication tips can boost interaction.
- **Encourage interaction**: Ask open-ended questions to spark conversation. For instance, invite followers to share their biggest leadership challenges. This not only encourages engagement but also provides insights into future content.
- **Curate valuable resources**: Don't just create original content. While this may sound counterintuitive, you should also share relevant articles, insights, or videos from other experts. Curating high-quality content positions you as a thought leader and provides additional value to your audience.
- **Create series or themes**: Develop content series like "Leadership Tip Tuesday" to give your followers a friendly, dependable spot to gather quick, helpful insights. To make it even more engaging, consider weaving in a few related themes—like innovation, communication, and teamwork—that can run together or in sequence. This way, your audience can look forward to a thoughtful journey through different topics, making your content feel more personal and approachable over time.
- **Use storytelling**: Share personal stories or anecdotes related to your content. For example, recounting a leadership challenge you faced and what you learned makes your messages more relatable and memorable.
- **Repurpose content**: Adapt your successful content into different formats. You can turn a blog post into a video, infographic, or social media series. This broadens your reach and engages diverse audience preferences.
- **Monitor analytics**: Regularly review engagement metrics such as likes, shares, comments, and click-through rates to see what resonates most. Use these insights to refine your content strategy over time.

As you continue to develop your leadership brand, it is important to think about how to build engagement into your content creation process (see Figure 10.1).

Step 4: Building and Maintaining a Community

Creating a strong community is key to fostering engagement and meaningful connections. By actively participating in conversations and using strategic hashtags, you can nurture relationships that enhance your influence within your industry.

Building Engagement

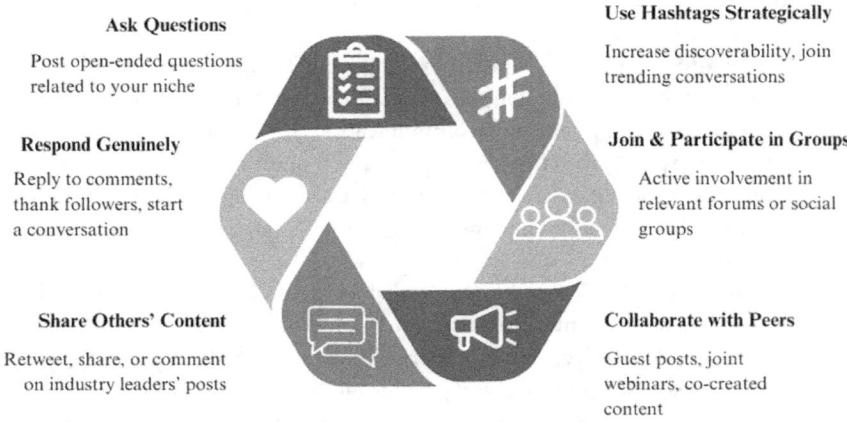

Figure 10.1 Effective engagement involves asking thoughtful questions, sharing authentic content, and building meaningful connections through collaboration and community.

Engage with Others

- **Foster conversation**: Encourage a two-way dialogue by asking questions. After sharing a leadership insight, ask, "What strategies have worked best for you?" This invites your audience to share their experiences and builds a sense of community.
- **Be responsive**: Make it a priority to reply to comments and questions. Quick, genuine responses show you value your audience's input and help deepen your connection. Dedicate time each day to engage and keep the conversation flowing.
- **Hashtags**: Research relevant hashtags that align with your industry and interests. For instance, using #CareerTips, #Leadership, or #PersonalDevelopment can increase the visibility of your posts and help you connect with a broader audience. Engage with others who use these hashtags by liking, commenting on, or sharing their posts to foster reciprocal relationships.

Staying Connected

- **Follow and engage with others**: Follow and engage with key figures in your field. Share their content, comment thoughtfully on their posts,

and mention them in your own discussions as a way to build relationships and increase your visibility within the industry.
- **Collaborate to create and promote**: Partner with influencers or peers through guest blogging, joint webinars, or social media campaigns. These collaborations bring fresh perspectives to your audience and introduce you to new followers who value your insights.
- **Participate**: Join relevant Facebook groups, LinkedIn groups, or industry-specific forums. Share your expertise, ask questions, and contribute to discussions. Being active in these spaces positions you as a knowledgeable and approachable leader in your industry (see Table 10.3).

Table 10.3 **Data and Trends: The Power of Consistent Sharing - Building Your Leadership Presence**

These statistics show that consistent, authentic content can greatly boost your leadership presence:
- 80–100% of social content is entertainment-driven for a quarter of organizations.[2]
- Edelman found that 63% of consumers and 58% of business decision-makers trust brands and leaders who regularly share authentic expertise.[3]
- LinkedIn reports that weekly content sharers are 7 times more likely to be seen as emerging industry leaders.[4]
- HubSpot found that posting weekly increases followers and engagement by up to 50%.[5]
- 93% of marketers see a strong ROI from video marketing—simple, phone videos can be highly effective.[6]

By posting consistently and using formats like video, you strengthen your authority and trust—key themes in this chapter to amplify your leadership voice.

Step 5: Measuring Success

Regularly reviewing your engagement metrics and website traffic provides valuable insights that can inform and improve your content strategy. Using data to guide your decisions helps you make thoughtful adjustments for greater impact.

Track Analytics

- **Engagement metrics**: Keep a close eye on likes, shares, and comments to see what resonates. Tools like Google Analytics and LinkedIn Analytics offer detailed data on your content's performance.
- **Social media interactions**: Observe how your audience engages. Are they commenting thoughtfully or just liking? Ask them questions about the topics they are interested in or what they would like to see next. Understanding their responses and behaviors allows you to tailor your content to their preferences.

- **Website traffic and conversions**: If you have a website or blog, monitor visitor numbers and conversion rates. Knowing where your traffic comes from and which content drives action helps refine your overall approach.

Adjust as Needed

- **Identify areas for improvement**. Use your analytics to pinpoint areas where your content may be falling short. For example, if a post gets low engagement, reflect on why and consider what changes could make it more appealing.

- **Test and refine**. Don't hesitate to experiment with new approaches. Try different types of content, posting times, or formats. Conduct A/B tests on headlines or visuals to see what resonates best. Use the results to refine your strategy and improve future engagement.

As you implement these strategies, remember that building a strong digital presence is an ongoing process that requires patience, consistency, and a willingness to adapt. Regularly analyzing your results will help you refine your approach, ensuring your efforts remain aligned with your goals and the audience's needs. By staying intentional and proactive, you will not only elevate your online visibility but also foster relationships that support your leadership journey. With this solid foundation, you are now ready to explore best practices that leverage technology even further, empowering you to amplify your leadership voice and make a lasting impact (see Table 10.4).

Table 10.4 Actionable Insights: Shaping Your Brand by Learning From Others

Not sure what your personal or leadership brand is yet? That's okay! Sometimes, the best way to start is by observing others you admire. Here's a quick guide:
1. Find People or Pages you Like
Look for leaders, content creators, or pages that catch your eye. What draws you to their style?
2. Ask Questions
What do I like about their content? Is it friendly, bold, or thoughtful? What values do they show?
3. Spot Patterns
What topics do they focus on? How do they communicate? What makes me want to follow or engage?
4. Get Inspired, Don't Copy
Pick out what feels authentic to you and think about how to incorporate it into your style.
5. Start Small
Share a story, a tip, or your opinion—no need to be perfect. Over time, you'll shape your genuine brand.
Remember, discovering your brand is a journey. By observing others and staying true to yourself, you're taking the first steps toward turning insight into action.

BEST PRACTICES

Now that you've learned the essentials—choosing the right platforms, creating engaging content, and building community—it's time to explore additional principles that will elevate your online interactions. The core principles of authenticity, consistency, and transparency translate seamlessly from face-to-face to online communication.

Throughout this book, we've discovered how these traits are foundational to effective communication. By integrating them into your online presence, you'll connect more genuinely, build trust, and foster meaningful relationships.

Authenticity

Being genuine in your communication is essential for building lasting connections with your audience. Authenticity fosters trust and strengthens relationships, making it crucial to present a true picture of who you are. When it comes to connecting genuinely with others, being authentic and transparent makes all the difference.

Table 10.5 presents some do's and don'ts to help you build trust and relatability.

Table 10.5 Authenticity builds trust: share real stories, lessons, and vulnerabilities.

What to Do: Be Authentic and Transparent	What NOT to Do: Be Inauthentic and Guarded
What to Do Lesson #1: Share Personal Stories and Challenges Being open about your journey, including setbacks, helps build trust. For example, "*After a project failed because I didn't listen enough, I learned to be a better listener and collaborator.*"	**What NOT to Do Lesson #1: Hide Struggles and Focus Only on Successes** Trying to portray constant success or suggesting that success is solely due to hard work can imply others aren't working hard enough or aren't good enough. This creates a disconnect and can make your audience doubt your sincerity.
What to Do Lesson #2: Show Vulnerability and Lessons Learned Share experiences like, "*I once missed an important deadline because I was overwhelmed, but I used that experience to improve my time management.*" Revealing your growth makes you relatable; sharing your new process makes you inspiring.	**What NOT to Do Lesson #2: Projecting a Perfect Image** Posting content that suggests you're immune to setbacks or mistakes isn't relatable or inspiring. Remember, people don't connect with perfection; they connect with authenticity.
What to Do Lesson #3: Use Real Examples and Honest Feedback Share specific stories like, "*Here's how I handled a difficult discussion with a client . . .*" Honest sharing positions you as a thought leader.	**What NOT to Do Lesson #3: Post Only Polished, Filtered Content** Over-curated images and messages that hide the real you can create a barrier. Authenticity is about showing the full picture, your wins AND your lessons. People want to connect with a human, not a perfect persona.

Consistency

Establishing a regular posting schedule is vital for keeping your audience engaged. Consistency helps your audience know when to expect content from you, reinforcing your presence in their feeds.

- **What to do**: Determine a sustainable posting frequency. This can be daily, weekly, bi-weekly, or even monthly. The most important thing is sticking with your schedule. Tools like Hootsuite or Buffer can help you schedule posts in advance, ensuring you maintain consistency even during busy periods. For instance, if you decide on a "Motivational Monday" theme where you share leadership tips every week, your audience can begin to look forward to starting their week with your insights.
- **What NOT to do**: Avoid erratic posting, such as a flurry of content one week followed by weeks of silence. This inconsistency can confuse your audience and lead to decreased engagement. It can also give the impression that you're not fully committed to your online presence. If you're just starting to build your online presence, consider biweekly posts as a way to dip a toe into this world.
- **Example to emulate**: Gary Gaynerchuk, CEO of VaynerMedia, consistently shares content across multiple platforms every week. His disciplined schedule reinforces his personal brand, positions him as a thought leader, and keeps his audience engaged.

Transparency

Openness about your experiences—your successes *and* challenges—makes you relatable and humanizes your brand. Transparency can inspire and encourage your audience to engage more meaningfully.

- **What to do:** Discuss the processes behind your decisions and the challenges you face. For example, when launching a new initiative, share the behind-the-scenes story of how it came to fruition, including the obstacles you encountered along the way. This narrative can resonate with your audience and create a sense of a shared experience.
- **What NOT to do:** Avoid glossing over failures, hurdles, or challenges. A company or thought leader who only showcases achievements without acknowledging struggles can come across as insincere or disconnected. A lack of transparency can lead to skepticism and undercut perceptions of authenticity.
- **Example to emulate:** Howard Schultz, former CEO of Starbucks, has been transparent about the company's challenges and its commitment to ethical sourcing and community engagement. His candid discussions about these issues, such as his decision to return to the role of CEO after poor sales, have garnered respect and loyalty.

By implementing best practices around authenticity, consistency, and transparency, you can build a powerful online presence. These strategies are not just theoretical; they are actionable insights drawn from the experiences of notable leaders and successful organizations. As you amplify your leadership voice, remember that each of these components works synergistically. Authenticity breeds trust, consistency solidifies relationships, and transparency nurtures community. By committing to these practices, you'll connect authentically with your audience while enhancing and amplifying your leadership journey.

> **READY TO PUT THIS INTO PRACTICE?**
>
> **Amplify Your Leadership Voice Further**
>
> For practical planning and strategy tips to amplify your digital presence and truly stand out, visit TheCommunicativeLeader.com.

KEY TAKEAWAYS

1. **Amplify Your Voice Through a Digital Presence:** In an interconnected world, leveraging technology to share your ideas is essential. By transitioning from limited channels to a robust digital presence, you can promote your values and engage meaningfully with a broader audience.
2. **Choose Platforms Wisely:** Understanding the demographics and unique strengths of different social media platforms is crucial. Align your platform choice with your goals and target audience to maximize engagement and impact, whether that's through professional networking on LinkedIn or community building on X or Facebook.
3. **Engage Meaningfully:** Craft content that invites conversation and encourages dialogue. By asking questions, responding to comments, and using feedback loops, you foster a sense of community, which in turn boosts your visibility and strengthens your connection with your audience.
4. **Commit to Consistency:** Establishing a regular posting schedule reinforces your digital presence. Consistency helps your audience know when to expect your content, making your insights more impactful and fostering deeper connections over time.
5. **Embrace Authenticity and Transparency:** Being genuine in your communication and open about your journey builds trust with your community. By sharing both your successes and your challenges, you create a relatable narrative that strengthens relationships and encourages engagement.

NOTES

1 Omilion-Hodges, L. (Host). (2024, February 12). Igniting your thought leadership brand: A conversation with Deevo Tindall [Audio podcast episode]. *The Communicative Leader Podcast.* https://www.thecommunicativeleader.com/podcast/episode/7b4156fc/igniting-your-thought-leadership-brand-a-conversation-with-deevo-tindall
2 Hootsuit. (2025). *Social media trends report.* https://blog.hootsuite.com/social-media-trends/
3 Edelman. (2020). *2020 Edelman trust barometer.* https://www.edelman.com/trustbarometer
4 LinkedIn. (2021). *The rise of social content sharing among professionals.* https://business.linkedin.com/learning
5 HubSpot. (2022). *The ultimate guide to personal branding.* https://blog.hubspot.com/marketing/personal-branding
6 Wyzowl. (2025). *Video marketing statistics 2025.* https://www.wyzowl.com/video-marketing-statistics/

Level 4

Sustain Your Leadership Voice

Chapter 11

Leadership Resilience
The Power of Self-Care and Reflection

WELCOME TO LEVEL 4: SUSTAIN YOUR LEADERSHIP VOICE

Welcome to the final stage of your leadership journey: sustaining your voice over the long term. This chapter highlights resilience through self-care, reflection, and ongoing growth. It's about nurturing your leadership voice so it remains vibrant, authentic, and impactful, no matter the challenges.

Think of this as exercising your leadership muscle regularly. When strengthened, it can carry you through any storm while inspiring others along the way.

- In this chapter, "Leadership Resilience," you'll discover strategies to build resilience, prioritize self-care, and reflect deeply, ensuring your voice remains a guiding force.
- Next, Chapter 12, "Your Leadership Voice as a Muscle," will provide practical daily habits to keep your voice strong, agile, and resilient so that you can continue to lead and communicate with confidence.

LEADERSHIP REQUIRES RESILIENCE

Leadership is often portrayed as a role of strength, vision, and focus. Yet, sustainable leadership begins with a foundational truth: caring for yourself. Effective leaders understand that prioritizing self-care and reflection isn't a sign of weakness, but a strategic imperative that boosts resilience, sharpens decision-making, and maintains your authentic voice. By nurturing your physical, emotional, mental, and spiritual health, you create a solid foundation for your leadership voice to thrive.

In this chapter, we will explore why self-care isn't a luxury, but rather an essential component of effective leadership, particularly during demanding seasons. We'll discuss how prioritizing your well-being can help you reduce burnout, avoid compassion fatigue, and maintain strong professional relationships. You will also find practical strategies for weaving self-care into your daily routine, from setting healthy boundaries to practicing mindfulness. Insights from licensed professional counselor Christine Sugg will help you stay balanced.

Reflection is also a key component of self-care. It keeps you connected to your purpose, helps you process experiences, and supports personal and professional growth. We will explore various reflection techniques and offer actionable steps to integrate them into your leadership journey. We will also address common obstacles, such as busy schedules or fear of vulnerability, and share strategies to overcome them.

Ultimately, this chapter demonstrates that self-care and reflection aren't optional; they're vital tools for sustaining your leadership voice, enabling you to communicate with clarity, compassion, and confidence for the long haul.

PRIORITIZING YOUR WELL-BEING

Prioritizing your well-being isn't just a personal choice; it is a professional imperative. By taking care of yourself, you show your team and organization that their well-being matters as well. Great leaders understand that self-care is not a luxury but a necessity for maintaining health. When you prioritize yourself, you build resilience, make smarter decisions, and model healthy behavior for others.

Research validates this. The American Psychological Association found that supportive leaders help reduce burnout and boost engagement.[1] Harvard Business Review[2] shows that leaders who practice self-care are more adaptable and build stronger relationships. What's more? It's not just good for you; it benefits your entire organization. The World Health Organization[3] reports that employees with a healthy work–life balance are more productive and are less likely to burn out. The Center for Creative Leadership[4] found that leaders who prioritize self-care foster positive cultures that increase engagement and retention.

Most importantly, taking care of yourself helps you lead with authenticity and integrity. When you are well, you are better equipped to handle challenges, make difficult calls, and connect with others on a deeper level.[5] Prioritizing your well-being demonstrates a commitment to yourself, your team, and your organization.

In the next sections, we will explore why self-care is so important and share practical ways to integrate it naturally into your daily routine. Figure 11.1 visualizes the impact and importance of self-care.

LEADERSHIP RESILIENCE

Figure 11.1 Centering Self-Care: Foundations for Sustainable Leadership.

THE IMPORTANCE OF SELF-CARE
Self-Care Is Not Optional

It is easy to get caught up in the whirlwind of full-time work and push through without pausing for a break. However, neglecting self-care has real consequences. When you consistently put your needs last, you risk increased stress, exhaustion, and decreased focus. Over time, this can lead to burnout—a state of physical, emotional, and mental depletion that impairs your ability to lead effectively. Burnout doesn't just affect you; it can also ripple through your team and your family, diminishing morale, productivity, and your reputation as a caring leader.

What Ignoring Self-Care Looks Like at Work

Ignoring self-care is a slippery slope that can manifest in several ways:

- **You're always "on"**: You're constantly skipping breaks, ignoring signs of fatigue, or working late into the night. This relentless pace leads

215

Leadership Resilience
The Power of Self-Care

STEP 1
Emotional Self-Care
To support your **emotional health** as a leader, practice stress management and develop emotional awareness.

STEP 2
Physical Self-Care
Prioritize nutrition, sleep, and exercise for overall well-being and **enhanced performance** in leadership roles.

STEP 3
Mental Self-Care
Engage in reflection and focus on mental clarity to **improve decision-making** and productivity.

STEP 4
Spiritual Self-Care
Connect with your values and purpose for **meaningful leadership** and personal fulfillment.

STEP 5
Practical Strategies
Incorporate mindfulness, set boundaries, and practice delegation to ensure well-rounded self-care for effective leadership. Here are some other practical strategies:

Prioritize sleep and rest
Use time-blocking and scheduling
Practice gratitude
Incorporate physical movement
Limit multitasking
Engage in creative and relaxing activities
Lean into your support system

Figure 11.2 Five key steps to build leadership resilience through self-care, reflection, and practical strategies for sustainable growth.

to a state of exhaustion that makes it impossible to perform at your best.
- **You're overextended**: You take on more than you can handle just to please others, constantly struggling to say no when you're already stretched thin.
- **You're in a vicious cycle**: The more you push through fatigue, the worse it gets, leading to poor decision-making and strained relationships. This creates a "self-care debt" that costs more time and energy to fix later on.

By recognizing these signs, you can proactively prioritize your well-being, protecting not only yourself but also the team you lead.

Self-care isn't a sign of weakness or laziness. It's a strategic act of strength that helps you lead with clarity and compassion. Prioritize small but impactful moments such as a quick walk, breathing exercises, or stepping away from your desk. These aren't optional; they are essential for recharging. Remember, small, consistent actions such as taking breaks, staying hydrated, and setting boundaries will strengthen your leadership foundation over time (see Figure 11.2).

Self-Care Involves Physical, Emotional, Mental, and Spiritual Well-Being

Neglecting any of the dimensions of self-care can have subtle yet serious impacts. Ignoring physical needs like poor nutrition, lack of exercise, or insufficient sleep can lead to fatigue, illness, and decreased resilience. Overlooking emotional health can result in increased stress, irritability, or difficulty managing conflicts. Failing to nurture mental well-being could cause burnout, difficulty concentrating, or a sense of stagnation. Dismissing spiritual or purpose-driven practices may leave you feeling disconnected from your values, diminishing your sense of fulfillment and clarity (see Table 11.1).

A leader who neglects self-care may work through weekends or suppress feelings of frustration, behaviors that undermine engagement and diminish empathy. The key is to avoid focusing exclusively on just one aspect, like only prioritizing physical health. Instead, strive for a balanced approach: take mindful pauses to breathe deeply (mental), schedule regular check-ins with yourself or others (emotional), and dedicate moments to reflect on your purpose (spiritual). Tending to all dimensions is necessary to keep your battery fully charged.

Table 11.1 Data and Trends: The Prevalence of Stress, Burnout, and the Neglect of Self-Care

Unfortunately, stress, burnout, and the neglect of self-care are incredibly common in the USA. Remember, prioritizing your well-being is not just personal; it's essential for maintaining your resilience.

- 60% of adults feel stressed or overwhelmed weekly.[6]
- Only 1 in 3 adults meets the weekly recommended 150 minutes of exercise.[7]
- Approximately 80% of workers face burnout at some point, impacting productivity and health.[8]
- Nearly 1 in 3 adults report insufficient sleep, which affects mental health and immunity.[9]

Holistic self-care is a strategic investment that strengthens your resilience and sharpens your ability to lead with sustained impact.

WHY EVERYONE (ESPECIALLY LEADERS) NEEDS SELF-CARE

Self-care influences how you relate to others, the decisions you make, and your overall growth. When you neglect your needs, you risk feeling overwhelmed, disconnected, or reactive. Small bumps can feel like mountains, derailing progress. Conversely, when you practice regular self-awareness and self-care, you are more present, empathetic, and capable of making thoughtful choices. Whether you are leading your family, volunteering in your community, or pursuing professional goals, the principles of self-care empower you to act with intention and authenticity.

Avoiding Burnout and Compassion Fatigue

Leadership often involves high levels of responsibility and emotional labor. Without proper self-care, leaders are at significant risk of burnout, a state characterized by emotional exhaustion, reduced motivation, and a sense of detachment. Satya Nadella, CEO of Microsoft, has spoken openly about the importance of mental health in maintaining resilience. He emphasizes that taking time for reflection helps him stay focused and effective during high-pressure periods.

Burnout does more than just diminish your personal well-being; it hampers your ability to inspire and support your colleagues. Compassion fatigue, the emotional exhaustion from constantly caring for others, can lead to decreased empathy, making it harder to connect meaningfully with others. Leaders like Nadella demonstrate that safeguarding your mental health is essential for sustainable leadership.

Impact on Relationships and Reputation

Your well-being directly influences your relationships with colleagues, clients, and stakeholders. When neglecting self-care, you may become irritable, less patient, or emotionally withdrawn, all of which can erode trust and rapport. Conversely, leaders who model healthy boundaries and self-awareness foster a positive, respectful environment. Consider Arianna Huffington, founder of Thrive Global, who has championed the importance of sleep and rest as vital components of leadership health. She rightfully asserts that leaders who take care of themselves build stronger relationships and a more resilient organizational culture. Failing to prioritize self-care can also lead others to perceive you as overwhelmed or disengaged, which may undermine your credibility and effectiveness.

Decision-Making and Judgment

Leadership demands sound decision-making, often under pressure. Chronic stress, fatigue, or emotional exhaustion impairs your ability to think clearly, evaluate options objectively, and exercise sound judgment. For instance, during the 2008 financial crisis, many leaders faced immense stress that clouded judgment, leading to risky decisions that contributed to the economic fallout. Regular self-care helps maintain mental clarity and emotional stability, ensuring that you approach decisions with a balanced perspective and confidence. Leaders like Sheryl Sandberg, founder of LeanIn.org, have emphasized the importance of self-awareness and emotional regulation in making strategic choices. When you are drained, you're more prone to impulsive choices or overlooking critical details—costly mistakes that can be avoided with better self-care.

STRATEGIES FOR PRIORITIZING SELF-CARE

Self-care doesn't have to be a grand gesture; it's about weaving small, intentional practices into your daily routine. In the workplace, you might set a calendar reminder to stretch every hour to avoid "tech neck." Even brief, regular breaks during the workday, like a cup of tea or short walk, can significantly reduce stress and improve productivity. Humming is another effective technique to stimulate your vagus nerve and calm your body. To help make these practices habits, use digital tools like Google Calendar, Habitica, or Loop to set reminders and track your self-care activities, ensuring that they become as routine as your meetings.

Practice Mindfulness

Mindfulness is a powerful way to cultivate present-moment awareness, which reduces stress and enhances clarity. Simple practices like focusing on your breath during a walk or pausing for a few deep breaths before responding to challenging emails can make a difference. Lupita Nyong'o, an actress and mental health advocate, credits mindfulness and meditation for helping her manage stress in her busy career. Apps like Headspace, Calm, or Insight Timer offer guided meditations tailored for busy schedules. Start small—just 5 minutes a day—and gradually extend your practice as you notice its calming effects.

Set Boundaries

Healthy boundaries are vital for protecting your energy and ensuring your actions align with your priorities. For example, a manager might block out "focus time" on their calendar or set a rule of "no meetings after 4 p.m." to minimize interruptions. You can establish your own limits by communicating, for instance, "I'll respond to non-urgent emails during business hours." Tools like calendar blockers or "Do Not Disturb" settings can help you maintain these boundaries. Not only do boundaries reduce burnout, but they also model healthy behavior for those around you.

Prioritize Tasks

Managing your energy effectively starts with clear priorities. Use tools like the Eisenhower Matrix to divide tasks into urgent/important, not urgent/important, etc., to focus on what truly advances your goals. For instance, instead of reacting to every email, identify three high-impact tasks each day. Marie Kondo, an organizing expert, advocates for decluttering your space and mental load to focus on what truly sparks joy. Apps like Todoist, Trello, or Asana can help you visualize and organize your priorities, making it easier to act with intention and avoid feeling overwhelmed. Leading with purpose ensures your efforts align with your core values.

Delegate

Delegation isn't just for managers; it's an essential act of self-leadership. In daily life, sharing chores or tasks with family members can lighten your load. Richard Branson, founder of Virgin Group, advocates for delegation, emphasizing the importance of trusting your team and empowering others to make decisions. Tools like Slack or Microsoft Teams can help you assign and track responsibilities effectively. Delegation not only empowers others but also preserves your energy, which is vital for maintaining balance and focus. Remember, asking for help is a sign of strength, not weakness.

Learn How to Say "No"

Saying "no" protects your time and energy for what truly matters. Chimamanda Ngozi Adichie speaks about the importance of setting boundaries to focus on her writing and personal priorities, emphasizing that "no" is an act of self-respect. Practice polite but firm responses like, *"Thank you, but I need to focus on my current commitments,"* and use tools like email templates or reminders to reinforce your limits. Cultivating the ability to say "no" allows you to say "yes" to your values and your well-being—fundamental acts of self-leadership.

Incorporating these practices into your life is more than just a strategy; it's about cultivating a mindset of intentionality and self-awareness. Use tools like habit trackers, mindfulness apps, and calendar blocks to support your efforts. Emulate those who prioritize their well-being and set boundaries, and over time, you'll find your capacity to lead yourself and others expanding. For more guidance, check out Table 11.2 where a licensed professional counselor, Christine Sugg, shares a powerful strategy to help you when you're feeling overwhelmed.

Table 11.2 Instant Impact: Leadership Takeaway from Licensed Professional Counselor, Christine Sugg

Conversations with Leaders: When You're Overwhelmed, STOP	Christine Sugg, a licensed professional counselor, shared a simple, 30-second strategy to boost well-being: the STOP technique: • Stop what you're doing at that moment. • Take deep breaths. Use belly breathing to move serotonin and calm your mind. • Observe. Notice your feelings, physical sensations, and self-talk. • Proceed mindfully. Clarify your goals and immediate next steps. Christine shared more tips, many that I use often. Listen to the full conversation on *The Communicative Leader*, Season 2, Episode 12.[10]

REFLECTION AS A KEY COMPONENT OF SELF-CARE

In leadership, action often takes center stage: making decisions, driving results, and inspiring teams. Yet, the most impactful leaders know that true growth begins with reflection. It's not just about looking back; it's an intentional practice of pausing to process, learn, and align your actions with your core values and goals. This is a vital form of self-care that nurtures clarity, resilience, and authenticity.

Why Reflection Is Your Competitive Advantage

Think of reflection as the mental and emotional hygiene that keeps your leadership voice healthy and strong (see Table 11.3). It's the essential practice that allows you to:

Table 11.3 Actionable Insights: Simple Reflections to Boost your Influence

> Reflection isn't just for leaders with titles; it's a practice everyone can use to become more centered and influential. You can transform insight into action by asking yourself a few simple questions:
> - What actions aligned with my values today?
> - When did I feel most confident and why?
> - What feedback did I receive?
> - Did I share my ideas?
> - How did I show trustworthiness?
> - What's one small step I can take to build rapport tomorrow?
>
> Reflection, in all its forms, is a powerful and essential practice that allows you to continually learn, grow, and strengthen your leadership from the inside out.

- Gain clarity on your priorities and values.
- Identify behavioral patterns to understand what is working and what is not.
- Cultivate resilience by understanding your reactions and emotions.
- Make more effective decisions, especially under pressure.

Different Types of Reflection

Reflection can take many forms, each serving a unique purpose in your professional growth.

1. **End-of-day reflection**: Briefly review what went well, what challenged you, and what you learned. For example, journaling for five minutes about your day helps you identify recurring themes, like stress triggers or moments of inspiration.
2. **Post-project reflection**: After completing an initiative, assess what contributed to success and what could be improved. A project leader might ask, "Did I communicate expectations clearly? How did my leadership communication support or hinder the team?"
3. **Crisis or challenge reflection**: During difficult times, reflect on your emotional responses and decision-making processes. This practice helps to build resilience and emotional intelligence.

4. **Periodic deep reflection**: Set aside time monthly to evaluate your progress toward your leadership goals, core values, and overall well-being.

Strategies for Incorporating Reflection

Making reflection a consistent part of your routine isn't about adding more to your plate; it's about integrating it meaningfully. Here are practical ways to do so:

Schedule It
- Block 10–15 minutes on your calendar, preferably at the start or end of your day. Treat this appointment with the same respect you would a meeting.

Create A Ritual
- Use a journal, voice memo, or digital app. At the end of each week, jot down three key insights: a success, a challenge, and a lesson learned.

Ask Powerful Questions
- Use prompts like:
  - What did I do today that aligned with my leadership values?
  - Where did I feel most energized or drained?
  - What feedback did I receive, and what does it reveal about my leadership?

Seek and Use Feedback
- Reflection isn't solely internal. Regularly ask trusted colleagues or mentors for honest feedback and reflect on their insights. After reflecting, identify a specific action or change to implement. For instance, if you notice you tend to interrupt others during meetings, commit to practicing active listening.

Practical Tips to Make Reflection a Habit

Consistent, intentional reflection is transformative for growth. It sharpens your focus, enhances your leadership voice, and accelerates your influence. See Figure 11.3 for more tips.

1. **Link it to an existing routine**: Reflect during your commute, after meetings, or before bed.
2. **Use technology**: Record voice memos or use apps to journal your thoughts.
3. **Share insights**: Discuss reflections with a trusted peer or mentor to deepen your learning.
4. **Celebrate progress**: Acknowledge small wins in your growth, such as finding it easier to speak up in a meeting or seeing your team defer to your expertise.

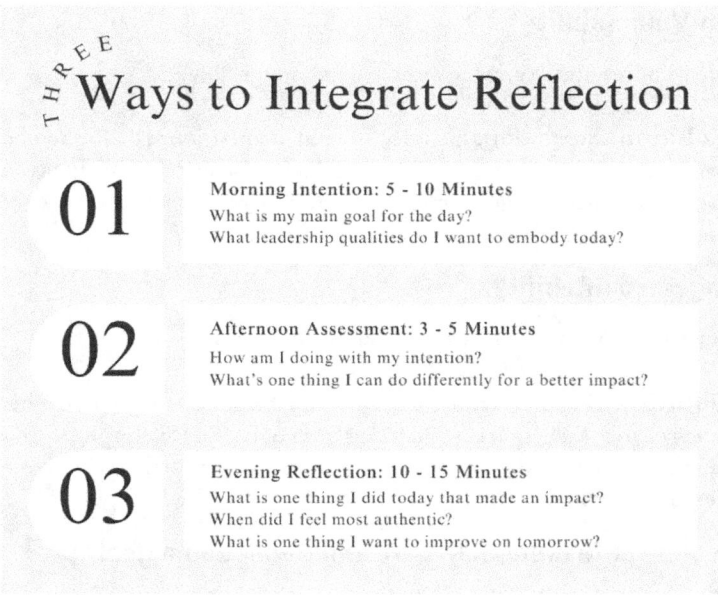

Figure 11.3 Daily reflection structure: A guided approach to setting intentions, assessing progress, and reflecting on impact.

OVERCOMING OBSTACLES TO SELF-CARE

Even with the best intentions, obstacles can block your path to meaningful self-care and reflection. Let's explore common barriers and concrete strategies to overcome them.

Time Constraints

Your schedule is packed, and self-care feels like a luxury.

- **Solution**: Start small. Dedicate just 3 minutes daily to ask yourself a single question like "What's one thing I learned today?" Over time, this habit will expand naturally.

Lack of Prioritization

Self-care isn't seen as essential.

- **Solution**: Recognize that self-care directly impacts your effectiveness. Use a visual cue, like a sticky note on your monitor, to remind yourself of its importance. Link reflection to your goals: "To maintain my focus on strategic planning, I need to block out 30 minutes for uninterrupted reflection."

Fear of Vulnerability

Self-care requires honesty, which can feel uncomfortable.

- **Solution**: Start with a private, nonjudgmental journal. Remember that vulnerability is a strength, not a weakness. Practice self-compassion and consider sharing insights gradually with a trusted mentor or peer to normalize the process.

Finding Accountability

Without accountability, self-care may fall by the wayside.

- **Solution**: Partner with a peer or coach. Schedule regular check-ins where you each share reflections or goals. For example, a manager might meet weekly with a peer to discuss leadership challenges and lessons learned.

Strategies for Making Self-Care and Reflection a Reality

- **Start small**: Commit to 5 minutes of self-care daily. This could be taking a mindful breath, stretching, or a brief walk. Focus on simple acts that help you to refuel your energy and reduce stress.
- **Prioritize rest and nutrition**: Schedule regular breaks, healthy meals, and sufficient sleep. Small adjustments like a brief rest or a nutritious snack can significantly boost your well-being.
- **Create a restorative environment**: Dedicate a quiet, comfortable space for self-care. Turn off notifications and give yourself permission to focus on your well-being without distractions.
- **Build support**: Connect with trusted colleagues, friends, or family members to share self-care goals. Supportive accountability can help you stay committed and motivated.
- **Practice mindfulness and relaxation**: Incorporate brief mindfulness exercises, deep breathing, or meditation into your day to help manage stress and increase resilience.
- **Make self-care non-negotiable**: Recognize that self-care isn't a luxury but a vital part of sustaining your energy and effectiveness. Schedule it into your daily routine just like any important meeting or task.

Remember, small, consistent steps lead to profound growth. As you deepen your self-awareness through reflection, you amplify your leadership making it more authentic, impactful, and aligned with your true purpose.

> **READY TO PUT THIS INTO PRACTICE?**
>
> **Amplify Your Leadership Voice Further**
>
> Amplify your leadership voice and build lasting resilience with the Amplifying Your Leadership Voice: Leadership Blueprint. Download your copy at TheCommunicativeLeader.com and start your journey today.

KEY TAKEAWAYS

1. **Sustainable Leadership Begins with Self-Care:** Prioritizing your physical, emotional, mental, and spiritual well-being is not a frill but a strategic imperative for effective leadership. It builds resilience, sharpens decision-making, and allows you to lead with clarity.
2. **Self-Care Is Essential for Avoiding Burnout and Maintaining Positive Impact:** Neglecting your well-being leads to burnout, compassion fatigue, and decreased effectiveness. Prioritizing self-care is crucial for maintaining healthy relationships, a positive reputation, and the ability to make sound decisions. This helps both you and your team.
3. **Integrate Intentional Self-Care Practices into Your Routine:** Weave intentional self-care practices into your routine. Consistent, small actions like short breaks, mindfulness, and setting healthy boundaries are vital for protecting your energy and aligning your actions with your priorities.
4. **Reflection Is a Powerful Tool for Growth and Authenticity:** Regularly pausing to process experiences, learn from challenges, and align your actions with your values is a key component of self-care. Intentional reflection nurtures self-awareness, enhances decision-making, and strengthens your leadership voice.
5. **Commit to Making Self-Care and Reflection Consistent Habits:** Overcome obstacles like time constraints and lack of prioritization by starting small, finding accountability, and recognizing the impact these practices have on your effectiveness and well-being. Consistent self-care and reflection are fundamental to leading yourself and others with resilience and compassion.

NOTES

1 American Psychological Association. (2023). *Workplaces as engines of psychological health and well-being: Work in America*™ *survey*. https://www.apa.org/pubs/reports/work-in-america/2023-workplace-health-well-being

2. Goleman, D. (2013). The focused leader: How emotional intelligence shapes leadership. *Harvard Business Review*, *91*(12), 78–85.
3. World Health Organization. (2019). *Mental health in the workplace: Information sheet.* https://www.who.int/news-room/fact-sheets/detail/mental-health-in-the-workplace
4. Center for Creative Leadership. (2024, May 17). *The keys to wellbeing and leadership.* https://www.ccl.org/articles/leading-effectively-articles/create-better-culture-the-keys-to-wellbeing-and-leadership/
5. Goleman, D. (1998). *Working with emotional intelligence.* Bantam Books.
6. American Psychological Association. (2021). *Stress in America™ 2021: Stress and decision-making.* https://www.apa.org/news/press/releases/stress/2021/decision-making-october-2021.pdf
7. Centers for Disease Control and Prevention. (2020). *Physical activity basics.* https://www.cdc.gov/physicalactivity/basics/index.htm
8. Wigert, B. (2020, March 13). Employee burnout: The biggest myth. *Gallup.* https://www.gallup.com/workplace/288539/employee-burnout-biggest-myth.aspx
9. National Heart, Lung, and Blood Institute. (n.d.). *What are sleep deprivation and deficiency?* NIH. https://www.nhlbi.nih.gov/health/sleep-deprivation
10. Omilion-Hodges, L. (Host). (2023, April 17). Leadership & self-care: A conversation with licensed professional counselor, Christine Sugg [Audio podcast episode]. *The Communicative Leader Podcast.* https://www.thecommunicativeleader.com/podcast/episode/79b4c716/leadership-and-self-care-a-conversation-with-licensed-professional-counselor-christine-sugg

Chapter 12

Your Leadership Muscle
Exercising and Strengthening Your Voice Daily

Level 4. Sustain Your Leadership Voice

Building on your resilience, this chapter offers daily practices to exercise and strengthen your leadership voice, ensuring it remains as powerful and authentic as ever.

KEEP THAT MOMENTUM GOING

We've reached the final chapter. We've covered communication, confidence, and connection. Now, let's focus on how to keep that momentum going.

Learning to lead is like riding a bike or playing an instrument; you don't master it in a day. It's an ongoing journey of consistent effort and practice. Your leadership voice is not a destination. In this chapter, we'll explore why regular practice matters, and how to make it a natural part of your leadership. We'll also bust some myths, like the idea that your leadership voice is fixed or that you must be perfect to make an impact. Spoiler: neither is true. Instead, we'll focus on embracing progress, leveraging your strengths, and staying committed to growth. Leadership communication is more important than ever, and I'll share practical tips to keep you inspired and moving forward.

WHY CONTINUOUS PRACTICE IS KEY

Let's talk about why sticking with practice is so vital for your leadership voice. You've probably heard of muscle memory—the way athletes or musicians perform complex moves effortlessly because they've repeated them so often. It's that ingrained ability to do something automatically after enough practice.

The good news? Muscle memory isn't just for physical skills; it applies to speaking up and leading too. Think back to a time in a meeting when you hesitated to share an idea. Perhaps your heart raced, doubt overshadowed your self-confidence, and you found yourself holding back. That's because your "leadership voice muscle" wasn't fully developed yet.

But here's the key: the more you practice speaking up—whether in team huddles, asking questions, or sharing your perspective—the stronger that muscle becomes. Over time, it gets easier to express your thoughts clearly, confidently, and quickly. Consistent practice turns once challenging moments into natural, instinctive leadership.

What NOT to Do

Sometimes it helps to consider what not to do.

- **Don't wait for "the perfect moment."** There's rarely a perfect time to speak up. The best time is usually when you have something valuable to share. Delaying only makes it harder later.
- **Don't be too hard on yourself**. Everyone stumbles or hesitates sometimes. This is normal. See it as a learning opportunity, not a failure.
- **Don't assume others are naturals**. Most confident communicators have worked at it. They've built their muscle memory through practice, just as you can.
- **Don't hold back thinking the moment isn't big enough**. Your leadership voice isn't just for major moments. Contributing small thoughts, asking questions, or offering support all count and help build that muscle for when the big moments arise.

What to Do

- **Start small and build**. Don't aim to give a TED Talk tomorrow. Share one relevant idea in your next team meeting, then add more over time.
- **Practice in low-pressure settings**. Rehearse what you want to say before meetings or explain complex ideas to a trusted colleague to get feedback first. The more you prepare, the easier it becomes.
- **Seek out chances to speak**. Volunteer to lead a part of a meeting, present findings, or jump into brainstorming sessions. Every opportunity strengthens your leadership voice.
- **Reflect afterward**. Think about what went well and what you can improve. Did you get your point across? Did you feel confident? Reflection helps refine your approach.

Remember, speaking up is a skill that improves with consistent practice. Each time you use your voice, you're strengthening that skill and making it more natural. It's about creating a habit that empowers you to contribute meaningfully and lead with confidence (see Table 12.1).

Table 12.1 Instant Impact: Leadership Takeaway from Leadership Coach, John Gallagher

	I recently had a great chat with John Gallagher on *The Communicative Leader*. Here are some of his top insights:
	Discipline Turns Good Intentions into Reality
Conversations with Leaders:	Even the best plans need discipline to truly happen. Staying committed, especially through challenges, makes all the difference.
Priorities and Legacy Building	**The Glass and Rubber Balls: Focus on What Truly Matters:** • **Glass**: Fragile, vital—family, close relationships. Protect these fiercely. • **Rubber**: Resilient, bounces back—work tasks, minor commitments. Knowing the difference helps you stay centered on what counts most.
	Tune in to the full conversation on The Communicative Leader podcast, season 7, episode 2.[1]

MINDSET SHIFT

While consistent action is crucial for building your leadership voice, your mindset plays an equally vital role. This section explores a fundamental shift in how you view your voice, challenging old beliefs and embracing a more empowering perspective.

Your Leadership Voice Is a Skill You Can Grow

One of the most freeing ideas you can accept is that your leadership voice isn't fixed or innate. Too often, we fall into the trap of thinking some people are "born leaders" or "natural communicators," believing we're out of luck if we don't see ourselves that way. But that's simply not true.

Your leadership voice is a skill—like learning a language or playing a sport. It improves with intentional effort and consistent practice. Viewing it this way gives you agency: you're not limited by some predetermined talent. Instead, you can learn, experiment, and refine your way of communicating and leading.

This mindset shift transforms your approach from feeling stuck or waiting for the 'right' moment to recognizing that growth is always possible. Your leadership voice is something you develop step by step, and embracing this truth places power firmly in your hands.

So how do you actually go about strengthening this crucial leadership muscle?

- **Get specific about your goals**. Instead of vague aims like "be a better speaker," identify exact areas such as structuring arguments clearly, using impactful language, or active listening. For example, if you tend to ramble when asked to speak off-the-cuff, practice summarizing key points concisely. Write down main ideas and rehearse with a timer to build clarity and confidence.
- **Seek learning opportunities**. Just like any new skill, you can improve your communication by exploring workshops, webinars, or books on public

speaking and leadership. Check if your organization offers training or use online platforms for practical tips on presentation, negotiation, and feedback.
- **Try different approaches**. Don't hesitate to experiment. What works in one situation might not in another, and that's okay. If you usually lead formal meetings, try a more conversational style. Switch from detailed emails to quick video messages or calls. The more approaches you try, the more adaptable your skills become.

Perfection Does Not Exist. Focus on Progress

Let's be real: chasing perfection in communication and leadership is paralyzing. The idea that you need a flawless presentation every time or a witty response on demand is not only unrealistic but also exhausting and discouraging. The truth? Perfection is an illusion. Pursuing it only leads to frustration and fear of trying.

A smarter, healthier approach is to focus on progress. That means accepting bumps along the way, like missed opportunities or messages that don't land. The goal isn't to be perfect, it's to keep learning, growing, and getting a little better each day.

Our mistakes remind others that we're human, which creates space for authenticity and reducing fear. So, embrace the mess-ups, keep practicing, and keep putting yourself out there, because that's where real growth happens. Here are some additional tips:

- **Set realistic expectations**. Cut yourself some slack. No one becomes a polished speaker overnight. Celebrate small wins, like making eye contact or cutting down filler words ("like, "um").
- **Turn mistakes into lessons**. When an interaction doesn't go as planned, don't dwell on it. Instead, ask, "What can I learn from this?" For example, if your feedback to a colleague didn't land well, reflect on why. Was it your tone, timing, or word choice? Be sure to circle back with your peer. Showing courage to revisit these moments demonstrates real commitment, authenticity, and growth.
- **Keep a "progress journal"**: Take a few minutes every week to reflect on your wins. Maybe you spoke up in a meeting, handled a tough conversation, or felt your leadership voice make a difference. Recognizing these moments, big or small, reminds you of how far you've come and keeps you motivated.

FOCUS ON STRENGTHS AND REMAIN COMMITTED TO GROWTH

Developing your leadership voice isn't about becoming someone you're not. That can feel fake and lead to burnout. Instead, focus on leveraging your existing strengths and being honest about where you can improve. Trying to imitate someone else's style isn't sustainable or authentic. Identify what you're already good at—whether it's clear communication, asking thoughtful questions, or empathetic leadership—and lean into those skills.

At the same time, a true growth mindset means being willing to acknowledge your limitations and actively work on those areas. It's not about dwelling on weaknesses; it's about recognizing opportunities to become a more effective, well-rounded leader. It's a balance of celebrating what you do well and being intentional about expanding your skills.

- **Leverage your strengths:** What do people compliment you on? Are you a great listener, someone others trust and open up to? Do you excel at breaking down complex ideas? Identify these strengths and lean into them. For example, if listening is your superpower, use it to build trust and gather insights before sharing your perspective.
- **Seek balanced feedback**: Don't just ask "How can I improve?" Also ask, "What do you think I do well when it comes to communication and leadership?" After a presentation, check in with a trusted colleague: "What worked well?" "Was my message clear?" and "What was a strength of mine in facilitating discussion?" Knowing what you do well is just as important as identifying growth opportunities.
- **Focus on growth that aligns with your goals.** You don't need to try to fix everything at once; that's overwhelming and unrealistic. Instead, choose areas that will have the biggest impact. If you want to be more influential, work on persuasive speaking. If you want to strengthen relationships, focus on active listening and empathy. Be strategic about where you invest your energy for growth.

By embracing these mindset shifts—seeing your leadership voice as a skill, prioritizing progress over perfection, and leveraging your strengths—you lay a strong foundation for ongoing development. It's about trusting the journey, being kind to yourself, and recognizing that every interaction is a chance to learn and refine your leadership voice (see Table 12.2).

Table 12.2 Data and Trends: Leadership Communication Skills in Demand

- 89% of HR professionals say that soft skills, such as communication, are just as important as technical skills for leadership success.[2]
- A survey by the World Economic Forum identified "emotional intelligence" and "leadership and social influence" as among the top skills needed for the future workforce.[3]
- According to a survey by Deloitte, 91% of executives say that leadership and communication skills are critical to organizational success, yet many organizations report a skills gap in these areas.[4]

By working on your communication skills, you're not just growing—you're also positioning yourself as a vital leader who can inspire and drive positive change. The future belongs to those who communicate with clarity, empathy, and purpose. You're well on your way.

AMPLIFYING YOUR LEADERSHIP VOICE

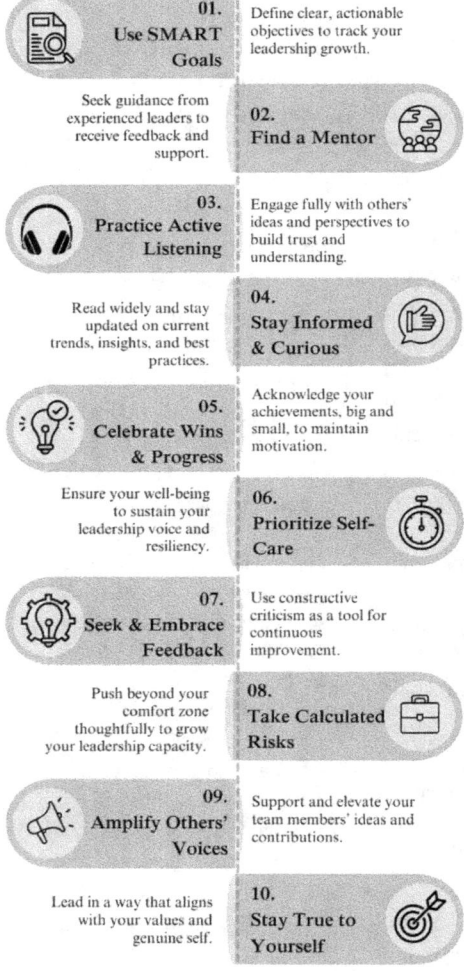

Figure 12.1 Ten essential steps to maintain your leadership voice and stay true to yourself.

TEN POWERFUL STRATEGIES TO KEEP YOUR LEADERSHIP VOICE SHARP

You have the foundation. Now, let's focus on sustaining your momentum. These ten powerful strategies are designed to help you keep your leadership voice sharp (see Figure 12.1). Consider them your final set of tools to ensure you continue to inspire, influence, and drive positive change throughout your career.

1. **Set SMART goals and track progress**: Stop dreaming in vague clouds of "someday." Make your goals **S**pecific, **M**easurable, **A**chievable, **R**elevant, and **T**ime-bound. Write them down and place them where you'll see them. Seeing your progress is a huge motivator.

Here's an example:

> **Vague goal**: I want to be better at my job.

SMART Goal Breakdown

- **Specific:** Improve my data analysis in Excel.
- **Measurable:** Complete an advanced course and score 85% or higher on the final.
- **Achievable:** Yes, the course is available, and I can dedicate 5 hours a week.

232

- **Relevant:** Better analysis skills will boost my current role and future prospects.
- **Time-bound:** Finish the course and pass the final by June 30.

2. **Find a mentor or coach**: Don't try to navigate the choppy waters alone. Find someone who's been through it and can offer real perspective, whether that's a mentor or coach. They won't solve everything, but they can give you honest feedback, push you when needed, and celebrate your wins. Their wisdom is a shortcut, so stay humble and eager to learn. Before reaching out, clarify what you need: are you after specific skills or general guidance? Knowing that will help you find the right person. Check out Table 12.3 for tips on landing a mentor or coach.

Table 12.3 Actionable Insights: Finding Your Guiding Star - How to Land a Mentor or Coach

You're ambitious and driven, but even the most seasoned navigators need a compass. Finding a mentor isn't a sign of weakness; it's a strategic power move to accelerate your growth. Here's how to make it happen:
Know What You Need
Before you start looking, clarify your goals. Do you want to grow your career? Acquire specific skills? Enhance your leadership presence? Pinpoint your focus. Also, think about what communication style works for you and find someone who speaks your language.
Scan Your Network
Start close to home. Who do you admire in your current or past circles? Reach out to trusted contacts, tap into alumni networks, or ask trusted contacts for information interviews. Instead of a direct "be my mentor" ask, request a chat to learn about their journey and gain insights. This builds a connection first.
Go Beyond Your Network
Expand your search beyond your immediate circle. Join professional industry groups, engage with associations in your field, or leverage online platforms like LinkedIn or dedicated mentorship sites.
Make the Ask Count
When you're ready to reach out, be specific. Clearly articulate why you admire them and what you hope to gain from their guidance. Start small by proposing a brief call or coffee. Show your initiative by sharing what you're already doing to learn and grow and always respect their time. Most importantly, say thank you.
Your Role as a Mentee
Finding a mentor is just the start. Be respectful of their time and insights, be open to feedback, follow through on your commitments, and always look for ways to offer value in return.

3. **Practice active listening**: Eliminate distractions. Look people in the eye. Really hear what they're saying, instead of waiting for your turn to speak. Active listening builds trust, gathers important information, and shows respect. Keep these tips in mind: eliminate distractions, lean in, listen to understand—not just respond. Be sure to summarize and paraphrase and acknowledge their perspective. Even if you don't agree, phrases like "*I hear what you're saying*" can open the door to better communication.

4. **Read and listen widely and stay informed**: The world is always changing, so stay curious and keep learning. Dive into books, articles, and news from a variety of sources because knowledge is power and staying informed keeps you relevant. Here are some suggestions:

    The Communicative Leader: My podcast is where I learn a ton from the impactful guests. It's all about simple, thoughtful communication changes that can boost your leadership and transform your work life.

    The Daily by The New York Times: A quick, insightful summary of the day's tops stories—perfect for staying current.

    Freakonomics Radio: Discover the hidden side of human behavior and society trends through economics. These episodes are great at challenging assumptions and sparking new thinking.

    Influence: The Psychology of Persuasion by Robert Cialdini: A classic that helps you understand how to communicate persuasively and resonate with others.

    Start with Why: How Great Leaders Inspire Everyone to Take Action by Simon Sinek: Learn how great leaders inspire action by articulating a clear purpose and compelling vision.

5. **Celebrate all wins**: Let's talk about celebration. You might think, "Do I really need to throw a party every time I check something off my list?" Not necessarily—no need for a parade. But dismissing your progress? That's a mistake. Recognize the momentum you're building. Did you crush that tough presentation? Take a moment to feel proud. It's not about ego; it's about acknowledging the effort and the success you've earned. These small wins are fuel for the long haul. Growth isn't a sprint; it's a marathon. Ignoring your progress can lead to burnout. So, next time you accomplish something, even if it seems minor, pause and celebrate. It's a simple practice but incredibly powerful for resilience and motivation.

6. **Prioritize self-care**: Let's be clear: self-care isn't optional. Burnout is the enemy of sustained success. You're a high-performance machine—would you run a race car without fuel or maintenance? Your mind and body are your top assets. Schedule downtime the way you schedule meetings, get enough sleep, fuel with good food, and move in ways you enjoy. You can't

pour from an empty cup. Leading and communicating effectively when depleted are like building a house without tools—ineffective and unsustainable. Your challenge: block out 30 minutes this week for something just for you, like going for a walk, reading a book, or listening to music. Treat it as a nonnegotiable appointment. Your best self will thank you.

7. **Seek feedback and embrace constructive criticism**: Let's talk about the F-word: Feedback. Yeah, it can sting. Nobody *loves* hearing they could do better, especially after pouring their heart into something. The instinct might be to get defensive, but resist that urge. Feedback, even the tough kind, is a gift. It highlights blind spots and guides growth. Next time someone offers feedback, listen without interrupting. Stay curious and ask clarifying questions if needed. Reflect: Is there truth here? Can I see their perspective? Then, use it. I changed my podcast lighting after a comment about distracting shadows, and now my conversations look clearer. Feedback is about growth, not criticism. Embrace it, learn from it, and watch yourself improve.

8. **Take calculated risks**: Growth rarely happens in your comfort zone. You have to be willing to step out, try new things, and push the boundaries. Calculated risks aren't reckless gambles; they're informed decisions with potential for a significant reward. Analyze the possibilities, weigh the odds, and then have the courage to jump. This doesn't mean attempting a high dive on day one. This can be sharing the idea you're kicking around in your mind during the meeting, rather than staying silent.

> **READY TO PUT THIS INTO PRACTICE?**
> **Amplify Your Leadership Voice Further**
>
> For more direction on taking calculated risks, explore the Amplifying Your Leadership Voice: Leadership Blueprint available at TheCommunicativeLeader.com.

9. **Amplify others' voices**: Listen up because this one's crucial. There's an old, tired idea that leadership is a zero-sum game—your win means someone else loses. That's simply not true. Operating with that mindset limits everyone's potential. True strength and leadership come from lifting others up. Be a champion for their ideas. Did someone on your team have a great suggestion? Don't just nod and move on—highlight it, give credit, and help them run with it. Did someone go above and beyond? Celebrate their contribution.

Supporting and empowering others isn't just kind; it's strategic. It creates a stronger, more collaborative environment where everyone feels valued and motivated. And guess what? It benefits you too. A team where people feel seen and supported is more engaged, innovative, and driven to achieve shared goals. Be a radiator, not a drain. Radiators give off warmth and energy, making the space better for everyone. Drains, on the other hand, absorb energy and leave others feeling depleted.

How do you make this happen? In your next team meeting, look for opportunities to highlight someone's contribution. Publicly acknowledge their effort and value.

10. **Stay authentic and true to yourself:** It might sound cliché, but it's true. In a world constantly shaping what it thinks a leader should be, your greatest strength is being yourself. Trying to be someone else is exhausting, unsustainable, and obvious: people can tell when you're faking it.

    Embrace your quirks, values, and unique perspective; these aren't weaknesses; they're assets. When you lead authentically, your decisions feel more aligned, your communication becomes more sincere, and your motivation stems from a deeper place than simply trying to fit in.

    Leadership isn't about copying others; it's about bringing your strengths forward. Staying true to your core builds trust because others see the real you. And trust is the foundation of effective leadership. Take a moment: what are your core values? How do they show up—or not—in your leadership? This week, find one small way to align your actions more closely with what matters most to you.

    There you have it—ten powerful principles to anchor your leadership journey. Keep these close, revisit them often, and remember progress is a marathon, not a sprint. Stay engaged, stay motivated, and keep pushing forward. The world is waiting for what you'll do next. Now, go make it happen.

EMBRACE YOUR LEADERSHIP COMMUNICATION EVOLUTION

Congratulations on this incredible journey. You've navigated discovery, refinement, amplification, and, now, sustainability. Each step has strengthened your authentic, confident, and resilient leadership voice.

Remember, leadership isn't a fixed trait; it's a dynamic muscle that grows stronger the more you use it. Your genuine voice has the power to inspire change, uplift others, and leave a lasting legacy. And this isn't the finish line; it's just the beginning of a lifelong practice.

As you move forward, carry the awareness that growth is ongoing. Prioritize self-care and reflection, nurture your resilience, and make exercising your leadership muscle a daily habit. Every challenge you face is an opportunity to deepen your impact and amplify your authentic voice.

And as we say on *The Communicative Leader* podcast, until next time, communicate with intention and lead with purpose.

KEY TAKEAWAYS

1. **Your Leadership Voice Is Built on Muscle Memory**: Just like mastering a physical skill, developing your leadership voice requires consistent practice to build that ingrained "muscle memory." Hesitation and fumbling decrease the more you intentionally speak up. Don't wait for the perfect moment; start small and consistently look for opportunities to contribute your thoughts and perspectives.
2. **View Your Leadership Voice as a Skill, not a Trait:** Stop believing that some people are just "born leaders" or "natural communicators." Your leadership voice is a dynamic skill that can be developed and strengthened with effort. Embracing this perspective gives you agency and control over your growth. Identify one specific communication skill you'd like to improve, such as explaining your ideas more clearly, and find a learning resource this month, like an article, video, or workshop, to help you develop it.
3. **Focus on Progress, Not Perfection:** The pursuit of perfection is an illusion that leads to paralysis and frustration. Embrace a mindset that values consistent learning and getting a little bit better each time, even when things don't go perfectly. Mistakes are opportunities to learn and refine your approach. After a conversation that doesn't go as planned, take a few minutes to reflect on future improvements, rather than dwelling on what went wrong.
4. **Leverage Your Strengths While Growing:** Effective leadership communication isn't about becoming someone you're not; it's about identifying and leaning into your natural communication strengths while also being proactive about developing growth areas. It's a balance of celebrating what you do well and expanding your skillset. Reflect on what communication strengths others have complimented you on. This week, use one of those strengths in the workplace.
5. **Stay Engaged and Prioritize Self-Care:** The journey of strengthening your leadership voice is ongoing, so staying engaged is key. This means setting clear goals, seeking support, and prioritizing your wellbeing. Burnout is the enemy of sustained progress. You can't effectively lead or communicate if you're running on empty. Look at your calendar for the next two weeks and schedule at least one block of time specifically for self-care.

NOTES

1. Omilion-Hodges, L. (Host). (2025, May 27). Unleashing uncommon leadership with John Gallagher [Audio podcast episode]. *The Communicative Leader Podcast.* https://www.thecommunicativeleader.com/podcast/episode/7ccd0f53/unleashing-uncommon-leadership-with-john-gallagher
2. LinkedIn Learning. (2019). *The most in-demand skills of 2019.* https://learning.linkedin.com/blog/top-skills-of-the-future/the-most-in-demand-skills-of-2019
3. World Economic Forum. (2020). *The future of jobs report 2020.* https://www.weforum.org/reports/the-future-of-jobs-report-2020
4. Deloitte. (2019). *Global human capital trends: Leading the social enterprise—reinvent with a human focus.* https://www2.deloitte.com/us/en/insights/focus/human-capital-trends/2019.html

Index

Note: Page numbers in *italics* indicate a figure, and page numbers in **bold** indicate a table on the corresponding page.

accountability 3, 100, 106, 167, 183; and self-care 224
advocacy *see* inclusivity and advocacy
achievement 56, 112, 132, 134–135; *vs.* ascription 136
active listening: CAT 33–34, 76; confrontational fear 116; engaging in 52, 114; improving 16, 38, 59, 71, 169–170, 234; mentoring 189; natural communication style **26**, 30–31; and nodding 83
active voice 93–94
adaptability 24, **26**, 30, 165
Adichie, C. 220
ambiversion 28–29
analytical thinking 166–167
analytics, digital: engagement metrics 205; social media interactions 205; website traffic and conversions 206
Angelou, M. 111
anxiety 57, 71, 114
Asana (project management tools) 106, 126, 219
ascription *vs.* achievement 136
assertiveness 24, **25**, 27, 30, 171
assessment: active listening 30–31; adaptability 30; assertiveness 30;

collaborative *vs.* avoidant conflict negotiation 29; emotional intelligence 29–30; feedback 31; interaction preferences 29; introversion/ambivert/extraversion 28–29; nonverbal communication 31
attention, commanding: audience engagement 185–186; communicating with intention 185; feedback loops 186–187; in face-to-face settings 191–195, *192*; in-person communication, impactful 187–190; leadership, elevated 180, *181*; messages, impactful 180–181; preparing 181–183; proactivity 186; stakeholders 190–191; storytelling 183–185
audience 90, 184–186, 199–200, 208
authenticity 10, 160, 161–162, 193–194; *vs.* inauthenticity *159*; leadership voice 50–51, **53**, 158–159; workplace 93; technology 207, **207**; written communication 93

body language: eye contact 84; facial expressions 83; gestures 84; haptics, touch 86; mirroring 85; and paralinguistic cues 85–86; personal

239

INDEX

space 85; posture 82–83; silence 86–87; tone 85–86
boundary setting 176, **177**
Branson, R. 188, 220
Brown, B. 188, 194
burnout 215, 218, 230, 234; boundary setting 219; and emotional drain 119, *159*; risks of 178, 218; signs of 176; and stress 17, 55, *217*
Butterfield, S. 191

career growth 1, *18*, 55, 198
Cialdini, R. 234
clarity 10; and conciseness 38–39; leadership voice 47–49, **53**; RACI model 48
Clark, D. 194
coaching 65, 126, 189
collaborative *vs.* avoidant conflict negotiation 29
collectivism 132
communication accommodation theory (CAT) 32; active listening 33–34; flexibility in style 34–35; principles of 37; feedback, soliciting 36–37
communication apprehension 14–15, **14**
communication, best practices: and body language 122–123; dialogue opportunities 123–124, **124**; language 120–123; resistance preparation 122; tone 122–123
communication skills 3, 23–24; clarity and conciseness 38–39; confidence in sharing ideas 66–69; confidence signaling, body language 81–87; conflict negotiation 39–40; conversations, mastering 71–72; difficult conversations 73–80; effective communicators, workplace 66; feedback (*see* feedback); meetings 72–73; nonverbal 81; public speaking 42; strengths and growth areas 43
communitarianism 134–135
community 203–205

compassion fatigue 214, 218, 225
conferences 35, 118, 188, 193
confidence 1, 157–158, 166, 168; active listening 16; lack of 13, 112–113; preparations 16; respectful discussions 16; in sharing ideas 66–67, **67**; sharing with 68–69; signaling (*see* body language)
confidence-building strategies: self-efficacy 173–174; internal and external self-awareness 171–172; positive self-talk 171–173; powerful language 174; reframing negative thoughts 174–175
conflict: navigating 76–77, **77**; negotiation 39–40; resolving 77–78
confrontational cultures 139
confrontational, fear of being 116–117; active listening and mutual goals 116; assertiveness 116; conflict management skills 117
consistency 200; audience engagement 208; profile alignment 202; regular updates 202; standardized tone 202; unified messaging 201–202; universalism 134; values in decision-making and communication 163
consistent messaging and behavior 193
content creation 202–203; headlines and captions 202; valuable content 203, *204*
control 54–55
conversations, difficult 73; constructive dissent 79–80; dissenting 78–79; handling pushback and criticism 74; navigating conflict 76–77; resolving conflict 77–78; strategies for responding to criticism 74–76
conversations, mastering 4, **14**, 41, **41**: conversation starters 71; active listening 71; effective conversations 71–72; wrapping up conversation 71–72
conviction 1, 9; boundary setting 176–177; growth mindset 176;

INDEX

leadership voice 49–50, **53**; mental preparation 177; stress management 176; values and goals 175
core values 172, 175, 236; authentic self 160, 161, **161**; and unique traits 192
creativity 15, **44**, 114, 160; analytical and strategic thinking 167; constructive dissent 79; psychological safety 60
critical thinking 117, 166
criticism/rejection, fear of 54, 114; conquering challenges 54; engaging in active listening 114; long-term stakes 54; preparing for conversations 114; reframe rejection 114; workplace example 54
criticism, overcoming 74–76
cultural competence 130, 152
Cultural Intelligence (CQ) 145–146
cultural leadership: Hofstede's cultural dimensions 131–133; Trompenaars' cultural dimensions 134–136
culture shaping communication **137**; cross-cultural communication **135**; Hall's high *vs.* low context 136–137; Meyer's cultural map 138–140, **140–142**
curiosity 59, 83, 152

decision-making: and communication *162*, 163; groupthink 120; and judgment 218; values in 163–165
dependability 166
digital communication skills: document collaboration platforms 106; feedback and signup tools 106–107; instant messaging tools 105; project management tools 106; toolkit for **108**; video call 103–105; video meeting tips 105; workflow overview **107**
digital presence 200, **201**; consistency across platforms 201–202; online presence 200–201
disruption, fear of 115–116

dissent, approaches to 144–145; constructive **78**, 79–80, 87; direct 144; dissent 144
documents 10, 96–102; collaboration platforms 106; emails 96–99; meeting minutes 100–101; newsletters 100; presentations 99–100; proposals 99; social media posts 101–102

Eber, K. 95, 96, 183
Edmondson, A. 60
egalitarian cultures 139
emails 96–99, **97–98**
emotional drain 119; *see also* burnout
emotional intelligence (EI) 29–30, 166; active listening 52; audience engagement 185; leadership voice **51**, 51–53; nonverbal cues 52; open-ended questions 52; pausing before responding 52
empathy 10, 35, 166
empowerment 166, 167
events 187–190
extraversion 28–29
eye contact 10, 34, 71, 84, 185

Facebook 198, 200, 205
face-to-face settings: authenticity and transparency 193–194; consistent messaging and behavior 193; core values and unique traits 192; dress and appearance 193; feedback and adaptation 194; legacy building 194–195; networking with purpose 193
facial expressions 83; genuine smile 83; monitoring eyebrows 83; neutral expression 83; nodding 83; raised eyebrows 83; relaxing facial muscles 83
fear, managing 57
fear of being confrontational *see* confrontational, fear of being
fear of being seen in negative light *see* negative light, fear of being seen in

INDEX

fear of misinterpretation *see* misinterpretation, fear of
fear of rejection or criticism *see* criticism/rejection, fear of
fear of disruption *see* disruption, fear of
fear of vulnerability *see* vulnerability, fear of
feedback 31, 40–41, **41**, 69–70; and adaptation 194; alternatives 70; assessment score 31; clarifying questions 70; digital 106–107; direct negative feedback *vs.* indirect 138; loop creation 186–187; mentorship and 112; misinterpretation, and 115; open-mindedness 69–70; peers 2; six-step approach to effective communication 187; soliciting 36–37; SurveyMonkey, Signup Genius, Qualtrics 106
femininity 132–133; *vs.* masculinity 132
Ferrazzi, K. 193
flexibility 34–35, 165
Ford, H. 173

Gaynerchuk, G. 208
gestures 84
Google Workspace 106
groupthink 120
growth mindset 176, 231

Haddad, A. 31
haptics 86
Harris, D. 61
hierarchical cultures 140
Hofstede, G. 131, 134, 139, 153; individualism *vs.* collectivism 132; masculinity *vs.* femininity 132–133; power distance 131–132; uncertainty avoidance 133
Holmes, E. 50
humor 35, 194

Icons8.com 198, **199**
imposter syndrome 13, 110–113

inclusivity and advocacy 151–153; inclusive group communication practices 146–147, **147**
individualism: *vs.* collectivism 132; *vs.* communitarianism 134–135
initiative 17, 48, 59, 68, 166–167
insecurity 53, 55; *see also* confidence
Instagram 198, 202
instant messaging tools 105
integrity 175, 192, 214; authentic confidence 158–160, 163, 214; personal attributes 166
intention 185
intersectionality 150–151
introversion 28–29
"I" Statements 120–122, **121–122**

jargon 91, 99, 101, 115, 185, 191
Jobs, S. 17, 159, 189
job satisfaction 1, 17
Jordan, M. 114

key messages 47, 89, 91–92, 94

leadership voice 2, **2–3**, 9–11, 21–22, 227; continuous practice 227–229; mentoring/coaching 233, **233**; mindset shift 229–230; SMART goal breakdown 232–236; speaking up (*see* speaking up); silent, staying (*see* silent, staying); strategies *232*, 232–236; strengths 230–231, **231**
learning 125–126
legacy 194–195
LinkedIn 125, 127, 198, 200–202
lists 94
lunch sessions 190

marginalized voices 149
Marie K. 219
masculinity *vs.* femininity 132
meeting minutes 100–101, **101**
meetings 72–73, 188

mentorship 19, 118, 149, 151–153; and coaching 189; and feedback 112
messages 38, 180–181; authenticity 93; documents 96; focusing on 91–92; quality *vs.* quantity of 200; "So What?" framework 183
Meyer, E. (Meyer's cultural map) 131; confrontational *vs.* avoiding confrontation 139; direct negative feedback *vs.* indirect 138; egalitarian *vs.* hierarchical 139–140; explicit *vs.* implicit 138; principles first *vs.* applications first 139; task-based *vs.* relationship-based 140–142
Microsoft 365 106
Microsoft Teams 105, 220
mindfulness practices 57, 219
mindset shift 229–230
minorities and underrepresented groups 148–151
mirroring 81, 85, 183
misinterpretation, fear of 114–115
mistakes 59, 110, 125–127, 230, 237
momentum 126–127

Nadella, S. 188, 218
natural communication style: assessment 24, **24–27**, *27*; assessment score 28–31; elements of 24, *27*; learning from others 32, **33**; for personal growth 28
negative light, fear of being seen in 149–150
negative self-talk, reframing 58, 59
networking 188, 193
neutral communication 136
newsletters 100
non-negotiables 160, 176
nonverbal communication: assessment score 31; CAT assessment score 31; communication styles 11; leadership communication 11; natural communication style assessment **31**; skills 81, *82*

nonverbal cues 143–144; active listening 33; emotional intelligence (EI) 52; eye contact 143; facial expressions and posture 144; gestures 144; practical tip 144
Nyong'o, L. 219

Obama, M. 189, 194
open-mindedness 69–70, 145
optimism 168
organizational skills 167
other-oriented focus 31

PACT Framework 194, **195**
panel discussions and roundtables 189
participation, encouraging 72–73
particularism 134
patience 76–78, 125, 128, 165, 206
perfectionism 46, 54–55, 126
perseverance 166–168
personal: attributes 165–166; goals 169–170; growth 167–168; mission statement 191, **191**
persuasiveness 38, 93, 166, 167
pitches 188–189
Porter, J. 171
positive body language 35, 81
positive self-talk 57–58, 171–173
positivity 166, 168
posture 82–83
power distance 131–132, 139
precision 123
presentations 2, 36, 47, 86, 96, 106, 169, 187–188; client 91; effective 99–100
proactivity 186
problem-solving 105, 160, 168, 198; group 75; leadership 166; reframing negative self-talk 59
professional goals 169–170
project management tools 106
proposals 99
proxemics, personal space 85

243

psychological safety: creating culture of 60–61; long-term benefits of 60–61; role in creating 59–60
public speaking 24, 42–43, **43**
purpose 181–183

Qualtrics 106–107

reframing: negative thoughts 174–175; self-talk 58, 59
rejection, fear of *see* criticism/rejection, fear of
relational skills 166
relationship-based culture 140
relationship-focused voice 171
reputation 218
resilience 59, 165, 213–214; importance of self-care 215–217; influences 217–218; overcoming obstacles to self-care 223–225; prioritizing well-being 214–215; reflection as component of self-care 221–223; prioritizing self-care 219–220, **220**; sustaining leadership voice 213
resourcefulness 167
Responsible, Accountable, Consulted, and Informed (RACI) model 48

Sandberg, S. 189, 218
Schultz, H. 189, 208
self-advocacy 144
self-awareness 171–172
self-care 215–217: accountability 224; competitive advantage 221, **221**; delegating 220; ignoring 215–216; lack of prioritization 223; leadership resilience *216*; mindfulness 219; overcoming obstacles to 223–225; practical tips 222–223, *223*; prioritize tasks 219; saying "No" 220; setting boundaries 219; strategies 219–220, 224–225; time constraints 223; types of reflection 221–222; vulnerability, fear of 224

self-discipline 165
self-doubt 13, 53–55, 57, 111, 228
self-efficacy 173–175
self-talk: positive (*see* positive self-talk); reframing negative 58, 59
sharing ideas: building and maintaining community 203–205; confidence in 66–67; with confidence 68–69; engaging content 202–203; preparation 67; presentation 68; professional digital presence 200–202; social media platforms 198–200; success 205–206, **206**
Signup Genius 106–107
silent, staying 12, 53–56, 86–87; *see also* communication apprehension; leadership voice; speaking up
Sinek, S. 234
skill learning challenges 125–126, **125**
Slack 94, 105, 191, 220, 230
social intelligence 166
social media platforms 198–200; aligning platform with purpose 198–199; knowing audience 199–200; quality *versus* quantity of messages 200
social media posts 101–102, **102**
"So What?" framework 183
speaking up 1, 15–16, **16**, 18–19; cultural context 117–118; emotional drain and burnout 119; fear of being seen as confrontational 116–117; fear of misinterpretation 114–115; fear of rejection or criticism 114; fear of disruption 115–116; groupthink 120; imposter syndrome 111–112; lack of confidence 112–113; lack of role models and support 118–119; *see also* silent, staying
stakeholders 190–191
storytelling 95–96, 183–185
strategic thinking 146, 166–168
strategies, leadership 232–236
strengths 165–170
success 205–206

Sugg, C. 214, 220
Sullivan, P. 163
SurveyMonkey 106–107

task-based culture 140
task-focused voice 170
teams 19, 31, 78, 144, 166, 203; communication across cultures **135**, 146; creating inclusive group communication practices 146–147; Cultural Intelligence (CQ) 145–146
technology: authenticity 207–209; ideas to share (*see* sharing ideas); integrating 11; intentional reflection 222; leveraging 206
The *Communicative Leader* podcast 4, **14**, **41**, **50**, **67**, **78**, **92**, 96, **124**, **160**, **201**, **229**, 237
TikTok 199
time: constraints 223, 225; management 72, 167, 168, 203
tone: and body language 122–123; and paralinguistic cues 85–86; standardized 202; variations 185
traditional leadership: intersectionality 150–151; negative light, fear of being seen in 149–150; marginalized voices 149; workplace biases 148, **149–150**
transparency: amplifying with tech 208–209; and authenticity 193–194
Trello 106, 126, 127, 219
Trompenaars' cultural dimensions: achievement *vs.* ascription 136; individualism *vs.* communitarianism 134–135; neutral *vs.* affective 136; specific *vs.* diffuse 135; universalism *vs.* particularism 134
trusting: adaptability 30; confidence 166; delegation 220; task-based *vs.* relationship-based 140–142

uncertainty avoidance 133
underrepresented voices 149–153
universalism 134

values: complementary 161–163, 165; core (*see* core values); in decision-making and communication 163–165, **164**; and goals 175
video call 102–105, 127
vision 42, 166, 167; clarity 47; conviction 49; personal attributes 166
visuals: clarity 39; eye-catching 101; incorporation of 94–95, 100; leveraging 203
volunteer engagements 190
vulnerability, fear of 214, 224

warmth 35, 42, 81, 85, 143
"We" Language 120–122
well-being 17, 127; and emotions 52; employee 119, 133; prioritizing 214, *215*; and self-care 127
"what if" approach 70
Winfrey, O. 190
workplace: authenticity 93; biases 148, **149–150**; cultural gaps 152
Wozniak, S. 17
wrapping up 71–72
written communication 5, 11; active voice 93–94; audience 90; authenticity 93; bullet points and lists 94; double checking 92–93; jargon, avoiding 91; key messages 91–92; language 91; visuals 94–95

X/Twitter 198

YouTube 199

For Product Safety Concerns and Information please contact our EU representative GPSR@taylorandfrancis.com
Taylor & Francis Verlag GmbH, Kaufingerstraße 24, 80331 München, Germany